WE DECLARE

LANDMARK DOCUMENTS IN IRELAND'S HISTORY

RICHARD ALDOUS & NIAMH PUIRSEIL

Quercus

Foreword by Fintan O'Toole

Historic documents are the vestiges of power. Irish historic documents are, for the most part, vestiges of someone else's power.

The texts collected here were written in Latin, French and English by Romano-Britons (Saint Patrick), Anglo-Normans, Dutch generals (Godert de Ginkel), English aristocrats, administrators and divines, and only latterly by Irish activists and politicians. Just one, Donall MacAmhlaigh's vibrant account of emigrant life in the 1950s, was written in what was, for most of the period covered by this book, the language of the majority of the Irish people – Gaelic.

It is striking that the earliest document in this collection actually written by an Irishman – Hugh O'Neill's statement of his aims in the native war against the Tudors – dates no earlier than November 1599. Even then, it is not written in the native Irish language, but in Latin, and it is aimed, not primarily at an Irish readership, but at the Pope in Rome. And it is not until another two centuries afterwards that we find another document written by authors – the founders of the United Irishmen – who could be called comfortably and self-consciously Irish.

This, however, is precisely where the drama of this collection lies. It is not, as an equivalent volume for most western European countries would be, an archive of fixed authority, of a settled power passing through different forms from one generation to another. It is rather the paper trail left by a continual tussle for authority. The Ireland it refers to is always a contested space, always up for grabs. What we encounter between these covers is a war of words, a series of struggles to control and define Ireland that is never definitively won or lost. Over the course of more than 1500 years, a public Irish voice struggles to emerge and, when it does emerge, struggles to be heard above the din of other, competing Irish voices. Instead of a dry remnant of past pronouncements, we have the sense of a living process in which even those with power can seldom hide their anxieties about its range and permanence.

This tension is rooted of course in the nature of Irish history, and the profound sense of unease that comes from the conjunction of an incomplete and only partly successful process of colonization with shifting, and for long doomed, strategies of resistance. But it is also shaped by the nature of language in Ireland. Whereas the companion volume, *Great Irish Speeches*, attests to the continuity between an old oral culture and the development of modern politics, the documentary record is profoundly affected by the other side of that coin – the wariness of an oral culture in relation to written texts.

Gaelic prose was not really invented until the 17th century. Even after that period, since much Irish political activity was clandestine and illegal or was undertaken by people of limited literacy, there was good reason to be wary of writing things down.

For large areas of Irish history – the cataclysmic abortive rising of 1798, for example – the documentary record is heavily weighted towards the State and away from those who opposed its power.

This, of course, is a common condition of the historical record everywhere, even if it is especially pronounced in the Irish case. What makes Ireland so intriguing, however, and what emerges so strikingly in these pages, is that the official record is itself so troubled and unsettled.

For English officialdom, State documents not only decreed the rules of order and civilization, but sought, in a sense, to embody them. In theory, the uniform, centralizing language of the official documents stood in contrast to the wildness of the Irish and what Henry VIII called 'the diversity that is betwixt them in tongue, language, order and habit, which by the eye deceiveth the multitude, and persuadeth unto them that they should be as it were of sundry sorts, or rather of sundry countries ... '. Good solid English writing could, in other words, help to make Ireland and England, not 'sundry countries' but a united kingdom. But in fact, at least from our perspective, those documents themselves are laden with an unease that belies that very belief.

Unease is indeed the keynote of these texts. Usually, historians rely on documents as the bedrock of truth, the primary guarantors of accuracy amid all the emotional and political uncertainties implicit in any engagement with the past. But the piquancy of these Irish documents is that they are so often themselves riven with uncertainty. They are full of strategies and manoeuvres, of bluster and wishful thinking, of thwarted expectations and tragic delusions. They remain, even after the passage of time, slippery to the touch.

St Patrick's Confession, a key Irish document that is rightly chosen to begin this collection, is at one level an extraordinarily vivid personal testament, an autobiographical narrative of a kind that is extremely rare for its time. Yet this great expression of personality is powerful precisely because it is so halting, so awkwardly written in a style of Latin that has none of the command and fluency of an educated Roman patrician. It begins, not as most documents of the pre-democratic age do, with a gesture of authority, but with a disavowal of status and learning: 'I Patrick, a sinner, very rustic, and very contemptible in the estimation of most people … '. And it is also painfully tantalizing in the way it gives us a glimpse of a man about whom we know precious little else. His surviving documents do not illuminate the surrounding darkness but are intriguing islands within it.

And this is not just a function of the long gap in time. Even more recent documents can have this tantalizing, enigmatic quality. The 1916 Proclamation of the Irish Republic is perhaps the most famous document in Irish history, but the process of its creation – who exactly wrote what? – remains somewhat opaque. Appropriately, perhaps, this uncertainty mirrors the status of the document to which, across the centuries, the proclamation replies. The infamous Papal Bull of Pope Adrian IV, legitimizing the English conquest of Ireland, is another keystone of Irish history. But it is also a shaky foundation for the subsequent narrative of '800 years of oppression'. In the form we have, it is probably, at least in part, a forgery. No original survives, and what we do have is derived from an obviously propagandistic context. It has, indeed, an eerily contemporary ring: the injunction to invade Ireland 'in order to subject its people to law and root out from them the weeds of vice' would not be hard to translate into a 21st-century context. Its fascination lies at least as much in its illustration of the long antecedents of sexed-up dossiers and the dubious spinning of pretexts for invasions as in its direct value as a witness to historical fact.

This sense that Irish historic documents can often occupy a no-man's-land between truth and fiction, the real and the unreal, is nowhere better exemplified than in Jonathan Swift's Drapier's Letters. There are few countries whose sober documentary history would have to include a work by a poet, novelist and satirist celebrated for his extreme, often surreal imagination and fecund invention. Fewer still would include such a document created by that writer while pretending to be someone else.

Twelve centuries after St Patrick, we find another churchman, keeper of the saint's cathedral, again adopting a humble, artless persona, apparently disavowing authority and swapping the dignity of the Dean for the allegedly unremarkable guise of an ordinary, honest shopkeeper, M.B. Drapier. He uses homely imagery: in the first letter he claims to have a 'pretty good shop of Irish Stuffs (tweeds) and Silks' and declares his intention to live by bartering with the butcher, the baker and the brewer rather than accept the debased coinage that is the object of Swift's attack. The whole thing is a brilliant linguistic performance, in which the broad political and philosophical arguments of the fourth letter, which is extracted here, have been built on a carefully calibrated language of 'common sense'. The arguments were stunningly effective, even though the public knew very well that they were expressed, essentially, through a lie (people knew that Drapier was really Swift) – a mark surely of the complex functioning of public documents in Irish history.

Conversely, while Swift could use fictional devices to get at the truth, we find Lord Widgery, three centuries later, using the cold, apparently authoritative language of hard fact to create a fiction. Widgery's official inquiry into the shooting dead by the British Army of 14 civilians in Derry in 1972 is a masterpiece of Olympian self-assurance. It is also a staggering case study in the use of linguistic devices – of the passive voice, of double negatives, of statements of the blindingly obvious as if they were profound findings – to suggest untruths without actually stating them. Statements like 'There would have been no deaths in Londonderry ... if those who organized the illegal march had not thereby created a highly dangerous situation ... ' or 'None of the deceased ... is proved to have been shot whilst handling a firearm or bomb' are positively Swiftian in their deadpan absurdity. And the very need to resort to such contortions betrays the anxiety that what could not have happened really did happen.

Even the most shocking, most brutal, and apparently most direct document in this collection, Oliver Cromwell's account to parliament of his massacre at Drogheda in 1649, has something about it of the same quality of artful performance in which a blunt, bluff no-nonsense persona is used to gain an audience's trust. Cromwell wrote with an immediate purpose – to ensure a flow of supplies for his army from the English parliament. His descriptions of the violence are at once more vivid than anything else in his extant letters and, simultaneously, coldly casual. The language of the direct narrative is deliberately offhand – 'I think that night they put to the sword 2,000 men'; 'their officers were knocked on the head'; 'all their friars were knocked on the head promiscuously'. But the language of Cromwell's justification is high-flown and apocalyptic: 'a righteous judgment of God on these barbarous wretches'. The two registers work together to depersonalize the massacre – it was just a matter of knocking some people on the head and anyway it was all God's doing.

But even here, in this carefully calibrated balance of vivid narrative and moral distancing, there is a moment when Cromwell's control falters and a cold shard of reality cuts through the surface of the text. Describing his burning of the steeple of St Peter's church with a hundred people inside, Cromwell suddenly and uniquely allows the voice of one of his victims to slip out into history: 'one of them was heard to say in the midst of the flames: "God damn me, God confound me; I burn, I burn."' He passes no comment, and moves briskly on, but it is hard not to feel that as he wrote he was hearing that scream in his head and losing, for just an instant, his absolute aura of command over Ireland and over himself. There is even a strange prefiguring of the other awful description of horror in these documents – N.M. Cummins's description of the famine in County Cork: 'Their demoniac yells are still ringing in my ears.' It is perhaps the strangest, most haunting moment in all of these documents, and one that shows, again, how hard it is for Irish public texts to retain their sense of authority.

A similar sense of instability clings to other crucial documents. Even expressions of the State's power often turn out to be rough guides to its relative impotence. The scheme for the Plantation of Ulster, vital to any understanding of Irish history up to the present day, is as much as a record of what didn't happen what did – its injunctions to undertakers were largely ignored, resulting not in a pure Protestant British colony but in an uneasy mix of native and settler.

The Treaty of Limerick is another of these documents that function almost as photographic negatives, shadowy reverse images of a reality that they were intended to represent, but that actually eludes them. Its official intent – a relatively generous settlement for the defeated Catholic forces in the Williamite wars – was to be lost in a miasma of missing and disputed clauses, penal legal manoeuvres, parliamentary obstruction and breaches of faith. Its placatory and civilized surface dissolved into cynicism and bitterness. Instead of guaranteeing peace, it would become a byword for betrayal and itself a war cry for future generations of Irish Catholics. Literally so: the Irish Brigade in the French armies used as its battle slogan the call to 'Remember Limerick'.

The same is, of course, true of many subsequent documents. We read the noble constitution of the Society of United Irishmen with its stirring call to end 'the intestine divisions among Irishmen' in the sober knowledge that the lasting effect of the society's doomed rebellion was to cement the very sectarian divisions it had hoped to abolish. We read the Act of Union – one of the effects of that rebellion – knowing that its grand gesture of declaring a day (New Year's Day, 1801) on which Ireland and Britain would forever 'be united into one kingdom' was in fact a grand illusion.

The best laid plans go agley. The scheme of Chief Secretary Edward Stanley for a national system of primary education, written in 1831, is fascinating in part as the genesis of a system that endures to this day. But it is just as fascinating for the fact that its central conception of a rigorously non-denominational system is actually still a part of a projected Irish future, discussed in the early 21st century as an idea whose time may have come. Stanley's notion that 'one of the main objects must be to unite in one system children of different creeds' would prove to be as much of an idealist's pipedream as the constitution of the United Irishmen. In this, the documents of colonial administrators and radical rebels can seem, in retrospect, far more like each other than either could have imagined. Neither side turns out to have the power to make what is written real.

Even the most absolute expression of authority here – the power, not over this world but the next – turns out to be wishful thinking. The 1922 Pastoral Letter of the Irish Catholic bishops condemning the anti-Treaty republican side in the civil war, is a potent work of rhetoric, written with a sense of command that goes beyond anything that even English kings could quite manage in their edicts on Ireland. It effectively excommunicates the republicans, denying them the Catholic sacraments and therefore condemning them to Hell in the next life. Yet far from lasting for all eternity, as the bishops undoubtedly imagined, their remit endured for barely a decade. Within ten years, the unrepentant republican leader would be the devout leader of an ostentatiously Catholic state. Within another ten, he would be the model of a great Catholic statesman.

Language itself, in these documents, is never just a transparent medium for conveying a message. It is almost always fraught with ironies and ambiguities. The Statute of Kilkenny, one the earliest documents collected here, is a case in point. It seems, on the surface, straightforwardly colonial, proscribing the native language and customs and prescribing the superior English modes. In fact, it is directed, not at the natives, but at the colonists – in a desperate attempt to stop them going native. It speaks, between the lines of its high legal language, not of power and arrogance, but of weakness and fear. And it contains another implicit commentary on the slipperiness of official discourse. While it wags a finger at the recalcitrant colonists for 'forsaking the English language', it was itself written in Norman French, and begins, in the original, 'Come a la conquest de la terre Direland ... '

At another extreme, language becomes self-consciously inadequate. In N.M. Cummins's letter to the Duke of Wellington, attempting to describe the famine scenes he had witnessed, the author is torn between the need to bear witness and the impossibility of conveying, in acceptable public discourse, what it is that he has witnessed: 'the scenes that presented themselves were such as no tongue or pen can convey the slightest idea of.' He draws attention to his own inability to say what he has must say: 'no words can describe' the 'frightful spectres' he has encountered. He is terrified that the obscenity of what he has witnessed will bleed into the language he is trying to use, rendering it unsuitable for public eyes: 'My heart sickens at the recital but I must go on … decency would forbid what follows, but it must be told.' But the bounds of what may be said and written must be broken: 'break the frigid and flimsy chain of official etiquette … '.

There is an irony in the way, in this collection, Cummins's rage at the boundaries of polite discourse rubs up against John Henry Newman's attempt to import into this same island the classic Victorian notion of gentility: 'a cultivated intellect, a delicate taste, a candid, equitable, dispassionate mind'. The matter of Ireland, as so many of the documents that share space in this book with Newman attest, could seldom be expressed equitably or dispassionately.

Yet what we see appearing in Newman's time in Ireland is nevertheless a new discourse, albeit one from which he was largely excluded. The documents that follow him in this collection chart the emergence of an internal Irish political discourse – an Irish political and cultural leadership addressing an Irish public in which mass literacy is coming to be taken for granted. The high, passionate, defiant rhetoric of the 1881 No Rent manifesto, signed by Charles Stewart Parnell, Michael Davitt and others, marks a decisive break with the dominant language of official civility. There is now a new imagined community of readers for these documents, the 'you' of the 'self-reliant nation' addressed by Parnell and Davitt, shading into the simple 'we' of Michael Cusack's document setting out the rules of hurling and Gaelic football and the luminously direct, representative 'I' of Donall MacAmhlaigh's account of his life on the building sites and in the foundries of England.

That 'we', of course, has barely entered the documentary record before it is contested by other, contradictory notions of collective identity: 'we whose names are under-written, men of Ulster, loyal subjects of His Gracious Majesty, King George V … '. Again, language itself becomes as much the message as the medium. The contrast between the informal, demotic tone and rhetorical flourish of many of the nationalist documents on the one hand and, on the other, the language of the Solemn League and Covenant, which draws on both the Scottish Presbyterian covenanting tradition and on the syntax of legal contracts, is not accidental. It expresses contrasting self-images – passionate rebels on the one side, respectable, orderly men on the other.

Yet one of the things we can trace in these documents is the way that Ulster's self-image, and indeed that contractual language, crosses over onto the other side and becomes the dominant syntax of Irish nationalism. De Valera's 1937 Constitution, as the editors remark, 'bore the indelible hallmark of British law'. His 1944 letter to the American ambassador, defending the practice of Irish neutrality during the Second World War, has as much righteous respectability as any Ulster covenanter could muster and indeed as much gentlemanly civility as even Cardinal Newman could desire. Even the epochal breakthrough of female voices, with the manifesto of the Irish Women's Liberation Movement, is strikingly civil and legalistic in its tone and content. A notion of how public documents function has become so widespread that even the rebels accept it.

Yet there is a nice irony in the way the cleverest, most carefully wrought, of all the documents collected here manages to combine that civil legalism with the older, stranger use of language. The Belfast Agreement reads, at one level, like any formal treaty. At another, though, it is weirdly consonant with the slipperiness that is such a feature of the documents that have gone before it. It disarms authority with its grammar of consent and parity. It is ingeniously ambiguous, telling two sides what each wants to hear. It never makes a statement without balancing it with another. It is as carefully constructed as a poem or a work of fiction. And, miraculously, it works. For once, in all the long history recorded here, shifty words function, not as a symptom of Ireland's troubles, but as a salve for them.

Introduction

'Black as ink, shot up 400 ft. into the sky, a giant column of writhing smoke and dust; black as ink, and not more than 50ft. in diameter at the base, it spread into mushroom form some 200 ft. up, and glared in the sun with lurid reds and browns, through which could be seen thousands of great white snow flakes, dipping, sidling, curtsying, circling, floating as snowflakes do . . . The great white snowstorm eddied ever upwards till, at a height of 500 feet, the west wind everbore the upward blast of the explosion and the drift of snow swept, high up in the air, down the quays in a slow slant towards Sackville Street.'

These 'thousands of great white snow flakes' were the contents of the Public Record Office, which had just been blown up. In April 1922 anti-Treaty republican forces had occupied the Four Courts complex in Dublin, using the Public Record Office as its munitions store. After a six-week stand-off, the National Army began shelling the Four Courts garrison before storming the building. An explosion in the PRO resulted in centuries-old documents being blown to shreds. Government appeals in the press for the return of documents yielded few returns.

The destruction of the documents was catastrophic. Historians then and since have lamented the loss of these papers which, ranging from administrative documents to census details, would otherwise have provided a keystone to understanding Ireland's past. However, even IRA 'intellectuals' such as Ernie O'Malley were unmoved at the incineration of such irreplaceable documents. Indeed, Tom Garvin has suggested that the obliteration of the records seemed a deliberate 'attempt to murder the nation as a collective entity with a collective memory'.

The nation was not a 'collective entity', however, and Ireland's documentary past reflects this. As Fintan O'Toole notes in his foreword, this collection is 'the paper trail left by a continual tussle for authority'. Many of the documents in this book are illustrations of state formation: early chapters show efforts by British monarchs and governments to establish a strong English state in Ireland and the efforts of Irishmen to resist. Later chapters record the creation of the newly independent Irish state, from its controversial beginnings following the signing of the Anglo-Irish Treaty to the 'dictionary republic' established under Bunreacht na hÉireann, and then the Act to establish a republic (done, in the end, in five lines).

Many of the documents included here helped to influence national identities and nation building on the island, ranging as they do from Dean Swift's form of 18th-century Irish patriotism to the cultural nationalism of Michael Cusack in establishing the Gaelic Athletic Association and the Protestant loyalism of the signatories of the Ulster Solemn League and Covenant. Others, such as the heart-rending account of the Famine in Cork, or Donall MacAmhlaigh's brilliant, un-mawkish description of his life as a labourer in post-war England, are compelling snapshots of their times. Also included, of course, are certain documents the titles of which have become well-known or even infamous, among them the Stanley Letter setting up the Irish National School system and the 'American Note' sent to de Valera during the Emergency, the texts of which perhaps few have had the chance to read.

Taken together these documents vividly represent the story of the emergence of modern Ireland – from St Patrick to Roy Keane.

St Patrick's Confessio

St Patrick's account of his vocation in Ireland, 5th century AD reland has long been proud of its Christian traditions and its writers. The most famous piece of writing from early Christian Ireland – and in one sense the beginning of Irish history – comes from the hand of the figure popularly credited with bringing Christianity to the island.

Born on the west coast of Roman Britain, Patrick, as a boy of 15, was taken from his home and brought as a slave to Ireland. The mid-5th century Ireland in which he found himself was radically different to the society Patrick had come from: it was rural, tribal and hierarchical, with a culture built on oral traditions and a druidic religion. After six years working as a herdsman, Patrick escaped from Ireland and returned to Britain. But a dream that the people of Ireland needed him to lead them to Christianity prompted his return as a priest.

In fact, Christian Ireland predated Patrick's arrival. By 431 there were sufficient numbers of 'Irish believing in Christ' for Pope Celestine to send Palladius to be their bishop. He served the Christians of Ireland well, by working to convert 'the barbarian island'. Despite this success, Palladius has become a mere footnote in Irish Christianity, leaving Patrick to take the glory as Ireland's patron saint.

Much of Patrick's pre-eminence comes from the power of the written word. Palladius left no record. Patrick, on the other hand, composed two very personal documents, his *Confessio* (*Confession*) and a *Letter to Coroticus* (both written in Latin), which represent the first Irish writings. In contrast to Palladius' ministry, we know a fair amount about Patrick's mission from his own accounts. He wrote his confession in response to public criticism, explaining how he came to be in Ireland and the nature of his mission: it is part apologia and part spiritual journey. Patrick writes that he is a reluctant author, ill-equipped to put his thoughts on paper and lacking in the formal education of his ecclesiastical peers. Predictably, this turns out to be false modesty.

The original document no longer exists, but a version of the confession remains in the *Book of Armagh*, the birthplace of the cult of St Patrick in the 7th century. Christians there probably used, perhaps even manipulated, Patrick's writings to legitimize their claim to primacy in the Irish church.

Patrick's confession became the basis of the hagiography that ultimately made his name. His own self-portrait is quite different from the one that later emerged through his 7th-century hagiographers Muirchú and Tírechán. Patrick presents himself as an ordinary Christian trying his best to fulfil his mission; the saint of the hagiographers is almost super-human as he takes on the might of druidic Ireland. Still, the combination of the original document with its later embellishment and the propagation of both for political means marked Patrick out as the man who brought Christ to the Irish.

I Patrick, 'a sinner', very rustic, and the least of all the faithful, and very contemptible in the estimation of most people, had as father a deacon named Calpornius, the son of Potitus, a priest, who was in the town Bannaventa Berniae; he had an estate nearby, where I was captured.

I was then almost 16 years of age. I was indeed ignorant of the true God, and I was taken in captivity to Ireland with so many thousands of people, and deservedly so, because 'we turned away from God' and 'we did not keep watch over his precepts', and we did not obey our priests, who kept warning us about our salvation, and the Lord 'poured down upon us the heat of his anger' where now my littleness is seen to be among an alien people. And there 'the Lord opened my heart to an awareness of my unbelief' so that, perhaps, I might at last remember my sins and that 'I might turn with all my heart to the Lord my God', who 'turned his gaze round on my lowliness' and had mercy on my youth and ignorance and kept watch over me before I knew him and before I was wise or could distinguish between good and evil and he protected me and comforted me as a father comforts a son.

'Whence moreover I cannot remain silent.'

Whence moreover I cannot remain silent, 'nor indeed is it expedient that I should', concerning such great benefits and the great grace which the Lord has been pleased to bestow on me 'in the land of my captivity', because this is what we can give in return after God corrects us and brings us to know him: 'to exalt and confess his wondrous deeds before every nation'.

… After I had come to Ireland, I was herding flocks daily, and many times a day I was praying. More and more the love of God and fear of him came to me, and my faith was being increased, the spirit was being moved, so that in one day I would say as many as a hundred prayers, and at night nearly the same, even while I was staying in woods and on the mountain; and before daybreak I was roused up to prayer, in snow, in frost, in rain; and I felt no ill-effects from it, nor was there any sluggishness in me, as I see now, because the spirit was fervent in me then. And there one night in a dream I heard a voice saying to me, 'It is well that you are fasting, soon you will go to your own country.' And again after a short time I heard the answer saying to me: 'Look, your ship is ready.' And it was not nearby, but was at a distance of perhaps two hundred miles; and I had never been there, nor did I know anybody there, and then later I took to flight, and I abandoned the person with whom I had stayed for six years, and I came in the power of God, who was directing my way unto good, and I was fearing nothing until I reached that ship. And on that day on which I arrived the ship had set out from its anchorage, and I said that I had the wherewithal to take passage with them; but the captain was not pleased, and answered sharply with indignation: 'By no means will you try to go with us.' And when I heard these things I left them, in order to return to the little hut where I was staying. And on the way back I began to pray; and before I had finished my prayer, I heard one of them, shouting out vigorously after me, 'Come quickly because these people are calling you.' And I returned immediately to them, and they began to say to me: 'Come, because we are receiving you on faith, make friends with us in whatever way you wish.' ... After three days we reached land, and for 28 days we travelled through deserted country, and food failed them, and 'hunger overcame them', and on the next day the captain began to say to me: 'How is this, Christian? You say your god is great and all powerful? Why then can you not pray for us? Because we are in danger of starving? It is indeed doubtful that we may ever see a human being again.' But I said to them with confidence: 'Be converted' in faith 'with all your heart to the Lord my God, because nothing is impossible to him', so that today he may send food to you until you have sufficient on your way, 'because there was abundance everywhere'.

And with the help of God it so came to pass. Look, a herd of pigs appeared on the road before our eyes, and they killed many of them ... and after this they rendered the highest thanks to God, and I became honourable in their eyes, and from that day on they had food in abundance.

... After a few years, I was in the Britains with my people, who received me as a son, and in faith besought me that now, at least after all the many hardships which I had endured, I should not ever depart from them. And there indeed 'I saw in a vision of the night' a man coming as if from Ireland, whose name was Victoricius, with countless letters, and he gave me one of them, and I read the beginning of the letter containing 'the Voice of the Irish', and as I was reading the beginning of the letter aloud I imagined I heard, at that moment, the voice of those very people who lived beside the Wood of Fochoill, which is near the Western Sea, and thus they cried out 'as if from one mouth', 'We request you, holy boy, that you come and walk once more among us.' And 'I was' truly 'cut to the heart', and I could read no further.

'Come and walk once more among us.'

... When I was tried by a number of my elders who came and cast up my sins as a charge against my laborious episcopate, on that day, assuredly, 'I was vigorously overwhelmed to the point of falling' here and for eternity, but the Lord spared the sojourner an exile because of his own kindly name, and he came powerfully to my support in this crushing under heel, so that, in disgrace and in shame, I did not come out badly. I pray God that 'it may not be reckoned to them as sin.' After 30 years 'they invented an occasion against me', a word which I had confessed before I was a deacon. In the anxiety of my troubled mind I disclosed to my dearest friend what I had done in my boyhood on one day, more precisely in one hour, because I had not yet gained self-control. 'I do not know, God knows' if I was then 15 years old; and

'There in Ireland I choose to spend my life.'

I did not believe in the living God nor had I believed in him from my infancy, but I remained in death and in unbelief until the time I was indeed castigated, 'and truly humiliated by hunger and nakedness', and that daily.

On the other hand I did not set out for Ireland of my own accord 'until the time' I had nearly perished. But this was rather to my advantage, since because of this I have been freed from fault by the Lord, and 'he has fitted me' so that today I may be what once was far beyond me, that I may be concerned or rather labouring for the salvation of others, whereas, as that time, I was not thinking even about myself.

There in Ireland I choose to spend my life until I die, if the Lord should grant that to me, because I am very much God's debtor, who has granted to me such great grace, that a multitude through me should be reborn to God and afterwards be confirmed and that clergy everywhere should be ordained for them, for a people coming recently to belief, whom the Lord has taken up from the ends of the earth, just as he had in times past promised through his prophets: to you will the pagans come from the ends of the earth, and say: 'Our ancestors established idols as worthless things, and there is no benefit in them.' And again: 'I have placed you as a light among the pagans, so that you may bring salvation to the ends of the earth'; and there I wish to wait in hope for the promise of him, who assuredly never deceives. … It is … our duty to fish well and diligently, as the Lord admonishes in advance and teaches, saying, 'Come after me and I will make you fishers of people.' … Whence moreover, it was especially fitting to spread our nets, so that 'a copious multitude and throng' should be taken for God, and that everywhere there should be clergy to baptize and exhort a needy and desiring people, as the Lord affirms in the Gospel, he admonishes and teaches, saying, 'Go therefore and teach all the pagans now, baptizing them in the name of the Father and of the Son and of the Holy Spirit, teaching them to observe everything that I have commanded you; and behold, I am with you all days, to the end of time.' And again he says: 'Go therefore into the entire world, proclaim the Gospel to every creature.'

Bull Laudabiliter

Pope Adrian IV's grant of Ireland to Henry II, c.1155

POPE ADRIAN IV (1100–59)

abbem. tā positum q̄ depositum. nec
non ⁊ Guiltm aldelini filiu̅. uocato
statu̅ apd Guatfordiam epoȝ sinodo.
in publica audiencia eide̅ puilegii
cum uniu̅sitati̅ assensu solempni̅
rectatō f̄ca fuit. ṅ u̅ ⁊ alter i puile
gii p eosde̅ t̄nsmissi qd ide̅ rex ab
adriano papa. alexandro decessore
antea pqu̅sierat p iohe̅m sa
riensem. post modu̅ epm̄ karnoten
sem. roma̅ ad li de
etia̅ ide̅ papa angloȝ regi a
aurei̅ in
taiit. Ol statim sim̄
in archiuu̅ wintonie reuocari̅ mat.
u̅ ⁊ u̅t̄riusq̄: puilegii te uote
miserere: s̄ superfluu̅ reputari̅.
Erat naq̄: pmu̅ ⁊ pmo i̅p̄cti li tenoȝ.

Adrian̄ epc seruus̄ seruoȝ di kino
in xpo filio illustri angloȝ regi salt.
⁊ apl̄ca b̄uctictione. Laudabilit̄
⁊ fructuose de gloso no̅e ppaga
do in t̄ris ⁊ eterne felicitati̅ p̄
mio cumulando in celis: tua mag
nificencia cogitat. cu̅ ad dilata̅
dos eccl̄e t̄minos. ad declaranda̅
indoctis ⁊ rudibȝ p̄pl̄i̅ xp̄iane
fidei u̅itate̅ ⁊ uicioȝ plantaria
de agro d̄ñico ext̄rpanda. sic
catholicus p̄nceps i̅tendis: ⁊
ad id c̄ueniencius exequendu̅.
c̄silium aplice seclis exigis ⁊ fauore̅.
In quo t̄co qu̅to altiori c̄silio. ⁊
maiori discretione pcedis: tātō
in eo feliciore pgressum te p̄state
diuo c̄fidim̄ habituru̅. eo qd ad

bonum exitū semp ⁊ fine soleant
attinge: que de ardore fidei ⁊ reli
gioni̅ amore p̄ncipiu̅ acceperu̅t.
Sane hybnia̅ ⁊ o̅s insulas quibȝ sol
iusticie xpo illux̄it. ⁊ q̄ docume̅ta
fidei xp̄iane ceper̄t: ad iu̅f beati pet
⁊ sacro s̄ce Romane eccl̄e qd tua etia̅
nobilitas recognos̄it: n̅ e̅ dubiu̅
p̄tite. Un tanto in eis lub̄encius
plantatione̅ fidele̅ ⁊ germen gratu̅
m̄um: quito id a nob i̅ t̄io
e̅iu̅ districti p̄ſ̄nciu̅ exige̅cia
e̅ m nob filiu̅
e̅ hybnie insula̅ ad subdendo̅
illum ipl̄m legibȝ ⁊ uicioȝ plantaria
e̅e ext̄rpanda. uelle i̅tiare. Et
de singlis domibȝ annua̅ uniu̅ dena
rii beato petro uelle solu̅e pensione.
⁊ tua eccl̄aru̅ ill̄ t̄re illibata ⁊ i̅
tegra c̄seruare. Nos itaq̄: piu̅ ⁊ lauda
bile desiderium tuu̅ cu̅ fauore c̄gruo
p̄sequentes ⁊ peticioni tue benig
nu̅ impendentes assensu̅: gratu̅
⁊ acceptu̅ habem̄. ut p dilatandi̅
eccl̄e t̄minis. p uicioȝ restri̅gedo
decursu. p corrigendis moribus uir
tutibȝ i̅serendis. p xp̄ne religioi̅
augme̅to: insulam illam i̅grediari̅.
Et q̄ ad honore̅ di ⁊ salute̅ ill̄ t̄re
spectauerint exequari̅. Et ill̄ t̄re
p̄pl̄s honorifice te recipiat: ⁊ sicut
d̄ñm ueneretur. Iure nimiru̅ eccl̄aȝ
illibato ⁊ i̅tegro pmanente ⁊ sal
ua beato pet ⁊ sacro s̄ce Rom̄e eccl̄e
de singlis domibȝ annua uniu̅s
denarii pensione. Si g̅ qd ceperi̅ti̅

The 12th-century Anglo-Norman intervention in Ireland profoundly changed the course of Irish history for centuries to come. The country was no stranger to invaders. During the ninth century the Vikings had found rich pickings on the east coast before they established settlements, including the town which would grow into the city of Dublin. But the arrival of the Normans represented the first time that Ireland's social–political structure had been disrupted so fundamentally, as military adventure turned into political conquest.

Before the Norman Conquest, Ireland consisted of 100–200 kingdoms of varying sizes. At the apex there was the high kingship, which was the source of claims and counter-claims by different provincial rulers. In the middle of the 12th century, there were two candidates for the kingship, backed by supporters who hoped to benefit from the winner's largesse. Between 1156 and 1166 the two sides fought savage campaigns until, in 1166, Rory O'Connor, king of Connaught, emerged victorious.

Among O'Connor's supporters was Tiernan O'Rourke of Breifne. O'Rourke had a long-standing score to settle with the king of Leinster, Dermot MacMurrough, after the latter had abducted and married his wife some 14 years earlier. Now that MacMurrough had backed the unsuccessful claimant for the high kingship, O'Rourke was in a position to exact revenge. He mounted a campaign against MacMurrough, forcing him to flee Ireland to seek support from the king of England, Henry II.

In return for MacMurrough's fealty, Henry II promised future assistance and allowed him to recruit Anglo-Norman mercenaries to regain his kingdom. The deposed king of Leinster returned to Ireland in 1167 and spent the next three years bolstering his army. The most notable addition was the Anglo-Norman lord Richard fitz Gilbert – known as Strongbow – who married MacMurrough's daughter Aoife. Shored up by Norman forces, MacMurrough successfully took back Leinster, but his death in 1171 meant that his kingdom passed through Aoife to Strongbow.

Henry II had always taken a dim view of Strongbow and had actually deprived the earl of his title in Wales when he became king in 1154. Fearing now that Strongbow was about to declare himself king of Ireland, Henry launched an expedition to take the up-start in hand. When Henry arrived in Ireland in September 1171, Strongbow capitulated without a fight. Thus began the process of foreign political control of Ireland.

Henry's assertion of his power was entirely pragmatic, but he also claimed a spiritual authority to bolster his claim. He brought with him the *Bull Laudabiliter*, a letter written in 1155 by Pope Adrian IV – the only English pope – that purportedly gave Ireland to Henry so that he might reform the Irish church.

As the letter used to legitimize the conquest of Ireland, *Laudabiliter* is one of the most contentious documents in Irish history. Over the years there have been serious questions as to its veracity, particularly as no copy of the original exists. Modern

opinion tends to believe that Adrian wrote a version of the bull, but not necessarily the one recorded by history. The earliest recorded copy, in the *Conquest of Ireland*, is unreliable because its author, Gerald of Wales, was the chief propagandist of the Anglo-Norman lordship and a vehement Hibernophobe.

Adrian's original grant was probably made at the behest of the church in Canterbury, which was trying to impose its authority on an Irish church that was growing in power. Despite receiving the bull in 1155, Henry only acted on it when necessity made it politically expedient. In addition to the challenge by Strongbow, the murder in 1170 of Thomas à Becket, archbishop of Canterbury, prompted Henry to leave the country and brandish his papal credentials.

Laudabiliter may or may not have been authentic, but it soon became an effective stick with which to beat the English. Arguing that foreign lordship had done little or nothing to advance the cause of the church in Ireland, Irish leaders – most famously in the so-called 'Remonstrance of the Irish Princes' to Pope John XXII in 1317 – claimed a breach in the terms of *Laudibiliter*. Thus it became just one of many ways to make the same point: the English had forfeited their claim to Ireland.

Adrian, bishop, servant of the servants of god, to our well beloved son in Christ the illustrious king of the English, greeting and apostolic benediction.

'You shall enter that island.'

Laudably and profitably does your majesty contemplate spreading the glory of your name on earth and laying up for yourself the reward of eternal happiness in heaven, in that, as becomes a catholic prince, you purpose to enlarge the boundaries of the Church, to proclaim the truths of the Christian religion to a rude and ignorant people, and to root out the growths of vice from the field of the Lord; and the better to accomplish this purpose you seek the counsel and goodwill of the apostolic see. In pursuing your object, the loftier your aim and the greater your discretion, the more prosperous, we are assured, with God's assistance, will be the progress you will make: for undertakings commenced in the zeal of faith and the love of religion are ever wont to attain to a good end and issue. Verily, as your excellency doth acknowledge, there is no doubt that Ireland and all islands on which Christ the sun of righteousness has shone, and which have accepted the doctrines of the Christian faith, belong to the jurisdiction of the blessed Peter and the Holy Roman Church; wherefore the more pleased are we to plant in them the seed of faith acceptable to God, inasmuch as our conscience warns us that in their case a stricter account will hereafter be required of us.

Whereas then, well-beloved son in Christ, you have expressed to us your desire to enter the island of Ireland in order to subject its people to law and to root out from them the weeds of vice, and your willingness to pay an annual tribute to the blessed Peter of one penny from every house, and to maintain the rights of the churches of that land whole and inviolate: We therefore, meeting your pious and laudable desire with due favour and according a gracious assent to your petition, do hereby declare our will and pleasure that, with a view to enlarging the boundaries of the Church, restraining the downward course of vice, correcting evil customs and planting virtue, and for the increase of the Christian religion, you shall enter that island and execute whatsoever may tend to the honour of God and the welfare of the land; and also that the people of that land shall receive you with honour and revere you as their lord: provided always that the rights of the churches remain whole and inviolate, and saving to the blessed Peter and the Holy Roman Church the annual tribute of one penny from every house. If then you should carry your project into effect, let it be your care to instruct that people in good ways of life, and so act, both in person and by agents whom you shall have found in faith, in word, and in deed fitted for the task, that the Church there may be adorned, that the Christian religion may take root and grow, and that all things appertaining to the honour of God and the salvation of souls may be so ordered that you may deserve at God's hands the fullness of an everlasting reward, and may obtain on earth a name renowned throughout the ages.

Statute of Kilkenny

*A Statute of the Fortieth Year
of King Edward III, enacted in
a parliament held in Kilkenny
before Lionel Duke of Clarence,
Lord Lieutenant of Ireland, 1366*

Despite the success of Henry II's 12th-century intervention in Ireland, a significant area of the country remained under the control of Gaelic chieftains. By the early 14th century it even seemed that this limited conquest might be under threat from an emerging Gaelic revival. Not only had the zones controlled by the colonists reduced in size, but the degree to which the newcomers had assimilated with the Gaelic Irish, becoming 'more Irish than the Irish themselves', had put not just their identity but even their loyalty in doubt.

The apparent fragility of the situation was a cause for concern in England. Yet while Edward III wanted to reassert control over his colony in Ireland, he was reluctant to devote the time or, more importantly, the resources. He tried issuing edicts, such as making it a requirement for holders of high legal office to be English born. The Anglo-Irish lords by and large ignored them – and him.

By the mid-1300s, however, those same lords found themselves in need of the king's protection. The Black Death had depleted their numbers and left them vulnerable to Gaelic Irish encroachments. Displacement caused by the plague had created an atmosphere of anarchy in the country. The king responded by sending his son, Lionel, earl of Ulster (later duke of Clarence), to Ireland as lieutenant in July 1361.

Clarence arrived with a point to prove – his famous brother, the Black Prince, out-shone him – and was militarily equipped to do so. His campaign proved successful, but while armed might was rampant, the Gaelic Irish way of life proved a more entrenched opponent. If the conquest was to survive, Clarence recognized, the Norman settlers would have to fight a cultural as well as military war. In 1366, preparing to leave Ireland, he formalized this by calling a parliament in Kilkenny. A statute was promulgated to provide for 'the good government of the land and the quiet of the people' and contained 36 clauses that effectively codified existing English law in Ireland. The statute's notoriety comes from these clauses and its preamble, which condemned any tendency towards the Gaelicization of the colonists and established a policy of apartheid to reverse and prohibit Gaelic Irish mores in culture or law.

The statute was largely unenforceable, but while its tenets were occasionally re-enacted over the centuries, it was not repealed until the early 17th century.

Whereas at the conquest of the land of Ireland and for a long time after, the English of the said land used the English language, mode of riding and apparel, and were governed and ruled, both they and their subjects called *Betaghes*, according to the English law; in which time God and Holy Church and their liberties according to their condition were maintained in due obedience. But now many English of the said land, forsaking the English language, fashion, mode of riding, laws and usages, live and govern themselves according to the manners, fashion, and language of the

Irish enemies, and also have made divers marriages and alliances between themselves and the Irish enemies aforesaid; whereby the said land, and the liege people thereof, the English language, the allegiance due to our lord the king, and the English laws there, are put in subjection and decayed, and the Irish enemies exalted and raised up, contrary to right. Now therefore our lord the King, considering the mischiefs aforesaid, in consequence of the grievous complaints of the commons of his said land, called to his parliament held at Kilkenny, the Thursday next after the day of Cinders *Ash Wednesday* in the fortieth year of his reign before his well-beloved son, Lionel, Duke of Clarence, his Lieutenant in Ireland, to the honour of God and his glorious Mother, and of Holy Church, and for the good government of the said land, and quiet of the people and for the better observation of the laws and punishment of evil doers there, are ordained and established by our said lord the King, and his said Lieutenant, and counsel there with the assent of the archbishops, bishops, abbots and priors (as to what appertains to them to assent to), the Earls, barons, and others the commons of the said land, at the said parliament there being and assembled, the ordinances and articles under written, to be held and kept perpetually upon the pains contained therein.

'Every Englishman shall use the English language and be named by an English name.'

First, it is ordained, agreed to, and established, that holy Church shall be free, and have all her franchises without injury, according to the franchises ordained and granted by our lord the king, or his progenitors, by *any* statute or ordinance made in England or in Ireland.

… Also it is ordained and established, that no alliance by marriage, gossipred, fostering of children, concubinage or by amour, nor in any other manner, be henceforth made between the English and Irish on the one side or on the other. And that no Englishman, nor other person being at peace shall give or sell to any Irish in time of peace or war horses or armour or any manner of victuals in time of war. And if any do to the contrary and thereof be attaint, that he shall have judgment of life and limb as a traitor to our lord the King.

Also it is ordained and established that every Englishman shall use the English language and be named by an English name, leaving off entirely the manner of naming used by the Irish; and that every Englishman use the English custom, fashion, mode of riding and apparel according to his estate; and if any English or Irish living amongst the English use the Irish language amongst themselves contrary to the ordinance and therof be attaint, his lands and tenements, if he have any, be seized into the hands of his immediate lord until he come to one of the places of our lord the King and find sufficient surety to adopt and use the English language and then that he have restitution of his said lands by writ to issue of the same place. In case that such person have not lands or tenements, then his body shall be taken by some of the officers of our lord the King and committed to the next gaol, there to remain until he or another in his name find sufficient surety in the manner aforesaid. And that no Englishman who has to the value of one hundred shillings of land or tenements or of rent by the year shall ride otherwise than on a saddle in the English fashion, and he that shall do the contrary and be thereof attaint his horse shall be forfeited to our lord the King and his body committed to prison until he make fine according to the King's pleasure for the contempt aforesaid. And also that beneficed persons of Holy Church living amongst the English shall use the English language; and if they do not, then their ordinaries shall have the issues of their benefices until they use the English language as aforesaid; and they shall have respite in order to learn the English language and to provide saddles between this and the feast of St Michael next coming.

'Use not henceforth the games which men call "hurlings".'

Also, whereas diversity of government and divers law in one land cause diversity of allegiance and disputes among the people it is agreed and established that no English having disputes with other English henceforth make distraint or take pledge, distress, or vengeance against any other whereby the people may be troubled, but that they shall sue each other at the common law, and that no English be governed in the settlement of their disputes by March or Brehon law, which by right ought not to be called law but bad custom; but that they be governed by the common law of the land as the lieges of our lord the King; and if they do to the contrary and thereof be attaint then he shall be taken and imprisoned and adjudged as a traitor. And that no difference of allegiance henceforth be made between the English born in Ireland and the English born in England by calling them 'English hobbe' or 'Irish dog', but that all shall be called by one name [viz.] the English lieges of our lord the King, and that any one found doing to the contrary shall be punished by imprisonment for a year and afterwards fined at the King's will.

… Also, whereas a land which is at war requires that every person do render himself able to defend himself, it is ordained and established that the commons of the said land of Ireland who are in divers marches of war use not henceforth the games which men call 'hurlings' with great clubs at ball upon the ground, from which great evils and maims have arisen to the weakening of the defence of the said land, and other games which men call 'coitings,' but that they apply and accustom themselves to use and draw bows and throw lances and other gentle games which appertain to arms, whereby the Irish enemies may be the better checked by the liege commons of these parts and if any do or practice the contrary and of this be attaint that he shall be taken and imprisoned and fined at the will of our lord the king.

Also, whereas divers wars have often heretofore been commenced and not continued or brought to a good termination but by the party taking from the enemies at their departure a small tribute, whereby the said enemies were and are the more emboldened to renew the war, it is agreed and established that any war which shall be commenced hereafter shall be undertaken by the Council of our lord the King, by advice of the lords, commons, and marchers of the county where the war shall arise, and shall be continued and finished by their advice and counsel, so that the Irish enemies shall not be admitted to peace until they are finally destroyed or shall make restitution fully of the costs and charges expended upon that war by their default and rebellion, and shall make reparation to those by whom the said charges and costs were incurred, and moreover shall make fine for the contempt at the King's will. And in case that hostages be taken and given to our lord the King or to his officers for keeping the peace by any of the Irish, that, if they renew the war contrary to the form of their peace, execution of their said hostages be made without delay or favour according to the ancient customs of the said land in such case used.

… Also, whereas the Irish minstrels coming among the English spy out the secrets, customs and policies of the English whereby great evils have often happened, it is agreed and forbidden that any Irish minstrels, that is to say tympanours, poets, story-tellers, babblers, rymours, harpers or any other Irish minstrels shall come amongst the English; and that no English receive them or make gift to them. And that he who does so and is thereof attaint, shall be taken and imprisoned, as well the Irish minstrels as the English that receive them or give them anything, and that afterwards they shall be fined at the King's will and the instruments of their minstrelsy forfeited to our lord the King.

> ### 'It is … forbidden that any Irish minstrels … shall come amongst the English.'

… Also our lord the Duke of Clarence, lieutenant of our said lord the King in Ireland, and the Council of our said lord the King there, the earls, barons, and commons of the land aforesaid at this present Parliament assembled, have requested the archbishops, bishops, abbots, priors and other persons of religion that they shall cause to be excommunicated and do excommunicate the persons contravening the statutes and ordinances aforesaid, and to fulminate other censures of Holy Church against them, if by any rebellion of heart act contrary to the statutes and ordinances aforementioned. And we, Thomas, archbishop of Dublin, Thomas, archbishop of Cashel, John, archbishop of Tuam, Thomas, bishop of Lismore and Waterford, Thomas, bishop of Killaloe, William, bishop of Ossary, John, bishop of Leighlin, and John, bishop of Cloyne, being present in the said parliament at the request of our said most gracious lord the Duke of Clarence, lieutenant of our lord the King in Ireland, ceding, do fulminate sentence of excommunication against those contravening the statutes or ordinances aforesaid, and do excommunicate them by this present writing, reserving and each of us reserving, the absolution of ourselves and of our subjects if they be in peril of death.

ATIS · · SVÆ · XLIX

An Act that the King and his Successors be Kings of Ireland

Henry VIII is declared King of Ireland, 1541

enry II had established the lordship of Ireland in the 12th century. By the later Middle Ages, that lordship had greatly decreased. Many of the Gaelic chieftains had reasserted themselves politically and militarily. Despite the terms laid down in the Statute of Kilkenny, the English settlers continued to assimilate and adopt Irish laws and customs. By the late 15th century, the English lordship's authority was limited to the Pale, a heavily fortified 30-mile strip of territory that ran between Dublin and Drogheda.

The Tudor monarchy was characterized by a quest to consolidate the crown's power. This would turn out to be as true of Ireland as it was of England and Wales. Henry VIII, crowned in 1509, had paid little attention to Ireland in the early years of his reign, but by 1515 his interest was growing. Advisers informed him of his limited power beyond the Pale, with 'Iryshe enymyes' who 'lyveyth onely by the swerde' and 'Englyshe rebelles' whose loyalty to the crown was in question. They suggested a huge military assault on the island to establish a new influx of colonizers. Henry, always watching his purse, rejected this approach in favour of a less costly political one.

The king's early efforts to rule directly had chaotic results and the situation in Ireland was made even more unstable that year by the king's domestic circumstances. Henry had broken with Rome over his desire to divorce and, through the 1534 Act of Supremacy, had established himself as Supreme Head of the Church of England. Two years later, the Dublin parliament conferred on him the title of Supreme Head of the Church of Ireland. The Henrician Reformation in Ireland would have obvious practical consequences, including the dissolution of the monasteries. But while church and state became Protestant, the majority of people in Ireland, whether of Gaelic or Norman descent, remained wedded to the Catholic faith.

In another effort to bring some political stability to Ireland, Henry's new deputy, Sir Anthony St Leger, introduced a scheme of 'surrender and regrant' in 1541. This involved Gaelic chiefs forgoing their traditional titles in return for ones granted by Henry as their acknowledged sovereign. The 'Kinges Iryshe enemyes' now became loyal subjects of the crown, many of them travelling to London to present themselves at court. It was suggested that the Irish would 'more gladder obey your highness by name of King of this your land, than by name of lord thereof'. The change of title had secondary advantages. Since the English crown notionally held the lordship of Ireland through a papal grant, the break with Rome had serious implications for Henry's authority in Ireland.

On 18 June 1541 the Irish parliament passed a bill by acclamation declaring Henry and his successors the kings of Ireland. In Dublin the news was greeted with popular rejoicing and bonfires. His kingship of Ireland changed little in a practical sense, but it was clearly the logical conclusion of the state building and consolidation policies he had pursued elsewhere.

By the time of his death in 1547, the conquest of Ireland, although far from complete, was more extensive than ever.

Forasmuch as the king our most gracious dread sovereign lord, and his grace's most noble progenitors, kings of England, have been lords of this land of Ireland, having all manner kingly jurisdiction, power, pre-eminence, and authority royal, belonging or appertaining to the royal estate and majesty of a king, by the name of lords of Ireland, where the king's majesty, and his most noble progenitors, justly and rightfully were, and of right ought to be kings of Ireland, and so to be reputed, taken, named and called, and for lack of naming the king's majesty and his noble progenitors kings of Ireland, according to their said true and just title, style and name therein, hath been great occasion that the Irish men and inhabitants within this realm of Ireland have not been so obedient to the king's highness and his most noble progenitors, and to their laws, as they of right, and according to their allegiance and bounden duties ought to have been. Wherefore, at the humble pursuit, petition, and request of the lords spiritual and temporal, and other the king's loving, faithful and obedient subjects of this his land of Ireland, and by their full assents, be it enacted, ordained, and established by authority of this present parliament, that the king's highness, his heirs and successors, kings of England, be always kings of this land of Ireland, and that his majesty, his heirs and successors, have the name, style, title, and honour of king of this land of Ireland, with all manner honours, pre-eminences, prerogatives, dignities, and other things whatsoever they be, to the estate and majesty of a king imperial appertaining or belonging; and that his majesty, his heirs and successors, be from henceforth named, called, accepted, reputed, and taken to be kings of this land of Ireland to have, hold, and enjoy the said style, title, majesty and honours of king of Ireland, with all manner pre-eminences, prerogatives, dignities and all other the premises, unto the king's highness, his heirs and successors for ever, as united and knit to the imperial crown of the realm of England.

'Proclamation shall be made.'

And be it further enacted by authority aforesaid, that on this side the first day of July next coming, proclamation shall be made in all shires within this land of Ireland, of the tenor and sentences of this act. And if any person or persons, of what estate, dignity, or condition, soever they or he be, subject or resident within this land of Ireland, after the said first day of July, by writing or imprinting, or by any exterior act or deed, maliciously procure or do, or cause to be procured or done any thing or things to the peril of the king's majesty's most royal person, or maliciously give occasion by writing, deed, print or act, whereby the king's majesty, his heirs or successors, or any of them might be disturbed or interrupted of the crown of this realm.

Hugh O'Neill's War Aims

Irish religious, legal and property demands during the Nine Years War, November 1599

HUGH O'NEILL (C. 1540–1616)

Conscientia mille t.

From 1534 the English crown regained control of Ireland through force, patronage and plantation. Now the task of ruling Ireland had become not only political and military, but also religious. While the Protestant Reformation was well under way in England, Ireland remained Catholic. Religion became intrinsically bound up with identity. Catholicism and Gaelic culture were two sides of the one coin. Faith and fatherland became a potent rallying cry.

The steadfast adherence of the Irish majority to Catholicism also had security implications for England. Catholic Spain, which had been planning an invasion of England since 1559, viewed Ireland as the soft underbelly of English power. Still, while the Reformation made little impact on Ireland, English military efforts were more successful. By the end of the century, the crown had seen off successive rebellions to the point that almost all of Ireland was under its effective control. Only Ulster remained as the last bastion of Gaelic Ireland.

An uneasy peace existed in Ulster. The Gaelic Irish chieftains were wary of English encroachments, while the English rulers were unhappy about leaving the Gaelic lords in place as a reminder of their limited power. In the end, an attempt by the lord deputy, Sir William FitzWilliam, to break up the MacMahon lordship in Cavan ended the stand-off. Fearing a similar fate, the Ulster chieftains launched a pre-emptive rebellion. What began as a local effort to keep the English out of Ulster eventually escalated to a nationwide rebellion against English rule in Ireland. The conflict that ensued became known as the Nine Years War.

The man who came to lead the rebellion was Hugh O'Neill, 2nd earl of Tyrone. O'Neill's political development was somewhat unusual. He had been brought up within the English Pale and indoctrinated in the ways of the court. He was on favourable terms with Elizabeth I, and during previous rebellions had fought on the side of the queen. For years he had seemed the epitome of the loyal servant to the crown. By the mid-1590s, however, this relationship had broken down as his strength in Ulster brought him into conflict with the English authorities. O'Neill began to emphasize his Gaelic authority by offering, covertly at first, his support to the Ulster rebels.

The Nine Years War, also known as O'Neill's Rebellion, began in Ulster in April 1594. O'Neill was a courageous and calculating military leader and his success on the battlefield came not only from his tactical ability but also from his careful training of men. In particular, his skilful deployment of musketeers and cavalry brought success. The rebels believed that outside help would be crucial, and the Ulster chieftains looked to Philip of Spain for help in a war to preserve Catholicism, even though an earlier attempt by the Spanish Armada in 1588 to breach England through Ireland had been a disaster. Although religion had not prompted the rebellion, its leaders hoped to sustain it by bringing the Old English into an alliance to make the conflict one about Catholicism rather than ethnicity or culture. O'Neill himself was unenthusiastic about this strategy, and this doubtless influenced the Old English, who failed to be persuaded.

By 1599, O'Neill had begun to organize diplomacy in Rome to win papal support. Later that year he started to emphasize the religious nature of the Irish conflict in a set of war aims. This strategy worked to a point: Pope Clement VIII gave his support to O'Neill and the Irish rebels, but refused to excommunicate the Catholics who continued to support the queen. This was vital in maintaining the Old English loyalty to the crown.

After abortive efforts to send Spanish fleets in 1596 and 1597, clement weather, at last, in December 1601 allowed them to reach Kinsale. Their luck did not last long. When Spanish forces landed, they were almost immediately beaten back by the English. The Battle of Kinsale was the decisive turning point in the war. O'Neill limped on for another 18 months before surrendering unconditionally in 1603. The Treaty of Mellifont, which followed the surrender, offered O'Neill and the other Gaelic chieftains remarkably generous terms. Not only were they pardoned, but they were not wholly dispossessed.

Nevertheless, there was an extraordinary and baffling coda some four years later. In September 1607, O'Neill and Rory O'Donnell, earl of Tyrconnell, led an exodus of the Ulster chieftains, setting sail for Europe from Rathmullen. The reason for this 'Flight of the Earls' has never been clear, but the impact – culturally, psychologically and practically – was immense. The collapse of this last bastion of power was a colossal blow to Gaelic Ireland. Desertion provided the crown with land that would be used for 'planting' British families. It was the end of one culture and the beginning of another.

With his emphasis on faith and country, O'Neill became an icon of nationalist Ireland during the 19th century. The Young Irelander John Mitchel wrote that he was the 'first for many a century, to conceive and almost to realize the grand thought of creating a new Irish nation'. Mitchel was wrong on the facts, but as an interpretation it was a powerful weapon in the propaganda war against English rule.

<hr />

1. That the catholic, apostolic, and Roman religion be openly preached and taught throughout all Ireland, as well in cities as borough towns, by bishops, seminary priests, Jesuits, and all other religious men.

2. That the Church of Ireland be wholly governed by the pope.

3. That all cathedrals and parish churches, abbeys, and all other religious houses, with all tithes and church lands, now in the hands of the English, be presently restored to the catholic churchmen.

4. That all Irish priests and religious men, now prisoners in England or Ireland, be presently set at liberty, with all temporal Irishmen, that are troubled for their conscience, and to go where they will, without further trouble.

5. That all Irish priests and religious men may freely pass and repass, by sea and land, to and from foreign countries.

6. That no Englishman may be a churchman in Ireland.

7. That there be erected an university upon the crown rents of Ireland, wherein all sciences shall be taught according to the manner of the catholic Roman church.

8. That the governor of Ireland be at least an earl, and of the privy council of England, bearing the name of viceroy.

9. That the lord chancellor, lord treasurer, lord admiral, the council of state, the justices of the laws, queen's attorney, queen's serjeant, and all other officers appertaining to the council and law of Ireland, be Irishmen.

10. That all principal governments of Ireland, as Connaught, Munster, etc., be governed by Irish noblemen.

11. That the master of ordnance, and half the soldiers with their officers resident in Ireland, be Irishmen.

12. That no Irishman's heirs shall lose their lands for the faults of their ancestors.

13. That no Irishman's heir under age shall fall in the queen's or her successors' hands, as a ward, but that the living be put to the heir's profit, and the advancement of his younger brethren, and marriages of his sisters, if he have any.

14. That no children nor any other friends be taken as pledges for the good abearing of their parents, and, if there be any such pledges now in the hands of the English, they must presently be released.

15. That all statutes made against the preferment of Irishmen as well in their own country as abroad, be presently recalled.

16. That the queen nor her successors may in no sort press an Irishman to serve them against his will.

17. That O'Neill, O'Donnell, the Earl of Desmond, with all their partakers may peacably enjoy all lands and privileges that did appertain to their predecessors 200 years past.

18. That all Irishmen, of what quality they be, may freely travel in foreign countries, for their better experience, without making any of the queen's officers acquainted withal.

19. That all Irishmen may freely travel and traffic all merchandises in England as Englishmen, paying the same rights and tributes as the English do.

20. That all Irishmen may freely traffic with all merchandises, that shall be thought necessary by the council of state of Ireland for the profit of their republic, with foreigners or in foreign countries, and that no Irishman shall be troubled for the passage of priests or other religious men.

21. That all Irishmen that will may learn, and use all occupations and arts whatsoever.

22. That all Irishmen may freely build ships of what burden they will, furnishing the same with artillery and all munition at their pleasure.

CONDITIONS TO

BE OBSERVED BY

the Brittiſh *Undertakers*

of the Eſcheated Lands in

VLSTER,&c.

---

1. What the *Brittiſh* Vn-
dertakers ſhall haue.

FIrſt, the Landes to be   The Præcincts.
vndertaken by them,
are diuided into ſun-
dry *Præcincts*, of different quantities.

    Euery *Præcinct* is   The Proportions
ſubdiuided into *Proportions* of three ſorts,
Great, *Middle*, and *Small*.

The great *Proportion* containeth 2000.
Engliſh Acres at the leaſt.

The middle *Proportion* cõtaineth 1500.
Acres at the leaſt.

        A 2   The

Ulster Plantation

*Conditions to be observed by the British undertakers
of the escheated lands in Ulster, etc., 1610*

Plantation was used by the Tudors to colonize, subdue and reform Ireland. English families were brought to Ireland in coherent settlements in the hope that their own manners and Protestantism would act as 'civilizing' influences on their Gaelic Irish neighbours. Small privately organized schemes were superseded by larger crown ones in Munster, Laois-Offaly and eventually Ulster, using land confiscated from Irish rebels. However, with settlers arriving in insufficient numbers, and those who did come uninterested in creating a new England in Ireland, these early plantations were largely not successful.

The Flight of the Earls in 1607 saw lands – amounting to some two million acres – forfeited or 'escheated' to the English crown. This provided an opportunity to impose English authority on an area that had hitherto vehemently and successfully resisted it. A succession of three commissions was established to survey the extent and nature of the lands available, which led between 1609 and 1610 to a plan for the plantation of Ulster.

Covering counties Armagh, Cavan, Donegal, Fermanagh, Coleraine (Derry) and Tyrone, the scheme involved a division of land into parcels of 2000, 1500 and 1000 acres. These would be granted to three different types: undertakers, servitors and 'natives'. Undertakers were English or Scottish, who would assume responsibility for building defences and defending the settlement. They were charged with settling 24 males for every thousand acres. Servitors were civil and military servants of the crown. 'Natives' were Irish who had assisted the crown during the Nine Years War. These last grants amounted to around 20 percent of land in the six counties involved. Unlike Munster, where the Irish tenants were scattered across the plantations, the Ulster plan designated specific areas where they would reside.

There were problems from the outset. Although the commissions managed to collect a degree of information on the areas at stake, the crown refused to pay for proper mapping. The result was that many of the settlers received more land than their grants stipulated, which encouraged them to leave their existing Irish tenants where they were rather than gather them together. Moreover, the Gaelic Irish proved able and willing to pay higher rents for land, which provided an incentive for settlers to keep them on as tenants.

New settlers, who were quite reasonably reluctant to move to a country that had been at war with the crown for almost a decade, were also hard to attract. Fear that O'Neill and his allies would return to reclaim their lands was a significant factor in limiting the appeal of plantation. By 1622, a little over ten years after the Ulster plantation began, only 13,000 English-born adults had settled in the planted areas. Perhaps the only notable success in fulfilling the terms of the grant had been the incorporation of four towns – Dungannon, Coleraine, Londonderry and Belfast.

For England, in the short term, the official plantation was neither a failure nor a great success. In fact, the real achievement occurred beyond the official scheme in counties Antrim and Down, which were planted privately around the same time. The proximity of Scotland by sea had facilitated a centuries-long tradition of migration between the two countries. By 1636 the numbers of Scots emigrating to Ireland was so great that they were prohibited from settling without a licence. Even if the official plantation had little impact, the process of planting as a whole changed the character of Ulster profoundly. Privatization succeeded where central government had failed.

1. WHAT THE BRITISH UNDERTAKERS SHALL HAVE.

First, the lands to be undertaken by them, are divided into sundry precincts of different quantities.

Every precinct is subdivided into proportions of three sorts, great, middle and small.

The great proportion containeth 2000 English acres at the least.

The middle proportion containeth 1500 acres at the least.

The small proportion containeth 1000 acres at the least.

Unto every of which proportions such bog and wood shall be allowed, as lieth within the same, for which no rent shall be reserved.

The precincts are by name distinguished, part for the English, and part for the Scottish, as appeareth by the table of distribution of the precincts.

Every precinct shall be assigned to one principal undertaker and his consort, as will appear by the table of assignation of the precincts.

The chief undertakers shall be allowed two middle proportions if they desire the same; otherwise no one undertaker is to be allowed above one great proportion.

They shall have an estate in fee simple to them and their heirs.

They shall have power to create manors, to hold courts baron twice every year and not oftener, and power to create tenures in socage to hold of themselves.

They, their heirs and assigns, for the space of 7 years next ensuing, shall have liberty to export out of Ireland all commodities growing or arising upon their own land undertaken, without paying custom or imposition.

They, their heirs and assigns, for the space of 5 years next ensuing, shall have freedom to import into Ireland out of Great Britain, victual and utensils for their households, materials and tools for their buildings and husbandry, and cattle to stock and manure the lands undertaken, without paying any custom or imposition; which shall not extend to any commodities transported by way of merchandise.

'Every of the said undertakers …
shall take the oath of supremacy.'

They shall have allowance of timber for their buildings to be erected upon their proportions, the same to be taken in any of the precincts, by the assignment of the commissioners, without paying anything for the same for the space of two years; and after that time expired every undertaker to hold to his own use the timber and woods remaining upon his own proportion.

The principal undertaker shall have one advowson within his precinct to him and his heirs.

2. WHAT THE SAID UNDERTAKERS SHALL FOR THEIR PART PERFORM.

They shall yearly yield unto his majesty for every proportion of 1000 acres, five pound six shillings eight pence English, and so rateably for the great proportions; the first half year's payment to begin at Michaelmas 1614.

Every of the said undertakers shall hold the lands so undertaken in free and common socage, as of the castle of Dublin, and by no greater service.

Every of the said undertakers of a great proportion, shall within 3 years to be accounted from Easter next, build thereupon a stone house, with a strong court or bawn about it; and every undertaker of a middle proportion shall within the same time build a stone or brick house thereupon, with a strong court or bawn about it; and every undertaker of a small proportion, shall within the same time make thereupon a strong court or bawn at least.

Every undertaker shall within three years, to be accounted from Easter next, plant or place upon a small proportion, the number of 24 able men of the age of 18 years or upwards, being English or inland Scottish; and so rateably upon the other proportions; which numbers shall be reduced into 10 families at least, to be settled upon every small proportion, and rateably upon the other proportions, in this manner, viz. the principal undertaker and his family to be settled upon a demesne of 300 acres, two fee-farmers upon 120 acres a piece, three leaseholders for three lives or 21 years upon 100 acres a piece, and upon the residue being 160 acres, four families or more of husbandmen, artificers or cottagers, their portions of land to be assigned by the principal undertaker at his discretion.

Every of the said undertakers shall draw their tenants to build houses for themselves and their families, not scattering, but together, near the principal house or bawn, as for their mutual defence and strength, as for the making of villages and townships.

The said undertakers, their heirs and assigns, shall have ready in the houses at all times, a convenient store of arms which may be viewed and mustered every half year according to the manner of England.

Every of the said undertakers before he be received to be an undertaker, shall take the oath of supremacy, either in the chancery of England or Scotland, or before the commissioners to be appointed for the establishment of the plantation, and shall also conform themselves in religion according to his majesty's laws; and every of their undertenants being chief of a family, shall take the like oath before the said commissioners or the justices of assize coming into the county, wherein the said tenants shall be placed, at the next assizes, after they shall sit down and inhabit in the said several counties. And they and their families shall be also conformable in religion, as aforesaid.

Every of the said undertakers for the space of five years, to be accounted from Michaelmas next, shall be resident himself in person upon his portion, or place some such other person thereupon, as shall be allowed by the state of England or Ireland, and shall take the oath of supremacy, and likewise be himself with his family conformable in religion as aforesaid, who shall be resident during the said five years, unless by reason of sickness or other important cause, he be licensed by the lord deputy and council of Ireland to absent himself for a time.

The said undertakers, their heirs and assigns, shall not alien or demise their portions or any part thereof to the mere Irish, or to such persons as will not take the said oath of supremacy, and to that end a proviso shall be insert in their letters patent, that the parcel of land so aliened shall be forfeited.

The said undertakers shall not alien their portions during five years to be accounted from Michaelmas next, but unto their under tenants in the form before expressed in the fourth article. The said undertakers shall not reserve any uncertain rent but the same shall be expressly set down without reference to the custom of the country.

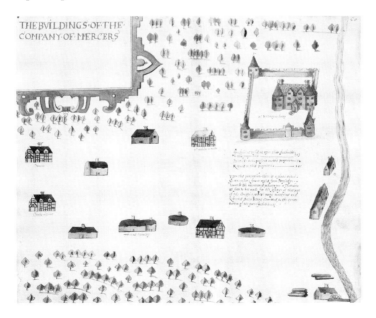

3. IN WHAT MANNER THE SAID PERFORMANCE SHALL BE.

The said undertakers either in person or by such agents as shall be allowed by the councils of estate of England or Scotland respectively, shall before midsummer day next, repair unto the realm of Ireland, and offer themselves to the lord deputy and the commissioners for the plantation, who shall take order with the said undertakers for the distribution of the proportions in their every precinct, either by agreement or lot, so as every undertaker shall know his portion if the same be not distributed here in England before.

The said undertakers by themselves or their said agents, shall take possession of their several portions, and sit upon down the same before Michaelmas next.

The said undertakers shall bring over into Ireland, and plant and place upon their several proportions, the several numbers of men and families aforesaid, viz. one third part before the feast of All Saints in the year of our Lord God 1611.

The said undertakers shall take out their letters patent either in England or Ireland at their election, before midsummer day next.

> ‘The said undertakers shall bring over into Ireland …
> the several numbers of men and families aforesaid.’

The said undertakers shall before the feast of All Saints next make their several courts or bawns upon their proportions, and erect habitations for one third part of the men and families which they are to plant thereupon; before the first day of May then next ensuing they shall erect habitations for the other third part, and provide and bring in place all the materials for building of their stone houses; and before the feast of All Saints 1611 following, they shall erect habitations for the residue of their men and families, and in the meantime proceed in the building of their stone houses, so as they may be fully finished within three years as aforesaid.

Every undertaker before the ensealing of their letters patent, shall enter into bond or recognizance with good sureties to his majesty's use in the office of his majesty's chief remembrancer in England or Ireland, or his majesty's exchequer or chancery in Scotland, to perform the aforesaid articles according to the several distinctions of building, planting, residence, alienation within five years, and making of certain estates to their tenants, viz. the undertakers of the greatest proportion to become bound in four hundred pounds, of the middle, in three hundred pounds, of the least, in two hundred pounds, which bonds or recognizances shall be delivered up after five years upon certificate of the L. deputy and the council, that the true meaning of the conditions thereof hath been performed.

Cromwell's Report to Parliament after Drogheda

Report to the Honourable William Lenthall, Esquire, speaker of the parliament, 17 September 1649

Oliver Cromwell (1599–1658)

The sense of grievance among Ulster Catholics caused by their dispossession remained very much alive in the first half of the early 17th century, while events in England and Scotland also created a climate of uncertainty. Radical Protestantism was in the ascendant and had established its power in the English parliament. For many Protestant MPs, Charles I's authoritarianism and his determination to enforce an almost Catholic style of worship in the churches in England and Scotland made him a monarch to be opposed almost at all costs.

Irish Catholics looked on this clash between the ultra-Protestant parliament and the crown with apprehension, since a parliamentary victory over the king could have profound effects on their rights to property and freedom of worship. Hoping to gain from English divisions (and fearing what might happen if they did not), the Irish in Ulster planned a rebellion to seize Dublin castle and reclaim their lands from settlers. In the event, things did not work out as intended. Instead of a full-scale rebellion, there was only a local uprising. On the night of 22 October 1641, settlers in Ulster came under attack from native Irish. Some 4000 planters died and a similar number fled to Britain. The violence was unquestionably horrific and was immediately seized upon by Protestant propagandists, who published lurid and spine-chilling accounts. At a time when radical Protestantism in Britain was at it most vehement, these 'Popish massacres' were offered as a bloody example of Catholic treachery.

The Ulster rebels were demanding stronger property rights and religious freedom, but they also stressed their loyalty to Charles I. The rebellion spread first across Ulster before moving south. In contrast to Hugh O'Neill's revolt decades earlier, this time the Old English of the Pale and beyond joined with the Gaelic Irish cause. Here was an insurgency of all Catholic Ireland. In May 1642, supported by the Catholic church in Ireland and on the Continent, these confederates formalized their alliance and structures in Kilkenny to establish a government for two-thirds of the country.

While events in Ireland were cause for concern in Scotland and England, naturally the conflict between crown and parliament, and the resulting civil war, were more pressing. By 1649 the crown had been defeated (leaving Charles I without his head) and replaced by a republican Commonwealth. Seen from London, Ireland was a country in chaos and one dominated by a Catholic force hostile to the British revolution. This was a situation that could not continue. To that end, parliament dispatched Oliver Cromwell as lord lieutenant of Ireland and commander of an army that would bring the country to order. Cromwell was a gentleman politician turned military organizer. Having undergone a Calvinist conversion almost 20 years earlier, he was a deeply committed Puritan, who regarded his mission in Ireland as one of religious right as much as regaining political control. He also saw it as a reckoning for the 1641 massacre of Ulster Protestants. He had at his disposal the New Model Army, the well resourced and disciplined parliamentary force established in 1645. Ominously for Ireland it had never suffered a significant defeat.

Landing unopposed in Dublin in mid-August 1649, Cromwell and his troops cut a swathe through the country, first heading north. On 10 September Cromwell summonsed the English Royalist governor of Drogheda to the effect that he had 24 hours to surrender the heavily fortressed town. Once news reached Cromwell that this had been rejected, he issued the order for bombardment to begin. Once the town had been breached, the New Model Army began carrying out Cromwell's order that no quarter should be given. Some contemporary accounts suggested his men killed every soldier, priest and civilian they came across. The level of violence was shocking even for the times. Perhaps most infamously, St Peter's church was razed and the 100 people who had sought sanctuary inside were burned alive.

Some have suggested that the brutality of Drogheda represents an early form of 'shock and awe'. Cromwell's strategy was that other towns, learning by example, would surrender quickly and peacefully. For the most part it worked; after Drogheda, only Wexford refused to surrender, and suffered a similar fate. Cromwell was a man of his time in that no quarter was given, should surrender be refused. Nevertheless, in his own reports to the speaker of the English parliament, he made it clear that there was more to the violence in Drogheda than mere military tactics. The Puritan in Cromwell wanted vengeance. It was warfare as retribution.

In the 40 weeks Cromwell was in Ireland, he 'accomplished a more complete control of Ireland than had been achieved under any English monarch'. Through physical force and the land settlements that followed, he changed the face of Ireland, perhaps more than any other individual in the country's history.

Sir, Your Army being safely arrived at Dublin; and the Enemy endeavouring to draw all his forces together about Trim and Tecroghan, as my intelligence gave … I resolved … to take the field. And accordingly, upon Friday the 30th of August last, rendezvoused with eight regiments of foot, six of horse and some troops of dragoons, three miles on the north side of Dublin. The design was, To endeavour the regaining of Tredah; or tempting the Enemy, upon his hazard of the loss of that place, to fight. Your Army came before the Town upon Monday following. Where having pitched, as speedy course was taken as could be to frame our batteries; which took up the more time because divers of the battering guns were on shipboard. Upon Monday the 9th of this instant, the batteries began to play. Whereupon I sent Sir Arthur Ashton, the then Governor, a summons, To deliver the Town to the use of the Parliament of England. To the which receiving no satisfactory answer, I proceeded that day to beat down the Steeple of the Church on the south side of the Town, and to beat down a Tower not far from the same place.

… Our guns not being able to do much that day, it was resolved to endeavour to do our utmost the next day to make breaches assaultable, and by the help of God to storm them. The place pitched up upon was that part of the Town-wall next a Church called St. Mary's; which was the rather chosen because we did hope that if we did enter and possess that Church, we should be the better able to keep it against their horse and foot until we could make way for the entrance of our horse; and we did not conceive that any part of the Town would afford the like advantage for that purpose with this. The batteries planted were two; one was for that part of the Wall against the east end of the said Church; the other against the Wall on the south side. Being somewhat long in battering, the Enemy made six retrenchments: three of them from the said Church to Duleek Gate; and three of them from the east end of the Church to the Town-wall and so backward. The guns, after some two or three hundred shot, beat down the corner Tower, and opened two reasonable good breaches in the east and south Wall.

'About five o'clock in the evening, we began the Storm.'

Upon Tuesday the 10th of this instant, about five o'clock in the evening, we began the Storm: and after some hot dispute we entered, about seven or eight hundred men; the Enemy disputing it very stiffly with us. And indeed, through the advantages of the place, and the courage God was pleased to give the defenders, our men were forced to retreat quite out of the breach, not without some considerable loss; Colonel Castle being there shot in the head, whereof he presently died; and divers officers and soldiers doing their duty killed and wounded. There was a Tenalia to flanker the south Wall of the Town, between Duleek Gate and the corner Tower before mentioned; – which our men entered, wherein they found some forty or fifty of the Enemy, which they put to the sword. And this 'Tenalia' they held: but it being without the Wall, and the sally-port through the Wall into that Tenalia being choked up with some of the Enemy which were killed in it, it proved of no use for an entrance into the Town that way.

Although our men that stormed the breaches were forced to recoil, as is before expressed; yet, being encouraged to recover their loss, they made a second attempt: wherein God was pleased so to animate them that they got ground of the Enemy, and by the goodness of God, forced him to quit his entrenchments. And after a very hot dispute, the Enemy having both horse and foot, and we only foot, within the Wall, – they gave ground, and our men became masters both of their retrenchments and of the Church; which indeed, although they made our entrance the more difficult, yet they proved of excellent use to us; so that the Enemy could not 'now' annoy us with their horse, but thereby we had advantage to make the ground, that so we might let in our own horse; which accordingly was done, though with much difficulty.

'I forbade them to spare any that were in arms in the Town.'

Divers of the Enemy retreated into the Mill-Mount: a place very strong and of difficult access; being exceedingly high, having a good graft, and strongly palisadoed. The Governor, Sir Arthur Ashton, and divers considerable Officers being there, our men getting up to them, were ordered by me to put them all to the sword. And indeed, being in the heat of action, I forbade them to spare any that were in arms in the Town: and, I think, that night they put to the sword about 2,000 men; – divers of the officers and soldiers being fled over the Bridge into the other part of the Town, where about 100 of them possessed St Peter's Church-steeple, some of the west Gate, and others a strong Round Tower next the Gate called St Sunday's. These being summoned to yield to mercy, refused. Whereupon I ordered the steeple of St Peter's Church to be fired, when one of them was heard to say in the midst of the flames: 'God damn me, God confound me; I burn, I burn.'

The next day, the other two Towers were summoned; in one of which was about six or seven score; but they refused to yield themselves: and we knowing that hunger

must compel them, set only good guards to secure them from running away until their stomachs were come down. From one of the said Towers, notwithstanding their condition, they killed and wounded some of our men. When they submitted, their officers were knocked on the head; and every tenth man of the soldiers killed; and the rest shipped for the Barbadoes. The soldiers in the other Tower were all spared, as to their lives only; and shipped likewise for the Barbadoes.

I am persuaded that this is a righteous judgment of God upon these barbarous wretches, who have imbrued their hands in so much innocent blood; and that it will tend to prevent the effusion of blood for the future. Which are the satisfactory grounds to such actions, which otherwise cannot but work remorse and regret.

… And now give me leave to say how it comes to pass that this work is wrought. It was set upon some of our hearts, That a great thing should be done, not by power or might, but by the Spirit of God. And is it not so, clearly? That which caused your men to storm so courageously, it was the Spirit of God, who gave your men courage, and took it away again; and gave the Enemy courage, and took it away again; and gave your men courage again, and therewith this happy success. And therefore it is good that God alone have all the glory.

It is remarkable that these people, at the first, set up the Mass in some places of the Town that had been monasteries; but afterwards grew so insolent that, the last Lord's day before the storm, the Protestants were thrust out of the great Church called St Peter's, and they had public Mass there: and in this very place near 1,000 of them were put to the sword, fleeing thither for safety. I believe all their friars were knocked on the head promiscuously but two; the one of which was Father Peter Taaff, brother to the Lord Taaff, whom the soldiers took, the next day, and made an end of. The other was taken in the Round Tower, under the repute of Lieutenant, and when he understood that the officers in the Tower had no quarter he confessed he was a Friar; but that did not save him.

'I most humbly pray the Parliament may be pleased.'

… I most humbly pray the Parliament may be pleased 'that' this Army may be maintained; and that a consideration may be had of them, and of the carrying on affairs here, 'such' as may give a speedy issue to this work. To which there seems to be a marvellous fair opportunity offered by God … And indeed if God please to finish it here as He hath done in England, the War is like to pay itself.

Treaty of Limerick

Terms of settlement following the Williamite war, 1691

Baron Godert de Ginkel (1630–1703)

The Commonwealth of England came to an end in 1660 with the restoration of the monarchy under Charles II, son of the executed Charles I. He made few concessions of style or substance to the feelings of his former opponents. He forged alliances with Catholic France and tried to remove anti-Catholic legislation, although his efforts were blocked by the English parliament and the monarchy, which remained resolutely Protestant. If relations between the two were tense, they broke down completely when Charles's brother, James II, ascended to the throne in 1685.

Where Charles had been well disposed towards Catholics, James had actually converted to Catholicism. Soon after he became king, James defied the Test Act, which forbade Catholics from holding public office, by appointing Catholics to the army. When the English parliament protested, he prorogued it. It would never meet again while he was king.

James's Catholicism increasingly alarmed British Protestants. Matters came to a head in June 1688 when his wife gave birth to a son. Until then the king's Protestant daughter, Mary, the wife of Prince William of Orange, had been first in line to the throne. A new Catholic heir raised the prospect that Britain would be permanently lost for Protestantism. On 30 June, seven Protestant noblemen invited Mary's husband to intervene and end the attack on 'their religion, liberties and properties'. William landed in England on 5 November – the anniversary of Guy Fawkes's failed Gunpowder Plot.

James fled to France, arriving in Paris on Christmas day, 1688. His ally Louis XIV had arranged lavish accommodation for James and his family, but made it clear that this was a temporary respite. James would have to retrieve his crown from William and restore the balance of power in Europe. Pushed back into the ring by Louis, the half-hearted James travelled to Ireland, which became the local theatre of a European war.

Irish Catholics enthusiastically welcomed James when he landed at Kinsale with war supplies and French troops in March 1689. Whatever the broader geopolitical implications, the war locally would be a battle for supremacy between Irish Catholics and Protestants.

The Williamite army made little progress until the summer of 1690. On 1 July those forces, led by William for the first time, won the Battle of the Boyne. Afterwards, James was among the first to flee to France. Despite his desertion, the 'war of the two kings' continued into the following year. Only after further Williamite victories at Aughrim and Galway in July 1691 was it clear that the tide had turned. With the last significant stronghold of Limerick under siege, the Jacobite leader, Patrick Sarsfield, opened talks with the Williamite Baron de Ginkel. The war ended with the Treaty of Limerick on 3 October.

Although he later became an icon for Irish Protestants, William cared little about Ireland. In an effort to conclude matters swiftly and ship out, his government offered the Jacobites exceptionally generous terms. To prevent a return to war, the military provisions allowed the soldiers of the Jacobite army to withdraw to France. Some 12,000 of these 'Wild Geese' travelled to the Continent, beginning a tradition of Irish brigades fighting in Continental armies. Agreement on the civil articles of the Treaty took longer. The first article guaranteed that 'the Roman Catholics of this kingdom shall enjoy such privileges in the exercise of their religion as are consistent with the laws of Ireland, or as they did enjoy in the reign of king Charles the second'. Initially only Sarsfield's men in Limerick were to have had guaranteed their rights to property, to practice their professions and to bear arms. Subsequently in the second draft, this was extended to include Galway, Mayo, Cork, Kerry and Clare. However, when the Treaty was sent to London, this latter clause was missing. William and Mary ordered the restoration of the missing clause the following February.

To Irish Protestants the Treaty was abhorrent. The terms were not only lenient but also positively dangerous. The Dublin parliament spent much of the 1690s avoiding enactment of the Treaty. When it finally passed in 1697, it only did so in a bastardized version that managed entirely to distort the spirit of the original. Worse still was the series of penal laws enacted against Catholics in the same period.

What purports to be the Treaty stone on which the document was signed remains on display in Limerick city to this day. It has endured better than the Treaty itself, which, it was said, was broken 'before the ink in which it was writ had dried'.

Articles agreed upon the third day of October; one thousand six hundred and ninety-one, between the right honourable sir Charles Porter, knight, and Thomas Coningsby, esq., lords justices of Ireland, and his excellency the baron de Ginkel, lieutenant-general, and commander in chief of the English army, on the one part, and the right honourable Patrick earl of Lucan, Piercy viscount Galmoy, colonel Nicholas Purcel, colonel Nicholas Cusack, sir Toby Butler, colonel Garret Dillon, and colonel John Brown, on the other part, in the behalf of the Irish inhabitants in the city and county of Limerick, the counties of Clare, Kerry, Cork, Sligo, and Mayo:

In consideration of the surrender of the city of Limerick, and other agreements made between the said lieutenant-general Ginkel, the governor of the city of Limerick, and the generals of the Irish army, bearing date with these presents, for the surrender of the said city and submission of the said army, it is agreed, that:

1. THE ROMAN CATHOLICS of this kingdom shall enjoy such privileges in the exercise of their religion as are consistent with the laws of Ireland, or as they did enjoy in the reign of king Charles the second: and their majesties, as soon as their affairs will permit them to summon a parliament in this kingdom, will endeavour to procure the said Roman Catholics such farther security in that particular, as may preserve them from any disturbance upon the account of their said religion.

2. ALL THE INHABITANTS or residents of Limerick, or any other garrison now in the possession of the Irish, and all officers and soldiers now in arms, under any commission of king James, or those authorized by him to grant the same, in the several counties of Limerick, Clare, Kerry, Cork, and Mayo, or any of them; and all the commissioned officers in their majesties' quarters that belong to the Irish regiments now in being, that are treated with, and who are not prisoners of war, or have taken protection and who shall return and submit to their majesties' obedience, and their and every of their heirs, shall hold, possess, and enjoy all and every their estates of freehold and inheritance, and all the rights, titles

---

VIII.

The Inhabitants and Residents in the City of *Lymerick*, and other Garrisons, shall be permitted to remove their Goods, Chattles, and Provisions, out of the same, without being viewed and searched, or paying any manner of Duties, and shall not be compelled to leave the Houses or Lodgings they now have, for the space of six weeks next ensuing the Date hereof.

IX.

The Oath to be administred to such *Roman Catholics* as submit to their Majesties Government, shall be the Oath abovesaid, and no other.

X.

No person or persons, who shall at any time hereafter break these Articles, or any of them, shall thereby make, or cause any other person or persons to forfeit or lose the benefit of the same.

XI.

The Lords Justices and General do promise to use their utmost Endeavours, that all the persons comprehended in the above-mentioned Articles, shall be protected and defended from all Arrests, and Executions for Debt or Damage, for the space of eight months, next ensuing the Date hereof.

XII.

Lastly, the Lords Justices and General do undertake, that their Majesties will Ratifie these Articles within the space of eight months, or sooner, and use their utmost Endeavours, that the same shall be ratified and confirmed in Parliament.

XIII.

And whereas Colonel *John Brown* stood indebted to several Protestants, by Judgments of Record ; which appearing to the late

---

and interests, privileges and immunities, which they and every or any of them held, enjoyed, or were rightfully and lawfully entitled to in the reign of king Charles II., or at any time since, by the laws and statutes that were in force in the said reign of king Charles II., and shall be put in possession, by order of the government, of such of them as are in the king's hands, or the hands of his tenants, without being put to any suit or trouble therein; and all such estates shall be freed and discharged from all arrears of crown-rents, quit-rents, and other public charges incurred and become

'All … shall hold, possess, and enjoy all and every their estates of freehold and inheritance'

The Civil Articles of Lymerick. 9

late Government, the Lord *Tyrconnel*, and Lord *Lucan*, took away the Effects the said *John Brown* had to answer the said Debts, and promised to clear the said *John Brown* of the said Debts; which effects were taken for the publick use of the *Irish*, and their Army: For freeing the said Lord *Lucan* of his said Engagement, past on their publick Account, for Payment of the said Protestants, and for preventing the ruine of the said *John Brown*, and for satisfaction of his Creditors, at the instance of the Lord *Lucan*, and the rest of the Persons aforesaid, it is agreed, That the said Lords Justices, and the said Baron *de Ginckle*, shall intercede with the King and Parliament, to have the Estates secured to *Roman-Catholicks*, by Articles and Capitulation in this Kingdom, charged with, and equally liable to the payment of so much of the said Debts, as the said Lord *Lucan*, upon stating Accompts with the said *John Brown*, shall certifie under his Hand, that the Effects taken from the said *Brown* amount unto; which Accompt is to be stated and the Ballance certified by the said Lord *Lucan* in one and twenty days after the Date hereof:

For the true performance hereof, We have hereunto set our Hands,

Char. Porter.
Tho. Coningsby.
Bar. De. Ginckle.

Prefent
Scravemore.
H. Maccay.
T. Talmafh.

ANd *whereas* the said City of *Limerick* hath been since, in pursuance of the said Articles, surrendred unto Us. *Now know ye*, that We having considered of the

D

due since Michaelmas, 1688, to the day of the date hereof: and all persons comprehended in this article shall have, hold, and enjoy all their goods and chattels, real and personal, to them or any of them belonging and remaining, either in their own hands or the hands of any persons whatsoever, in trust for or for the use of them or any of them: and all and every the said persons, of what profession, trade or calling soever they be, shall and may use, exercise, and practise their several and respective professions, trades, and callings as freely as they did use, exercise, and enjoy the same in the reign of king Charles II., provided that nothing in this article contained be construed to extend to or restore any forfeiting person now out of the kingdom, except what are hereafter comprized: provided also, that no person whatsoever shall have or enjoy the benefit of this article, that shall neglect or refuse to take the oath of allegiance, made by act of parliament in England, in the first year of the reign of their present majesties, when thereunto required.

3. ALL MERCHANTS or reputed merchants of the city of Limerick, or of any other garrison now possessed by the Irish, or of any town or place in the counties of Clare or Kerry, who are absent beyond the seas, that not bore arms since their majesties' declaration in February, 1688, shall have the benefit of the second article in the same manner as if they were present, provided such merchants and reputed merchants do repair into this kingdom within the space of eight months from the date hereof.

4. THE FOLLOWING OFFICERS, viz., colonel Simon Lutterel, captain Rowland White, Maurice Eustace, of Yeomanstown, Chievers of Maystown, commonly called Mount Leinster, now belonging to the regiments in the aforesaid garrisons and quarters of the Irish army, who were beyond the seas, and sent thither upon affairs of their respective regiments or the army in general, shall have the benefit and advantage of the second article, provided they return hither within the space of eight months from the date of these presents, and submit to their majesties' government and take the above-mentioned oath.

'A general pardon of all attainders, outlawries, treasons … and other crimes.'

5. THAT ALL AND SINGULAR the said persons comprized in the second and third articles, shall have a general pardon of all attainders, outlawries, treasons, misprisions of treason, premunires, felonies, trespasses, and other crimes and misdemeanours whatsoever by them or any of them committed since the beginning of the reign of king James II.; and if any of them are attainted by parliament, the lords justices and general will use their best endeavours to get the same repealed by parliament and the outlawries to be reversed gratis, all but writing clerks' fees.

6. AND WHEREAS these present wars have drawn on great violences on both parts, and that if leave were given to the bringing all sorts of private actions, the animosities would probably continue that have been too long on foot, and the public disturbances last; for the quieting and settling, therefore, of this kingdom, and avoiding those inconveniences which would be the necessary consequence of the contrary, no person or persons whatsoever comprized in the foregoing articles shall be sued, molested, or impleaded at the suit of any party or parties whatsoever, for any trespasses by them committed, or for any arms, horses, money, goods, chattels, merchandizes, or provisions whatsoever by them seized or taken during the time of the war. And no person or persons whatsoever in the second or third articles comprized shall be sued, impleaded, or made accountable for the rents or mean rates of any lands, tenements, or houses by him or them received or enjoyed in this kingdom, since the beginning of the present war to the day of the date hereof, nor for any waste or trespass by him or them committed in any such lands, tenements, or houses; and it is also agreed that this article shall be mutual and reciprocal on both sides.

7. EVERY NOBLEMAN and gentleman comprized in the said second and third article, shall have liberty to ride with a sword and case of pistols, if they think fit, and keep a gun in their houses for the defence of the same, or for fowling.

8. THE INHABITANTS and residents in the city of Limerick, and other garrisons, shall be permitted to remove their goods, chattels, and provisions out of the same, without being viewed and searched, or paying any manner of duties, and shall not be compelled to leave the houses or lodgings they now have for the space of six weeks next ensuing the date hereof.

'Their majesties will ratify these articles within the space of eight months.'

9. THE OATH to be administered to such Roman Catholics as submit to their majesties' government, shall be the oath abovesaid and no other.

10. NO PERSON or persons who shall at any time hereafter break these articles, or any of them, shall thereby make, or cause any other person or persons to forfeit or lose the benefit of the same.

11. THE LORDS JUSTICES and general do promise to use their utmost endeavours, that all the persons comprehended in the above-mentioned articles shall be protected and defended from all arrests and executions for debt or damage, for the space of eight months next ensuing the date hereof.

12. LASTLY, THE LORDS JUSTICES and general do undertake that their majesties will ratify these articles within the space of eight months, or sooner, and use their utmost endeavours that the same shall be ratified and confirmed in parliament.

13. AND WHEREAS colonel John Brown stood indebted to several Protestants by judgments of record, which appearing to the late government, the lord Tyrconnell and lord Lucan took away the effects the said John Brown had to answer the said debts, and promised to clear the said John Brown of the said debts, which effects were taken for the public use of the Irish and their army: for freeing the said lord Lucan of his said engagement, past on their public account, for payment of the said Protestants, and for preventing the ruin of the said John Brown, and for satisfaction of his creditors, at the instance of the lord Lucan and the rest of the persons aforesaid, it is agreed that the said lords justices and the said baron de Ginkel, shall intercede with the king and parliament to have the estates secured to Roman Catholics by articles and capitulation in this kingdom charged with and equally liable to the payment of so much of the said debts as the said lord Lucan, upon stating accounts with the said John Brown, shall certify under his hand that the effects taken from the said John Brown amount unto; which account is to be stated, and the balance certified by the said lord Lucan in one and twenty days after the date hereof. For the true performance hereof we have hereunto set our hands:

Charles Porter, Thomas Coningsby, Baron de Ginkel. –
Present: *Scravemoer, H. Mackay, T. Talmach.*

A Letter to the Whole People of Ireland

From Drapier's Letters, *13 October 1724*

M.B. DRAPIER (JONATHAN SWIFT; 1667–1745)

The Williamite Settlement had established the Protestant Ascendancy in Ireland, but if Irish society was now built on a foundation of inequality, so too was the relationship between Ireland and Britain. While the view of Irish Protestants was that Ireland existed as a separate kingdom equal to Britain, British legislators cited Poynings's Law, passed in the 15th century, which declared that no legislation could be introduced or passed in an Irish parliament without crown consent.

The British parliament had passed some legislation designed to hinder the development of Irish trade and manufacturing, including a ban on the export of Irish woollen goods. The strong opposition of Protestant 'Patriots', such as William Molyneux, had had little effect. In fact the Irish position worsened when the Declaratory Act was passed in 1720 'for better securing the dependence of Ireland [on Britain]'.

A potent example of Ireland's inferior position came in the decision to grant William Wood, an ironmaster from Wolverhampton, a patent to coin more than £100,000 of small change for Ireland. There was no apparent need for the coinage and contemporary opinion was that the patent had been purchased from George I's mistress, the duchess of Kendal. There was trenchant opposition to the coinage in Ireland by merchants who feared that the economy would be flooded with worthless money. The introduction of 'Wood's Halfpence' in 1722 became a symbol of British contempt for Ireland and provoked a flood of pamphlets. The most famous of these were by M.B. Drapier, a Protestant linen draper. Drapier was, in fact, a pseudonym for Jonathan Swift, the dean of St Patrick's Cathedral in Dublin. It was a barely disguised ruse known about by most in the city.

By the time he came to write *Drapier's Letters*, Dean Swift was already an established political journalist and satirist. He had been born in Dublin in 1667. His English father was an officer in the King's Inns. After taking his degree in Trinity College Dublin, Swift left for England. He began to move in elite circles, acting as secretary to Sir William Temple – the politician and diplomat who had negotiated the marriage of King William III and Queen Mary II. He then abandoned a political career for one in the church, returning briefly to Ireland for ordination in 1695. His life in London as Sir William's secretary involved ecclesiastical affairs, political intrigue and journalism. Swift developed that distinctively acerbic style which he used to great effect in satires on London politics and even matters religious. Ultimately, his writing and his political dalliances saw him fall out of favour with the government; posted to Dublin as dean of St Patrick's Cathedral, Swift believed he had been sent into exile.

Swift always saw himself as a member of the Protestant elite. The circumstances of his unwilling return did little to suggest the creative energy that his time in Dublin would inspire. However, Swift was scandalized by the poverty he saw on his doorstep and infuriated by the injustice of Britain's treatment of Ireland. His first notable pamphlet on this subject was the 'Proposal for the universal use of Irish manufacture' (1720), in which he attacked the mercantilist trade laws that Britain used to hinder the growth of Irish industries. 'Burn everything English but their coal,' he urged. *Drapier's Letters* were in a similar vein and satirically attacked Wood's halfpenny in language that was accessible to many ordinary people. The first three letters focused on the mechanics of the coinage. In the fourth, published in October 1724, Drapier broadened his critique. Addressing the 'whole people of Ireland', he questioned the right of an English parliament to legislate for Ireland. He cited Molyneux, who had argued that 'government without the consent of the governed is the very definition of slavery'. This was radical stuff. His call for a boycott of the coin turned the fourth letter into something close to sedition.

The author was proclaimed and the printer arrested. A £300 reward was offered for discovering the origin of the letters. While it was well known that Swift had penned them, proving this was almost impossible. Two grand juries refused to find him guilty of seditious libel. In the event, Wood's patent was cancelled in September 1725. *Drapier's Letters* were widely regarded as the crucial factor in the campaign against the new coin. Swift, the reluctant Irishman, won widespread public acclaim. He was lauded as a great patriot not just by his contemporaries but also by later generations of Irish nationalists. Perhaps Alexander Pope summed this up best when he wrote:

> Let Ireland tell, how Wit upheld her cause,
> Her Trade supported, and supply'd her Laws;
> And leave on SWIFT this grateful verse ingrav'd,
> The Rights a Court attack'd, a Poet saved.

Having already written three Letters, upon so disagreeable a subject as Mr Wood and his halfpence; I conceived my task was at an end: but, I find that cordials must be frequently applied to weak constitutions, political as well as natural. A people long used to hardships, lose by degrees the very notions of liberty; they look upon themselves as creatures at mercy; and that all impositions laid on them by a stronger hand, are, in the phrase of the report, legal and obligatory. Hence proceed that poverty and lowness of spirit, to which a kingdom may be subject, as well as a particular person. And when Esau came fainting from the field, at the point to die, it is no wonder that he sold his birth-right for a mess of pottage.

'Who would leave a hundred pounds a year in England … to be paid a thousand in Ireland?'

… There is one comfortable circumstance in this universal opposition to Mr Wood, that the people sent over hither from England, to fill up our vacancies, ecclesiastical, civil and military, are on our side: money, the great divider of the world, hath by a strange revolution, been the great uniter of a most divided people. Who would leave a hundred pounds a year in England, (a country of freedom) to be paid a thousand in Ireland out of Wood's exchequer? The gentleman they have lately made primate, would never quit his seat in an English house of lords and his preferments at Oxford and Bristol, worth twelve hundred pounds a year, for four times the denomination here, but not half the value: therefore, I expect to hear he will be as good an Irishman, at least, upon this one article, as any of his bretheren; or even of us, who have had the misfortune to be born in this island. For those who, in the common phrase, do not come hither to learn the language, would never change a better country for worse, to receive brass instead of gold.

Another slander spread by Wood and his emissaries is that, by opposing him, we discover an inclination to shake off our dependence

(3)

A Letter, &c.

My Dear Countrymen,

H*AVING* already written Three *Letters* upon so disagreeable a Subject as Mr. *Wood* and his *Half-pence*; I conceived my Task was at an End: But I find, that Cordials must be frequently apply'd to weak Constitutions, *Political* as well as *Natural*. A People long used to Hardships, lose by Degrees the very Notions of *Liberty*, they look upon themselves as Creatures at Mercy, and that all Impositions laid on them by a stronger Hand, are, in the Phrase of the *Report*, *Legal* and *Obligatory*. Hence proceeds that *Poverty* and *Lowness of Spirit*, to which a *Kingdom* may be subject as well as a *Particular Person*. And when *Esau came fainting from the Field at the Point to Die*, it is no wonder that he *Sold his Birth-Right for a Mess of Pottage*:

I thought I had sufficiently shewn to all who could want Instruction, by what Methods they might safely proceed, whenever this *Coyn* should be offered to them: And I believe there hath not been for many Ages an Example of any Kingdom so firmly united in a Point of great Importance, as this of Ours is at present, against that detestable Fraud. But however, it so happens that some weak People begin to be allarmed a-new, by Rumours industriously spread. *Wood* prescribes to the News-Mongers in *London* what they are

upon the crown of England. Pray observe, how important a person is this same William Wood; and how the publick weal of two kingdoms, is involved in his private interest. First all those who refuse to take his coin are papists; for he tells us, that none but the papists are associated against him. Secondly, they dispute the King's prerogative. Thirdly, they are ripe for rebellion. And fourthly, they are going to shake off their dependence upon the crown of England; that is to say, they are going to chuse another King: for there can be no other meaning in this expression, however some may pretend to strain it.

'Those who come over hither to us …
tell us, that Ireland is a depending kingdom.'

And this gives me an opportunity of explaining, to those who are ignorant, another point, which hath often swelled in my breast. Those who come over hither to us from England, and some weak people among ourselves, whenever, in discourse, we make mention of liberty and property, shake their heads, and tell us, that Ireland is a depending kingdom; as if they would seem, by this phrase, to intend, that the people of Ireland is in some state of slavery or dependence, different from those of England: whereas, a depending kingdom is a modern term of art, unknown, as I have heard, to all antient civilians, and writers upon government; and Ireland is, on the contrary, called in some statues an imperial crown, as held only from God; which is as high a style, as any kingdom is capable of receiving. Therefore by this expression, a depending kingdom, there is no more understood, than that by a statute made here, in the 33rd year of Henry VIII, the king and his successors, are to be kings imperial of this realm, as united and knit to the imperial crown of England. I have looked over all the English and Irish statutes, without finding any law that makes Ireland depend upon England; any more than England doth upon Ireland. We have, indeed, obliged ourselves to have the same king with them; and consequently they are obliged to have the same king with us. For the law was made by our own parliament; and our ancestors then were not such fools (whatever they were in the preceding reign) to bring themselves under I know not what dependence, which is now talked of, without any ground of law, reason, or common sense.

'The remedy is wholly in your own hands.'

… It is true, indeed, that within the memory of man, the parliaments of England have sometimes assumed the power of binding this kingdom, by laws enacted there; wherein they were, at first, openly opposed (as far as truth, reason and justice are capable of opposing) by the famous Mr Molineaux, an English gentleman born here; as well as by several of the greatest patriots, and best Whigs in England; but the love and torrent of power prevailed. Indeed, the arguments on both sides were invincible. For in reason, all government without the consent of the governed, is the very definition of slavery: but in fact, eleven men well armed, will certainly subdue one single man in his shirt. But I have done. For those who have used power to cramp liberty, have gone so far as to resent even the liberty of complaining; although a Man upon the Rack, was never known to be refused the Liberty of roaring as loud as he thought fit.

… The remedy is wholly in your own hands … by the laws of God, of nature, of nations, and of your own country, you are and ought to be as free a people as your brethren in England.

Aims and Organization of the United Irishmen

The declaration, resolutions and constitution of the societies of United Irishmen, 1797

England's political and economic subjugation of Ireland remained a source of considerable and widespread resentment throughout the 18th century. The spirit of Molyneux and Swift was invoked by a minority of Protestant 'Patriots' such as Henry Flood and Henry Grattan as they endeavoured to free the Irish parliament from the shackles imposed by Britain. By the 1780s, the Patriots had gone beyond parliamentary campaigns to become a popular Protestant movement.

The Volunteers, an association that began as a militia but developed into a political campaign for greater autonomy for the Irish parliament, successfully pushed London into enacting legislative reforms known as the 'constitution of 1782'. This ushered in the years of 'Grattan's parliament', regarded later by many nationalists as a golden era of Irish parliamentary independence.

The reality was less positive. Parliament remained corrupt and unrepresentative. The inequality of legal status that lay at the heart of Ascendancy Ireland – a society where Anglicans enjoyed full rights, dissenters (Presbyterians) limited rights, and the majority Catholic population fewer still – remained unchanged.

Founded in Belfast on 18 October 1791, the Society of the United Irishmen was established as an organization to campaign to reform this situation. Influenced by the politics of the American and French Revolutions as well as by the philosophy of the European and Scottish enlightenments, its founders were middle-class Presbyterian radicals frustrated by the lack of civil rights available to them. They were joined by a Dublin Anglican, Theobald Wolfe Tone, who had recently published the pamphlet *An Argument on Behalf of the Catholics of Ireland*. This called on Protestant radicals to extend their commitment to political liberty beyond members of the reformed churches; its sales in Ireland were second only to those of Thomas Paine's *The Rights of Man*.

Based in Belfast and Dublin, the society began as a reform club, dedicated to amending the Irish constitution to extend civil and religious liberties. Believing that sectarian divisions in Ireland were the result of a policy by England to divide and conquer, the United Irishmen proposed that Ireland's strength would come, as Wolfe Tone put it, by marrying 'protestant, Catholic and dissenter under the common name of Irishman'. The United Irishmen's newspaper, the *Northern Star,* described the society's aim as being to make every Irishman a citizen and every citizen an Irishman.

What had started as a reform club had by the mid-1790s become a revolutionary conspiracy. With England at war with France, even political radicalism was seen as potentially seditious. In 1794 the society was banned. Re-formed as a secret oath-bound organization, the United Irishmen in Belfast adopted a new constitution in May 1795, followed by the Dublin society the next year. Their mission was to destroy the connection with England.

Through Wolfe Tone, the society successfully won French military support, but an invasion led by Admiral Hoche in December 1796 was aborted following terrible storms. Eighteen months later, the United Irishmen tried again, but the insurrection was localized in areas of Leinster and Ulster. It was effectively put down within four weeks. It succeeded only in killing thousands, inflaming sectarian hatred and convincing English politicians of the need to keep Ireland on a tight rein.

The United Irishmen's constitution was a dead letter. The society's oaths of secrecy had not prevented it becoming riddled with spies and informers. Its call for the uniting of faiths and denominations had too often been cast aside in favour of sectarian violence. Yet while failing on its own terms, the spirit of the society remained a potent force in Irish nationalism. As founders of the first modern separatist group, the United Irishmen would be revered as the fathers of Irish republicanism, setting an agenda for equality, unity and civil rights that remains potent today.

'We do pledge ourselves to our country, and mutually to each other.'

In the present era of reform, when unjust governments are falling in every quarter of Europe, when religious persecution is compelled to abjure her tyranny over conscience, when the rights of men are ascertained in theory, and that theory substantiated by practice, when antiquity can no longer defend absurd and oppressive forms, against the common sense and common interest of mankind, when all governments are acknowledged to originate from the people, and to be so far only obligatory, as they protect their rights, and promote their welfare, we think it our duty, as Irishmen, to come forward, and state what we feel to be our heavy grievance, and what we know to be its effectual remedy. We have no national government, we are ruled by Englishmen, and the servants of Englishmen, whose object is the interest of another country, whose instrument is corruption, and whose strength is the weakness of Ireland; and these men have the whole of the power and patronage of the country, as means to seduce and subdue the honesty of her representatives in the legislature. Such an extrinsic power, acting with uniform force, in a direction too frequently opposite to the true line of our obvious interest, can be resisted with effect solely by unanimity, decision, and spirit in the people, qualities which may be exerted most legally, constitutionally, and efficaciously, by that great measure, essential to the prosperity and freedom of Ireland, an equal representation of all the people in parliament.

Impressed with these sentiments, we have agreed to form an association, to be called the Society of United Irishmen, and we do pledge ourselves to our country, and mutually to each other, that we will steadily support, and endeavour by all due means to carry into effect the following resolutions:

1st. Resolved, That the weight of English influence in the government of this country is so great, as to require a cordial union among all the people of Ireland, to maintain that balance which is essential to the preservation of our liberties, and extension of our commerce.

2nd. That the sole constitutional mode by which this influence can be opposed is by a complete and radical reform of the representation of the people in parliament.

3rd. That no reform is practicable, efficacious, or just, which shall not include Irishmen of every religious persuasion.

'We submit our resolutions to the nation.'

Satisfied, as we are, that the intestine divisions among Irishmen have too often given encouragement and impunity to profligate, audacious, and corrupt administrations, in measures which, but for these divisions, they durst not have attempted, we submit our resolutions to the nation, as the basis of our political faith. We have gone to what we conceived to be the root of the evil. We have stated what we conceive to be the remedy. With a parliament thus formed, everything is easy – without it, nothing can be done – and we do call on, and most earnestly exhort our countrymen in general to follow our example, and to form similar societies in every quarter of the kingdom, for the promotion of constitutional knowledge, the abolition of bigotry in religion and politics, and the equal distribution of the rights of man throughout all sects and denominations of Irishmen. The people, when thus collected, will feel their own weight, and secure that power which theory has already admitted as their portion, and to which, if they be not aroused by their present provocations to vindicate it, they deserve to forfeit their pretensions for ever.

1st. This society is constituted for the purpose of forwarding a brotherhood of affection, a community of rights, and a union of power among Irishmen of every religious persuasion; and thereby to obtain a complete reform in the legislature, founded on the principles of civil, political and religious liberty.

2nd. Every candidate for admission into this society shall be proposed by one member and seconded by another, both of whom shall vouch for his character and principles. The candidate to be balloted for on the society's subsequent meeting, and if one of the beans shall be black, he shall stand rejected.

3rd. Each society shall fix upon a weekly subscription suited to the circumstances and convenience of its numbers, which they shall regularly return to their baronial by the proper officer.

4th. The officers of this society shall be a secretary and treasurer, who shall be appointed by ballot every three months, on every first meeting in November, February, May and August.

5th. A society shall consist of no more than twelve members, and those as nearly as possible of the same street or neighbourhood, whereby they may be all thoroughly known to each other, and their conduct be subject to the censorial check of all.

6th. Every person elected a member of the society shall, previous to his admission, take the following test. But in order to diminish risk, it shall be taken in a separate apartment, in the presence of the persons who proposed and seconded him only, after which the new member shall be brought into the body of the society, and there vouched for by the same.

TEST

In the awful presence of God, I, A.B., do voluntarily declare, that I will persevere in endeavouring to form a brotherhood of affection among Irishmen of every religious persuasion, and that I will also persevere in my endeavours to obtain an equal, full, and adequate representation of all the people of Ireland. I do further declare, that neither hopes, fears, rewards, or punishments, shall ever induce me, directly or indirectly, to inform on, or give evidence against, any member or members of this or similar societies for any act or expression of theirs, done or made collectively or individually in or out of this society, in pursuance of the spirit of this obligation.

7th. No person, though he should have taken the test, will be considered a United Irishman until he has contributed to the funds of the institution, or longer than he shall continue to pay such contribution.

8th. No communication relating to the business of the institution shall be made to any United Irishman on any pretence whatever, except in his own society or committee, or by some member of his own society or committee.

9th. When the society shall amount to the number of twelve members, it shall be equally divided by lot (societies in country places to divide as may best suit their local situation), that is, the names of all the members shall be put into a hat or box, the secretary or treasurer shall draw out six individually, which six shall be considered the senior society, and the remaining six the junior who shall apply to the baronial committee, through the delegates of the senior society, for a number. This mode shall be pursued until the whole neighbourhood is organized.

TEST FOR SECRETARIES
OF SOCIETIES OR COMMITTEES

In the awful presence of God I, A.B., do voluntarily declare that as long as I shall hold the office of secretary to this I will, to the utmost of my abilities faithfully discharge the duties thereof.

That all papers or documents received by me as secretary I will in safety keep; I will not give any of them, or any copy or copies of them, to any person or persons, members or others, but by a vote of this ____ and that I will, at the expiration of my secretaryship deliver up to this ____ all such papers as may be in my possession.

The Act of Union
(Ireland)

The Act uniting the Irish and British parliaments, 1800

The 'constitution of 1782' had to some extent resolved the question of Ireland's political inferiority to Britain by giving the Irish parliament an unprecedented degree of independence from Westminster. This had been granted only reluctantly. Britain, having just lost the war with the American colonies, needed to conciliate Ireland to avoid a similar confrontation closer to home. Worryingly for Britain, the Irish parliament showed an alarming tendency to flex its legislative muscles. It refused to cooperate either on economic regulation between the two kingdoms or on constitutional matters.

Relations were particularly strained during the 'Regency crisis' of 1788–9 caused by the apparent madness of George III. While British politicians clashed over whether the Prince of Wales should become regent, the parliament in Dublin voted in favour of asking the Prince of Wales to assume the regency of Ireland. It was a symbolic gesture because the king recovered, but the episode provided the British government with a salient lesson. If the Irish parliament was going to use its independence, then that autonomy must be removed. When the United Irishmen launched their unsuccessful rebellion in the summer of 1798, it merely confirmed what the British prime minister, William Pitt, already knew. First, the Irish parliament had failed to govern the country effectively. Second, that failure was a threat to British security.

Irish attitudes towards legislative union with Britain had undergone profound change over the course of the 18th century. When the Scottish and English parliaments had combined in 1707, the Irish parliament had requested unsuccessfully to be part of the union. By the end of the century, not least after the battle to secure its independence in 1782, the Irish parliament was loath to give up its powers. Many Irish Catholics, on the other hand, saw little to be gained from retaining an unrepresentative assembly in Dublin that legislated on behalf of the Protestant minority. Pitt had even encouraged them to believe that Catholic emancipation would be introduced at Westminster.

Unlike the Act of Union with Scotland, there were no negotiations between Britain and Ireland on the terms of the agreement drawn up by Pitt and his advisers. That lack of consultation mattered little. To most opponents, it was the principle rather than the application of union that was contested. For, as the Irish MP George Ponsonby proclaimed, it was 'the undoubted birthright of the people of Ireland to have a free and independent legislature'.

On 22 January 1799, following more than 20 hours of continuous debate, the Irish House of Commons rejected the principle of a legislative union. Over the next year, the British government cajoled and bribed Irish MPs in order to build a majority. When the bill came before the Irish parliament for the second time the following year, it passed easily through both houses. Henry Grattan accused proponents of the union of attempting to 'buy what cannot be sold – liberty'. For most Irish MPs and Lords, however, liberty did have a price – they asked and the British government gladly paid.

Royal assent was given to the Act of Union on 1 August 1800 and the Irish parliament was dissolved. The union came into effect on 1 January 1801. Far from solving the problematic relationship between Britain and Ireland, the union would become the single most contested issue between the two countries for the next hundred years and beyond.

The parliaments of Great Britain and Ireland have resolved to concur in measures for uniting the two kingdoms:

Whereas in pursuance of his Majesty's most gracious recommendation to the two houses of parliament in Great Britain and Ireland respectively, to consider of such measures as might best tend to strengthen and consolidate the connexion between the two kingdoms, the two houses of the parliament of Great Britain, and the two houses of the parliament of Ireland have severally agreed and resolved, that in order to promote and secure the essential interests of Great Britain and Ireland, and to consolidate the strength, power, and resources of the British empire, it will be advisable to concur in such measures as may best tend to unite the two kingdoms of Great Britain and Ireland, into one kingdom, in such manner, and on such terms and conditions, as may be established by the acts of the respective parliaments of Great Britain and Ireland.

'The said kingdoms of Great Britain and Ireland shall ... be united.'

And whereas in furtherance of the said resolution, both houses of the said two parliaments respectively have likewise agreed upon certain articles for effectuating and establishing the said purposes in the tenor following:

ARTICLE FIRST.
That it be the first article of the union of the kingdoms of Great Britain and Ireland, that the said kingdoms of Great Britain and Ireland shall, upon the first day of January, which shall be in the year of our lord one thousand eight hundred and one, and for ever, be united into one kingdom, by the name of 'the united kingdom of Great Britain and Ireland,' and that the royal stile and titles appertaining to the imperial crown of the said united kingdom and its dependencies, and also the ensigns, armourial flags and banners thereof, shall be such as his Majesty by his royal proclamation under the great seal of the united kingdom shall be pleased to appoint.

ARTICLE SECOND.
That it be the second article of union, that the succession to the imperial crown of the said united kingdom, and of the dominions thereunto belonging, shall continue limited and settled in the same manner as the succession to the imperial crown of the

said kingdoms of Great Britain and Ireland now stands limited and settled, according to the existing laws, and to the terms of union between England and Scotland.

'The parliament of the united kingdom of Great Britain and Ireland.'

ARTICLE THIRD.

That it be the third article of union, that the said united kingdom be represented in one and the same parliament, to be stiled 'The parliament of the united kingdom of Great Britain and Ireland.'

ARTICLE FOURTH.

That it be the fourth article of union that four lords spiritual of Ireland, by rotation of sessions, and twenty-eight lords temporal of Ireland, elected for life by the peers of Ireland, shall be the number to sit and vote on the part of Ireland in the house of lords of the parliament of the united kingdom, and one hundred commoners (two for each county of Ireland, two for the city of Dublin, two for the city of Cork, one for the university of Trinity college, and one for each of the thirty-one most considerable cities, towns, and boroughs) be the number to sit and vote on the part of Ireland in the house of commons of the parliament of the united kingdom.

… That any person holding any peerage of Ireland now subsisting, or hereafter to be created, shall not thereby be disqualified from being elected to serve, if he shall so think fit, or from serving, or continuing to serve, if he shall so think fit, for any county, city, or borough of Great Britain, in the house of commons of the united kingdom, unless he shall have been previously elected as above to sit in the house of lords of the united kingdom, but that so long as such peer of Ireland shall not be entitled to the privilege of peerage, nor be capable of being elected to serve as a peer on the part of Ireland, or of voting at any such election… .

ARTICLE FIFTH.

That it be the fifth article of union, that the churches of England and Ireland, as now by law established, be united into one protestant episcopal church, to be called 'the united church of England and Ireland,' and that the doctrine, worship, discipline and government of the said united church shall be, and shall remain in full force for ever, as the same are now by law established for the church of England; and that the continuance and preservation of the said united church, as the established church of England and Ireland, shall be deemed and taken to be an essential and fundamental part of the union; and that in like manner the doctrine, worship, discipline and government of the church of Scotland shall remain, and be preserved as the same are now established by law, and by the acts for the union of the two kingdoms of England and Scotland.

'One protestant episcopal church, to be called
"the united church of England and Ireland".'

ARTICLE SIXTH.

That it be the sixth article of union, that his Majesty's subjects of Great Britain and
Ireland shall, from and after the first day of January, one thousand eight hundred
and one, be entitled to the same privileges, and be on the same footing as to
encouragements and bounties on the like articles, being the growth, produce, or
manufacture of either country respectively, and generally in respect of trade and
navigation in all ports and places in the united kingdom and its dependencies; and
that in all treaties made by his Majesty, his heirs, and successors, with any foreign
power, his Majesty's subjects in Ireland shall have the same privileges, and be on the
same footing as his Majesty's subjects of Great Britain.

That from the first day of January, one thousand eight hundred and one, all
prohibitions and bounties on the export of articles the growth, produce, or

manufacture of either country to the other, shall cease and determine; and that the said articles shall thenceforth be exported from one country to the other, without duty or bounty on such export.

That all articles the growth, produce, or manufacture of either country, (not herein-after enumerated as subject to specific duties) shall from thenceforth be imported into each country from the other free from duty, other than such countervailing duty … and that for the period of twenty years from the union, the articles enumerated in the schedule, no. II hereunto annexed, shall be subject on importation into each country from the other, to the duties specified.

'Articles shall thenceforth be exported …
without duty or bounty.'

ARTICLE SEVENTH.

That it be the seventh article of union that the charge arising from the payment of the interest and the sinking fund for the reduction of the principal of the debt incurred in either kingdom before the union shall continue to be separately defrayed by Great Britain and Ireland respectively, except as here-in provided.

That for the space of twenty years after the union shall take place, the contribution of Great Britain and Ireland respectively towards the expenditure of the united kingdom in each year shall be defrayed in the proportion of fifteen parts for Great Britain and two parts of Ireland, that at the expiration of the said twenty years the future expenditure of the united kingdom (other than the interest and charges of the debt to which either country shall be separately liable) shall be defrayed in each proportion as the parliament of the united kingdom shall deem just and reasonable, upon a comparison of the real value of the exports and imports of the respective countries upon an average of three years next preceding the period of revision, or on a comparison of the value of the quantities of the following articles consumed within the respective countries on a similar average, viz. beer, spirits, sugar, wine, tea, tobacco and malt, or according to the aggregate proportion resulting from both these considerations combined, or on a comparison of the amount of income considerations combined, or on a comparison of the amount of income in each country estimated from the produce for the same period of a general tax, if such shall have been imposed on the same descriptions of income in both countries … .

ARTICLE EIGHTH.

That it be the eighth article of union, that all laws in force at the time of the union, and all the courts of civil and ecclesiastical jurisdiction within the respective kingdoms, shall remain as now by law established within the same, subject only to such alterations and regulations from time to time as circumstances may appear to the parliament of the united kingdom to require, provided that all writs of error and appeals depending at the time of the union, or hereafter to be brought, and which might now be finally decided by the house of lords of either kingdom, shall from and after the union be finally decided by the house of lords of the united kingdom, and provided that from and after the union there shall remain in Ireland an instance court of admiralty for the determination of causes civil and maritime only … and that all laws at present in force in either kingdom, which shall be contrary to any of the provisions which may be enacted by any act for carrying these articles into effect, be from and after the union repealed… .

ARTICLE TENTH.

And be it enacted, that the great seal of Ireland, may, if his majesty shall so think fit, after the union be used in like manner as before the union, except where it is otherwise provided by the foregoing articles, within that part of the united kingdom called Ireland, and that his majesty may, so long as he shall think fit, continue the privy council of Ireland, to be his privy council for that part of the united kingdom called Ireland.

'All laws … shall remain as now by law established.'

EDUCATION, IRELAND.

COPY of a LETTER from the CHIEF SECRETARY for *Ireland*, to His Grace the DUKE OF LEINSTER, on the Formation of a BOARD OF COMMISSIONERS FOR EDUCATION in *Ireland*.

MY LORD,   Irish Office, London, October 1831.

HIS MAJESTY'S GOVERNMENT having come to the determination of empowering the Lord Lieutenant to constitute a Board for the superintendence of a system of National Education in Ireland, and Parliament having so far sanctioned the arrangement as to appropriate a sum of money in the present year as an experiment of the probable success of the proposed system, I am directed by his Excellency to acquaint your Grace, that it is his intention, with your consent, to constitute you the President of the new Board: and I have it further in command to lay before your Grace the motives of the Government in constituting this Board, the powers which it is intended to confer upon it, and the objects which it is expected that it will bear in view, and carry into effect.

The Commissioners, in 1812, recommended the appointment of a Board of this description to superintend a system of Education from which should be banished even the suspicion of proselytism, and which, admitting children of all religious persuasions, should not interfere with the peculiar tenets of any. The Government of the day imagined that they had found a superintending body, acting upon a system such as was recommended, and intrusted the distribution of the national grants to the care of the Kildare-street Society. His Majesty's present Government are of opinion, that no private society, deriving a part, however small, of their annual income from private sources, and only made the channel of the munificence of the Legislature, without being subject to any direct responsiblity, could adequately and satisfactorily accomplish the end proposed; and while they do full justice to the liberal views with which that Society was originally instituted, they cannot but be sensible that one of its leading principles was calculated to defeat its avowed objects, as experience has subsequently proved that it has. • The determination to enforce in all their schools the reading of the Holy Scriptures without note or comment was undoubtedly taken with the purest motives; with the wish at once to connect religious with moral and literary education, and at the same time not to run the risk of wounding the peculiar feelings of any sect by catechetical instruction or comments which might tend to subjects of clerical controversy. But it seems to have been overlooked, that the principles of the Roman-catholic Church, (to which, in any system intended for general diffusion throughout Ireland, the bulk of the pupils must necessarily belong,) were totally at variance with this principle; and that the indiscriminate reading of the Holy Scriptures without note or comment, by children, must be peculiarly obnoxious to a church which denies, even to adults, the right of unaided private interpretation of the Sacred Volume with respect to articles of religious belief.

Shortly after its institution, although the Society prospered and extended its operations under the countenance of the Legislature, this vital defect began to be noticed, and the Roman-catholic clergy began to exert themselves with

Religious tensions became increasingly acute in the early years of the union. Catholics had been led to believe that their interests would be accommodated under the new settlement, but it soon became clear that Catholic emancipation was not on the parliamentary agenda. The gap between expectation and reality offered fertile ground for disillusion and resentment. By the 1820s, Irish Catholics, now organized under Daniel O'Connell's Catholic Association, became increasingly vocal in their grievances and demands. Educational reform was high on their list of demands.

Elementary schooling in Ireland was disorganized. By the early 19th century, most education was provided by voluntary societies, which were aided by state funds. These were usually Protestant, such as the charter schools run by the Incorporated Society in Dublin for Promoting English Protestant Schools in Ireland. They were established to teach English and instruct the liturgy of the Church of Ireland to 'the children of the Popish and other poor natives'. Many Catholic parents found this too high a price to pay for their children's education. As a result, only a tiny proportion of Catholic children of school-going age regularly received basic education.

For around half a million children, unregulated 'hedge schools' filled the gap. Better than nothing, these were hardly adequate, and, while Catholic teaching orders such as the Presentation Nuns (1793) and the Christian Brothers (1802) helped the situation, pressure in Britain and Ireland grew for the state to take the lead. In 1812, a committee of inquiry recommended a centralized state-controlled system, but the Tory government rejected this. Instead, they decided to give a subsidy to the Kildare Place Society, which had been founded to provide non-denominational education. The only religious education provided in the schools would be Bible readings, which would be conducted without comment to avoid sectarian disagreements. Steering clear of such controversy was never going to be easy. The Kildare Place Society schools were accused of proselytizing anyway and, within ten years of the schools being set up, Catholics were being instructed not to send their children to them.

The Chief Secretary for Ireland at the time was the future prime minister Edward Stanley (subsequently the 14th earl of Derby). His approach was one of carrot and stick. He entered office in November 1830 convinced that Ireland was on the brink of rebellion. He took a firm line against O'Connell in parliament and his movement in the country, introducing legislation to suppress meetings and declare martial law in disturbed districts. Alongside these coercive measures he brought in significant reforms. The most important and enduring was his scheme to establish a board of commissioners for education in Ireland. Influenced by a pamphlet entitled 'Thoughts and Suggestions on the Education of the Peasantry of Ireland' by Anthony Blake (1820), Stanley's scheme established a board that would centrally administer elementary education in Ireland and ensure a non-denominational system of schooling. It would provide finance for school buildings and teacher salaries, training and inspection, and lay down a curriculum of secular education with religious instruction.

Inevitably, there were complaints from all denominations. The Catholic hierarchy, although initially well disposed to the board, was swayed by Archbishop McHale's attacks on the secular curriculum and the presence of Protestants on the board. 'Better enter Heaven possessed of no earthly learning than go to Hell possessing the knowledge of a Socrates, an Aristotle or a Cicero,' he said. For others, knowledge of Greek and Roman philosophers was fine, but the Anglicizing effect of the schools was not. Children were learning English language, literature and history, which later would see the schools blamed for their role in nearly extinguishing the Irish language. In many ways exemplars of 19th-century English manners and customs, the schools aimed to turn good Irish children into model British subjects.

Despite strong opposition from the churches, the scheme survived. The Catholic Church would turn out to be an effective pressure group in undermining the non-denominational character of the schools, which was stealthily dissolved over time. Nevertheless, the structure of elementary education laid down by Stanley in 1831 remains virtually unchanged to this day.

His Majesty's Government having come to the determination of empowering the Lord Lieutenant to constitute a Board for the superintendence of a system of National Education in Ireland, and Parliament having so far sanctioned the arrangement as to appropriate a sum of money in the present year as an experiment of the probable success of the proposed system, I am directed by his Excellency to acquaint your Grace, that it is his intention, with your consent, to constitute you the President of the new Board: and I have it further in command to lay before your Grace the motives of the Government in constituting this Board, the powers which it is intended to confer upon it, and the objects which it is expected that it will bear in view, and carry into effect.

'No private society ... could adequately and satisfactorily accomplish the end proposed.'

The Commissioners, in 1812, recommended the appointment of a Board of this description to superintend a system of Education from which should be banished even the suspicion of proselytism, and which, admitting children of all religious persuasions, should not interfere with the peculiar tenets of any. The Government of the day imagined that they had found a superintending body, acting upon a system such as was recommended, and intrusted the distribution of the national grants to the care of the Kildare Street Society. His Majesty's present Government are of the opinion, that no private society, deriving a part, however small, of their annual income from private sources, and only made the channel of the munificence of the

Legislature, without being subject to any direct responsibilities, could adequately and satisfactorily accomplish the end proposed; and while they do full justice to the liberal views with which that Society was originally instituted, they cannot but be sensible that one of its leading principles was calculated to defeat its avowed objects, as experience has subsequently proved that it has. The determination to enforce in all their schools the readings of the Holy Scriptures without note or comment was undoubtedly taken with the purest motives; with the wish at once to connect religious with moral and literary education, and at the same time not to run the risk of wounding the peculiar feelings of any sect by catechetical instruction or comments which might tend to subjects of polemical controversy. But it seems to have been overlooked, that the principles of the Roman-catholic Church (to which, in any system intended for general diffusion throughout Ireland, the bulk of the pupils must necessarily belong) were totally at variance with this principle; and that the indiscriminate readings of the Holy Scriptures without note or comment, by children, must be peculiarly obnoxious to a church which denies, even to adults, the right of unaided private interpretation of the Sacred Volume with respect to articles of religious belief.

Shortly after its institution, although the Society proposed and extended its operations under the fostering care of the Legislature, this vital defect began to be noticed, and the Roman-catholic clergy began to exert themselves with energy and success, against a system to which they were on principle opposed, and which they feared might lead in its results to proselytism, even although no such object were contemplated by its promoters. When this opposition arose, founded on such grounds, it soon became manifest that the system could not become one of National Education.

'It was soon found that these schemes were impractical.'

Commissioners of Education, in 1824-5, sensible of the defects of the system, and of the ground as well as the strength of the objection taken, recommended the appointment of two teachers in every school, one Protestant and the other Roman-catholic, to superintend separately the religious education of the children; and they hoped to have been able to agree upon a selection from the Scriptures which might have been generally acquiesced in by both persuasions. But it was soon found that these schemes were impractical; and, in 1828, a Committee of the House of Commons, to which were referred the various reports of the Commissioners of Education, recommended a system to be adopted which should afford, if possible, a combined literary, and a separate religious education, and should be capable of being so far adapted to the views of the religious persuasions which prevail in Ireland as to render it, in truth, a system of national education for the poorer classes of the community.

'The Board should exercise a complete control.'

For the success of the undertaking much must depend upon the character of the individuals who compose the Board, and upon the security thereby afforded to the country, that while the interests of religion are not overlooked, the most scrupulous care should be taken not to interfere with the peculiar tenets of any description of Christian pupils.

To attain the first object, it appears essential that the Board should be composed of men of high personal character, including individuals of exalted station in the Church; to attain the latter, that it should consist of persons professing different religious opinions.

It is the intention of the Government that the Board should exercise a complete control over the various schools which may be erected under its auspices, or which, having been already established, may hereafter place themselves under its management, and submit to its regulations. Subject to these, applications for aid will be admissible from Christians of all denominations; but as one of the main objects must be to unite in one system children of different creeds, and as much must depend upon the co-operation of the resident clergy, the Board will probably look with peculiar favour upon applications proceeding either from,

1st The Protestant and Roman-catholic clergy of the Parish; or

2d One of the clergymen, and a certain number of parishioners professing the opposite creed; or

3d Parishioners of both denominations.

Where the application proceeds from Protestants or exclusively from Roman-Catholics, it will be proper for the Board to make inquiry as to the circumstances which lead to the absence of any names of the persuasion which does not appear.

The Board will note all applications for aid, whether granted or refused, with the grounds of decision, and annually submit to Parliament a report of their proceedings.

They will invariably require, as a condition not to be departed from, that local funds shall be raised, upon which any aid from the Public will be dependent.

They will refuse all applications in which the following objects are not locally provided for,

1st A fund sufficient for the annual repairs of the school-house and furniture.

2d A permanent salary for the master.

3d A sum sufficient to purchase books and school-requisites at half price.

4th Where aid is sought from the Commissioners for building a school-house, it is required that at least one-third of the estimated expense be subscribed, a site for the building, to be approved of by the Commissioners, be granted for the purpose, and that the school-house, when furnished, be vested in trustees, to be also approved of by them.

They will require that the schools be kept open for a certain number of hours, on four or five days of the week, at the discretion of the Commissioners, for moral and literary education only; and that the remaining one or two days in the week be set apart for giving, separately; such religious education to the children as may be approved by the clergy of their respective persuasions.

They will also permit and encourage the clergy to give religious instruction to the children of their respective persuasions, either before or after the ordinary school hours, on the other days of the week.

'They will exercise
the most entire control over all books.'

They will exercise the most entire control over all books to be used in the schools, whether in the combined moral and literary, or separate religious, instruction; none to be employed in the first except under the sanction of the Board, nor in the latter but with the appointment of those members of the Board who are of the same religious persuasion with those for whose use they are intended: Although it is not designed to exclude from the list of Books for the combined instruction, such portions of sacred history, or of religious and moral teaching as may be approved of by the Board, it is to be understood that this is by no means intended to convey a perfect and sufficient religious education, or to supersede the necessity of separate religious instruction on the day set apart for the purpose.

They will require that a register shall be kept in the schools in which shall be entered the attendance or non-attendance of each child on Divine worship on Sundays.

They will, at various times, either by themselves, or by their inspectors, visit and examine into the state of each school, and report their observations to the Board.

They will allow to the individuals or bodies applying for aid the appointment of their own teacher, subject to the following restrictions and regulations:

1st He (or she) shall be liable to be fined, suspended, or removed altogether, by the authority of the Commissioners, who shall, however, record their reasons.

2d He shall have received previous instruction in a model school in Dublin, to be sanctioned by the Board.
N. B. It is not intended that this regulation should apply to prevent the admission of masters or mistresses of schools already established, who may be approved of by the Commissioners.

3d He shall have received testimonials of good conduct, and of general fitness for the situation, for the Board.

The Board will be instructed with the absolute control over the funds which may be annually voted by Parliament, which they shall apply to the following purposes:

1st Granting aid for the erection of schools, subject to the conditions here-in – before specified.

2d Paying inspectors for visiting and reporting upon schools.

3d Gratuities to teachers of schools conducted under the rules laid down.

4th Establishing and maintaining a model school in Dublin, and training teachers for country schools.

5th Editing and printing such books of moral and literary education as may be approved of for the use of the schools, and supplying them and school-necessaries at not lower than half price.

6th Defraying all necessary contingent expenses of the Board.

I have thus stated the objects which His Majesty's Government have in view, and the principal regulations by which they think those objects may be most effectually promoted; and I am directed by the Lord Lieutenant to express his Excellency's earnest wish that the one and the other may be found such as to procure for the Board the sanction of your Grace's name, and the benefit of your Grace's attendance.

A full power will of course be given to the Board to make such regulations upon matters of detail, not inconsistent with the spirit of these instructions, as they may judge best qualified to carry into effect the intentions of the Government and of the Legislature. Parliament has already placed at his Excellency's disposal a sum which may be available even in the course of the present year; and as soon as the Board can be formed, it will be highly desirable that no time should be lost, with a view to the estimates of the ensuing year, in enabling such schools already established, as are willing to subscribe to the conditions imposed, to put in their claims for protection and assistance; and in receiving applications from parties desirous to avail themselves of the munificence of the Legislature in founding new schools under your regulations.

'It will be highly desirable that no time should be lost.'

On Conditions during the Great Famine

*Letter to the Duke of Wellington,
17 December 1846*

N.M. CUMMINS, ABSENTEE LANDLORD
AND JUSTICE OF THE PEACE IN CORK

The Great Famine in Ireland has been described as 'the most appalling calamity to affect any Western European country in peacetime since the Black Death of the fourteenth century'. Indeed, as the economic historian Cormac Ó Gráda has noted, the Irish famine killed a greater proportion of the total population of the country than any in modern times, including Ukraine under Stalin in the 1930s, Bengal in the 1940s, and Ethiopia and Somalia in the 1980s.

The famine had a cataclysmic effect on Ireland's population. Around eight and a half million people lived in Ireland on the eve of the famine. The figure recorded in the 1851 census was six and a half million. Ireland's four provinces were not affected in equal measure: Connaught and Munster lost nearly 30 percent of their populations to death or emigration; Leinster and Ulster lost around half that figure.

By 1845 potatoes were the main food source for more than half the population of Ireland. Around one third were almost entirely reliant on them. This dependency had arisen from a variety of factors, not least the capacity of the potato to give subsistence to families living on tiny land holdings. With potatoes producing abundant nutritious crops for nine months of the year, even the poorest rural family might keep itself in food all year around.

When the potatoes were good, they were very good, but they could also be unreliable and susceptible to blight. In 1845 the crop failed. It was not the first time this had happened. In the previous 30 years there had on average been a full or partial failure every two years. This latest instance was particularly devastating because three harvests out of four failed in a row. What turned shortage into famine, however, was the fiasco of inadequate relief mechanisms to deal with the effects of the crisis. 'The Almighty sent the potato blight,' noted the Young Irelander John Mitchel, 'but the English created the famine.' A mixture of incompetence, paralysis and unbending Malthusian principles left the British government unwilling and unable to act. Some even believed the famine was the result of Providence.

The Conservative government led by Sir Robert Peel responded with a three-strand approach, importing Indian maize from the United States (although wheat and cattle were still being exported from Ireland), establishing local relief committees to raise funds and distribute food, and the inauguration of work schemes. When Peel resigned in the summer of 1846, Lord John Russell's administration rolled back even these inadequate relief efforts. It was not until early in 1847 that Russell conceded that public works schemes were failing and agreed to introduce soup kitchens. These served a thin gruel of maize, rice and oats called stirabout to some three million people until they were closed down in August that year. Many private organizations, notably the Society of Friends, did their best to provide relief, but their capacity to do so was often limited by their size and lack of resources.

An estimated one million people died as a result of starvation or disease, with typhus and relapsing fever, enteric fever, scurvy, dysentery, influenza, pneumonia, smallpox, cholera and tuberculosis among the most common illnesses. Hunger or disease killed almost one person in eight. A similar number emigrated.

Among the famine's many consequences was the deepening of Irish resentment against Britain at home and among those who fled the island for America and elsewhere. The resentment was justified. As the historian of empire Niall Ferguson observes: 'Not even the most jingoistic Brit could deny that in the mid-1840s the British not only failed to alleviate, but actually exacerbated, one of the great catastrophes of the 19th century.'

On the 150th anniversary of the Famine, the newly elected British prime minister, Tony Blair, expressed his regret that 'Those who governed England at the time failed their people by standing by while a crop failure turned into a massive human tragedy.'

⁘

My Lord Duke, Without apology or preface, I presume so far to trespass on your Grace as to state to you, and, by the use of your illustrious name, to present to the British Public the following statement of what *I have myself seen within the last three days:* –

Having for many years been intimately connected with the western portion of the County of Cork, and possessing some small property there I thought it right personally to investigate the truth of the several lamentable accounts which had reached me of the appalling state of misery to which that part of the county was reduced. I accordingly went on the 15th inst. to Skibbereen, and to give the instance of one townland which I visited as an example of the state of the entire coast district, I shall state simply what I saw there. It is situated on the eastern side of Castlehaven Harbour, and is named South Reen, in the parish of Myross. Being aware that I should have to witness scenes of frightful hunger, I provided myself with as much bread as five men could carry, and on reaching the spot I was surprised to find the wretched hamlet apparently deserted. I entered some of the hovels to ascertain the cause, and the scenes that presented themselves were such as no tongue or pen can convey the slightest idea of. In the first six famished and ghastly skeletons, to all appearance dead, were huddled in a corner on some filthy straw, their sole covering what seemed a ragged horse-cloth, and their wretched legs hanging about, naked above the knees. I approached in horror, and found by a low moaning they were alive; *they were in fever* – four children, a woman, and what had once been a man.

It is impossible to go through the details – suffice it to say that in a few minutes I was surrounded by at least 200 of such phantoms, such frightful spectres as no words can describe. By far the greater number were delirious, either from famine or from fever.

'Their horrible images are fixed upon my brain.'

Their demoniac yells are still ringing in my ears, and their horrible images are fixed upon my brain. My heart sickens at the recital, but I must go on. In another case – decency would forbid what follows, but it must be told – my clothes were nearly torn off in my endeavours to escape from the throng of pestilence around, when my neck-cloth was seized from behind by a grip which compelled me to turn. I found myself grasped by a woman with an infant, *just born*, in her arms, and the remains of a filthy sack across her loins – the sole covering of herself and babe. The same morning the police opened a house on the adjoining lands, which was observed shut for many days, and two frozen corpses were found lying upon the mud floor, *half devoured by rats*.

A mother, herself in fever, was seen the same day to drag out the corpse of her child, a girl about twelve, perfectly naked, and leave it half covered with stones. In another house within 500 yards of the cavalry station at Skibbereen, the dispensary doctor found seven wretches lying, unable to move, under the same cloak – *one had been dead many hours, but the others were unable to move either themselves or the corpse.*

'I hungered and ye gave Me no meat.'

To what purpose should I multiply such cases? If these be not sufficient, neither would they hear who have the power to send relief, and do not, even 'though one came from the dead.'

Let them, however, believe and tremble that they shall one day hear the Judge of all the Earth pronounce their tremendous doom, with the addition, "I hungered and ye gave Me no meat; thirsty and ye gave Me no drink; naked and ye clothed Me not." But I forget to whom this is addressed. My Lord, you are an old and justly honoured man. It is yet in your power to add another honour to your age, to fix another star and that the brightest in your galaxy of glory. You have access to our young and gracious Queen – lay these things before her. She is a woman, she will not allow decency to be outraged. She has at her command the means of at least mitigating the sufferings of the wretched survivors of this tragedy. They will soon be few, indeed, in the district I speak of, if help be longer withheld. Once more, my Lord Duke, in the name of starving thousands, I implore you, break the frigid and flimsy chain of official etiquette, and save the land of your birth – the kindred of that gallant Irish blood which you have so often seen lavished to support the honour of the British name – and let there be inscribed upon your tomb, *Servata Hibernia* ('Ireland was preserved by me').

THE IDEA OF A UNIVERSITY

DEFINED AND ILLUSTRATED

I. IN NINE DISCOURSES ADDRESSED TO THE CATHOLICS OF
DUBLIN

II. IN OCCASIONAL LECTURES AND ESSAYS ADDRESSED TO THE
MEMBERS OF THE CATHOLIC UNIVERSITY

BY

JOHN HENRY NEWMAN, D.D.

OF THE ORATORY

THIRD EDITION

LONDON
BASIL MONTAGU PICKERING
196, PICCADILLY
1873

162 b

e Idea of a University

*University teaching considered in
nine discourses, Discourse V.,
'Knowledge its own end', 1852*

JOHN HENRY NEWMAN (1801–90)

University education had become a contentious issue for middle-class Catholic Ireland by the end of the 18th century. Trinity College Dublin was Ireland's only university, but it was an institution of the Protestant Ascendancy. Although Trinity opened its doors to Catholics in 1793, religious tests remained until 1873. Catholic bishops vehemently opposed Catholics attending the college, but a Catholic university was needed to provide a suitable alternative. Similarly, Presbyterians, who had to go to Scotland for a university education, wanted their own institution.

The foundation of a Catholic university was one of the key demands of Daniel O'Connell's repeal movement. The British prime minister, Robert Peel, had no intention of repealing the Act of Union, but he thought new universities might appease the Catholic church and people. He planned for the establishment of the Queen's University, with constituent colleges in Cork, Galway and Belfast. These colleges would be state-backed, non-denominational and non-residential (in line with the contemporary red-brick universities in England). Although Peel hoped his plan would enjoy reasonable support among the Catholic hierarchy, he failed to account for opposition from the more militant Catholic bishops, not least the archbishop of Armagh, Paul Cullen. The Queen's colleges opened their doors for the first time in 1849. A year later the synod of Thurles warned the laity against attending these 'Godless colleges'.

Cullen immediately turned his attention towards establishing a Catholic university along the same lines as Louvain in Belgium. He turned for advice to John Henry Newman, English Catholicism's most famous convert. In November 1851, Newman agreed to become the Catholic University's first rector (although it would not admit students for another three years). In order to set an agenda for the new institution, he delivered a series of nine discourses the following year on his ideas about the nature of university education. These went beyond merely explaining the need for a new Catholic university. He also made a compelling case for teaching the liberal arts. These were under attack from some educationalists in Victorian Britain who thought students should concentrate on learning facts and figures rather than cultivating their intellects or broadening their horizons. As Dickens's schoolteacher, Mr Gradgrind, commands in *Hard Times* (1854): 'Teach these boys and girls nothing but Facts. Facts alone are wanted in life. Plant nothing else, and root out everything else. You can only form the mind of reasoning animals upon Facts: nothing else will ever be of any service to them.'

Newman's skilful and powerful defence of the university and the liberal arts was published as *The Discourses on the Scope and Nature of University Education* (1852), which made up the first half of *The Idea of a University* (1873). It became an instant classic.

The Catholic University, later University College Dublin, opened its doors for the first time on 3 November 1854, with 17 students on the register. They were the first of many to study the liberal arts at the original home of the 'idea of the university'.

A UNIVERSITY may be considered with reference either to its Students or to its Studies; and the principle, that all Knowledge is a whole and the separate Sciences parts of one, which I have hitherto been using in behalf of its studies, is equally important when we direct our attention to its students. Now then I turn to the students, and shall consider the education which, by virtue of this principle, a University will give them; and thus I shall be introduced, Gentlemen, to the second question, which I proposed to discuss, viz., whether and in what sense its teaching, viewed relatively to the taught, carries the attribute of Utility along with it.

1.

I have said that all branches of knowledge are connected together, because the subject-matter of knowledge is intimately united in itself, as being the acts and the work of the Creator. Hence it is that the Sciences, into which our knowledge may be said to be cast, have multiplied bearings one on another, and an internal sympathy, and admit, or rather demand, comparison and adjustment. They complete, correct, balance each other. This consideration, if well-founded, must be taken into account, not only as regards the attainment of truth, which is their common end, but as regards the influence which they exercise upon those whose education consists in the study of them. I have said already, that to give undue prominence to one is to be unjust to another; to neglect or supersede these is to divert those from their proper object. It is to unsettle the boundary lines between science and science, to disturb their action, to destroy the harmony which binds them together. Such a proceeding will have a corresponding effect when introduced into a place of education. There is no science but tells a different tale, when viewed as a portion of a whole, from what it is likely to suggest when taken by itself, without the safeguard, as I may call it, of others.

'The drift and meaning of a branch of knowledge varies with the company in which it is introduced.'

Let me make use of an illustration. In the combination of colours, very different effects are produced by a difference in their selection and juxtaposition; red, green, and white, change their shades, according to the contrast to which they are submitted. And, in like manner, the drift and meaning of a branch of knowledge varies with the company in which it is introduced to the student. If his reading is confined simply to one subject, however such division of labour may favour the advancement of a particular pursuit, a point into which I do not here enter, certainly it has a tendency to contract his mind. If it is incorporated with others, it depends on those others as to the kind of influence which it exerts upon him.

… It is a great point then to enlarge the range of studies which a University professes, even for the sake of the students; and, though they cannot pursue every subject which is open to them, they will be the gainers by living among those and under those who represent the whole circle. This I conceive to be the advantage of a seat of universal learning, considered as a place of education. An assemblage of learned men, zealous for their own sciences, and rivals of each other, are brought, by familiar intercourse and for the sake of intellectual peace, to adjust together the claims and relations of their respective subjects of investigation. They learn to respect, to consult, to aid each other. Thus is created a pure and clear atmosphere of thought, which the student also breathes, though in his own case he only pursues a few sciences out of the multitude. He profits by an intellectual tradition, which is independent of particular teachers, which guides him in his choice of subjects, and duly interprets for him those which he chooses. He apprehends the great outlines of knowledge, the principles on which it rests, the scale of its parts, its lights and its shades, its great points and its little, as he otherwise cannot apprehend them. Hence it is that his education is called 'Liberal'. A habit of mind is formed which lasts through life, of which the attributes are, freedom, equitableness, calmness, moderation, and wisdom; or what in a former Discourse I have ventured to call a philosophical habit. This then I would assign as the special fruit of the education furnished at a University, as contrasted with other places of teaching or modes of teaching. This is the main purpose of a University in its treatment of its students.

'What is the use of it?'

And now the question is asked me, What is the *use* of it? and my answer will constitute the main subject of the Discourses which are to follow.

2.

Cautious and practical thinkers, I say, will ask of me, what, after all, is the gain of this Philosophy, of which I make such account, and from which I promise so much. Even supposing it to enable us to exercise the degree of trust exactly due to every science respectively, and to estimate precisely the value of every truth which is anywhere to be found, how are we better for this master view of things, which I have been extolling? Does it not reverse the principle of the division of labour? will practical objects be obtained better or worse by its cultivation? to what then does it lead? where does it end? what does it do? how does it profit? what does it promise? Particular sciences are respectively the basis of definite arts, which carry on to results tangible and beneficial the truths which are the subjects of the knowledge attained; what is the Art of this science of sciences? what is the fruit of such a Philosophy? what are we proposing to effect, what inducements do we hold out to the Catholic community, when we set about the enterprise of founding a University?

I am asked what is the end of University Education, and of the Liberal or Philosophical Knowledge which I conceive it to impart: I answer, that what I have already said has been sufficient to show that it has a very tangible, real, and sufficient end, though the end cannot be divided from that knowledge itself. Knowledge is capable of being its own end. Such is the constitution of the human mind, that any kind of knowledge, if it be really such, is its own reward. And if this is true of all knowledge, it is true also of that special Philosophy, which I have made to consist in a comprehensive view of truth in all its branches, of the relations of science to science, of their mutual bearings, and their respective values. What the worth of such an acquirement is, compared with other objects which we seek, – wealth or power or honour or the conveniences and comforts of life, I do not profess here to discuss; but I would maintain, and mean to show, that it is an object, in its own nature so really and undeniably good, as to be the compensation of a great deal of thought in the compassing, and a great deal of trouble in the attaining.

… Hence it is that Cicero, in enumerating the various heads of mental excellence, lays down the pursuit of Knowledge for its own sake, as the first of them. 'This pertains most of all to human nature,' he says, 'for we are all of us drawn to the pursuit of Knowledge; in which to excel we consider excellent, whereas to mistake, to err, to be ignorant, to be deceived, is both an evil and a disgrace.' And he considers Knowledge the very first object to which we are attracted, after the supply of our physical wants. After the calls and duties of our animal existence, as they may be termed, as regards ourselves, our family, and our neighbours, follows, he tells us, 'the search after truth. Accordingly, as soon as we escape from the pressure of necessary cares, forthwith we desire to see, to hear, and to learn; and consider the knowledge of what is hidden or is wonderful a condition of our happiness' … .

'Knowledge is one thing, virtue is another.'

9.

Useful Knowledge then, I grant, has done its work; and Liberal Knowledge as certainly has not done its work, – that is, supposing, as the objectors assume, its direct end, like Religious Knowledge, is to make men better; but this I will not for an instant allow, and, unless I allow it, those objectors have said nothing to the purpose. I admit, rather I maintain, what they have been urging, for I consider Knowledge to have its end in itself. For all its friends, or its enemies, may say, I insist upon it, that it is as real a mistake to burden it with virtue or religion as with the mechanical arts. Its direct business is not to steel the soul against temptation or to console it in affliction, any more than to set the loom in motion, or to direct the steam carriage; be it ever so much the means or the condition of both material and moral advancement, still, taken by and in itself, it as little mends our hearts as it improves our temporal circumstances. And if its eulogists claim for it such a power, they commit the very same kind of encroachment on a province not their own as the political economist who should maintain that his science educated him for casuistry or diplomacy. Knowledge is one thing, virtue is another; good sense is not conscience, refinement is not humility, nor is largeness and justness of view faith. Philosophy, however enlightened, however profound, gives no command over the passions, no influential motives, no vivifying principles. Liberal Education makes not the Christian, not the Catholic, but the gentleman. It is well to be a gentleman, it is well to have a cultivated intellect, a delicate taste, a candid, equitable, dispassionate mind, a noble and courteous bearing in the conduct of life; – these are the connatural qualities of a large knowledge; they are the objects of a University; I am advocating, I shall illustrate and insist upon them; but still, I repeat, they are no guarantee for sanctity or even for conscientiousness, they may attach to the man of the world, to the profligate, to the heartless, – pleasant, alas, and attractive as he shows when decked out in them. Taken by themselves, they do but seem to be what they are not; they look like virtue at a distance, but they are detected by close observers, and on the long run; and hence it is that they are popularly accused of pretence and hypocrisy, not, I repeat, from their own fault, but because their professors and their admirers persist in taking them for what they are not, and are officious in arrogating for them a praise to which they have no claim. Quarry the granite rock with razors, or moor the vessel with a thread of silk; then may you hope with such keen and delicate instruments as human knowledge and human reason to contend against those giants, the passion and the pride of man.

'We perfect our nature … by adding to it what is more than nature, and directing it towards aims higher than its own.'

… Your cities are beautiful, your palaces, your public buildings, your territorial mansions, your churches; and their beauty leads to nothing beyond itself. There is a physical beauty and a moral: there is a beauty of person, there is a beauty of our moral being, which is natural virtue; and in like manner there is a beauty, there is a perfection, of the intellect. There is an ideal perfection in these various subject-matters, towards which individual instances are seen to rise, and which are the standards for all instances whatever. … To open the mind, to correct it, to refine it, to enable it to know, and to digest, master, rule, and use its knowledge, to give it power over its own faculties, application, flexibility, method, critical exactness, sagacity, resource, address, eloquent expression, is an object as intelligible (for here we are inquiring, not what the object of a Liberal Education is worth, nor what use the Church makes of it, but what it is in itself), I say, an object as intelligible as the cultivation of virtue, while, at the same time, it is absolutely distinct from it.

… We attain to heaven by using this world well, though it is to pass away; we perfect our nature, not by undoing it, but by adding to it what is more than nature, and directing it towards aims higher than its own.

No Rent Manifesto

The Land League calls for a rent strike against landlords, 18 October 1881

CHARLES STEWART PARNELL (1846–91) AND OTHERS

Irish politics had been in disarray after the famine. The establishment in 1870 of what eventually became the Home Rule Party changed this. Under the leadership of founder Isaac Butt, the Home Rule Party held a deliberately vague policy of self-government for Ireland. While it won support from the majority of nationalist voters when fighting its first elections, the party lacked either the cohesion or dynamism to be a genuinely popular movement. Home Rule was all very well, but it involved looking for 'jam tomorrow'.

Most Irish people, particularly tenant farmers, were more occupied with immediate daily concerns. The second half of the 1870s had seen another agricultural crisis, with poor potato crops and the collapse of international grain prices. The drop in rural incomes caused serious hardship. The failure of the potato crop, with all its dreadful connotations, stirred up a climate of fear. With wages falling and evictions in the west on the increase (rising to 1238 in 1879), tenants began demanding rent abatements. This, in 1879, marked the beginning of the Land War.

One person who was all too aware of the Home Rule Party's shortcomings was the young MP for Meath, Charles Stewart Parnell. An Ascendancy landlord born into a life of privilege, he was a rising star of the parliamentary party. In contrast with the more genteel Butt, Parnell was a militant 'obstructionist' whose radical tactics went far beyond the Palace of Westminster. In June 1879, following discussions with the Fenians John Devoy and Michael Davitt, he sponsored the 'New Departure' to marry land agitation and Home Rule.

Davitt and Parnell founded the Irish National Land League in October 1879. Under their leadership, the Land League successfully merged radical action on the ground with parliamentary engagement. In 1880, Parnell became leader of the Home Rule Party. Although he was closely identified with advanced nationalists and land reform-ers, he was initially careful to walk the thin line between appearing radical enough to win support in Ireland and retaining his constitutional credentials in London.

By 1881, however, Parnell was moved to abandon the balancing act for a more orthodox policy. In part, this was a response to the Irish policies of the prime minister, William Gladstone. Around this time, parliament passed the second of Gladstone's land acts. This legislated for the core demands of tenants – the 'three Fs' of fair rent, fixity of tenure and free sale – as well as providing funds for occupier purchase. Parnell conceded privately the Land Act was a huge advance, but could not say so publicly. Instead, he provocatively called on tenants to 'test the act' to prove its inadequacy. This resulted in the government imprisoning him in Kilmainham jail, along with several of his lieutenants. Militants, including Michael Davitt, had been calling for a rent strike for some time. Parnell and the other Home Rulers had previously ignored them. Now imprisoned, he sought a way to burnish his militant credentials by embracing the idea. On 18 October Parnell issued a 'no rent manifesto'. Two days later, the government banned the Land League.

During this period, as Parnell had predicted before his arrest, outrages on the land increased significantly. By the summer of 1882, Gladstone decided to negotiate directly with Parnell. The resulting Kilmainham 'Treaty' of 25 April 1882 gave Parnell a figurative and literal 'get out of jail' card. The government agreed to expand the 1881 Land Act to cover tenants in arrears and to phase out coercion. Parnell agreed to withdraw the 'no rent manifesto', to cooperate with Liberal reforms and to bring violence to an end. Although hugely unpopular with radicals, the Kilmainham Treaty marked a profound change in Irish politics. Parnell had enacted a decisive shift away from radical land reform towards a purely constitutional campaign for Home Rule.

F ELLOW CITIZENS: The hour to try your souls and to redeem your pledges has arrived. The executive of the National Land League, forced to abandon its policy of testing the Land act, feels bound to advise the tenant farmers of Ireland from this day forth to pay no rents under any circumstances to their landlords until Government relinquishes the existing system of terrorism and restores the constitutional rights of the people. Do not be daunted by the removal of your leaders. Do not let yourselves be intimidated by threats of military violence. It is as lawful to refuse to pay rents as it is to receive them. Against the passive resistance of the entire population military power has no weapon. Funds will be poured out unstintedly for the support of all who may endure eviction in the course of the struggle. Our exiled brothers in America may be relied upon to contribute, if necessary, as many millions of money as they have contributed thousands to starve out landlordism and bring English tyranny to its knees. You have only to show that you are not unworthy of their boundless sacrifices of your imprisoned brothers.

'Stand together in face of the brutal, cowardly enemies of your race!'

One more struggle in which you have the hope of happy homes and national freedom to inspire you, one more heroic effort to destroy landlordism, and the system which was and is the curse of your race will have disappeared forever. Stand together in face of the brutal, cowardly enemies of your race! Pay no rent under any pretext! Stand passively, firmly, fearlessly by, while the armies of England may be engaged in their hopeless struggle against the spirit which their weapons cannot touch, and the Government, with its bayonets, will learn in a single Winter how powerless are armed forces against the will of a united determined, and self-reliant nation.

Charles S. Parnell   *Michael Davitt*
Thomas Brennan   *Patrick Eagan*
A.J. Kettle   *John Dillon*
Thomas Sexton

Rules of Football and Hurling

Rules agreed by the Gaelic Athletic Association (GAA), Dublin, 17 January 1885

MICHAEL CUSACK (1847–1906) AND OTHERS

By the middle of the 19th century, organized sports such as rugby and soccer were on the rise in Ireland. Rugby had been played in Ireland since the 1850s. Soccer was introduced in the late 1870s, with the first international match played in 1882. Ireland lost 13–0 to England. Another import, cricket, became increasingly popular in urban areas. While the new games were arriving, traditional Irish ones seemed to be on the way out.

Hurling was particularly at risk. Versions of the game had been played in Ireland since at least the time of the Brehon laws. By the time of the Statute of Kilkenny, English colonists were banned from playing 'the games which men call "hurlings". By the 18th century there were two types of hurling: one version, similar to the Scottish game of shinty, was played in the north during winter; the other, a summer game played in the south, more closely resembled the modern game. The southern code of *baire* or *iomán*, patronized by landlords, was a popular spectator and gambling sport. Over the first half of the 19th century, however, it went into decline. The game lost its benefactors after the 1798 rebellion and was later opposed by the Royal Irish Constabulary (RIC). More influentially, the Catholic church condemned it for encouraging moral and public disorder. These factors, combined with the impact of the famine, meant the game withered away until it was only played in certain areas of Galway, Cork and Wexford.

The seemingly inevitable extinction of hurling alarmed some nationalists, notably a schoolteacher named Michael Cusack. He believed that the culture surrounding imported games was too exclusive and foreign. He wanted to encourage ordinary people to play traditional Irish games in an effort to revive the physical and cultural life of the nation. Cusack had organized athletics in Dublin and had taught in such schools as Clongowes and Blackrock College. He was aware of the fashion for codifying sport and establishing sporting associations, such as the English Football Association (FA) (1863). Similar moves were afoot in some of the public schools in Ireland and in Trinity College Dublin, whose hurling club set out the first rules of the game in 1870.

The game played by the Trinity students, including the young Edward Carson, was more like hockey. During the early 1880s, Cusack and some Dublin hurlers tried to formulate a game that fused the traditional style with the newer version. When this proved unsuccessful, he decided on a more ambitious approach: a new organization to regulate athletics and revive hurling. Cusack's earlier record of establishing such bodies was less than impressive, and the turnout of a dozen or so at its first meeting did not augur well. Nevertheless, on 1 November 1884, Cumann Lúthchleass Gael, or the Gaelic Athletic Association (GAA), was established at Hayes Hotel in Thurles, with the aim of preserving and cultivating the national pastimes of Ireland.

Weeks later, on 17 January 1885, the association met again to draw up a code for hurling, Gaelic football and athletics, including weight throwing and racing – and to establish the rules of the association. Some of these regulations were controversial at the time, and would remain so, notably the ban on members of the GAA competing in non-GAA (i.e. 'foreign') games. This was augmented two years later with a ban on members of the RIC joining. These strict rules were rigorously enforced, although they did little to diminish the GAA's early popularity.

Michael Cusack was as unbending as the rules he helped formulate. His robust personality cost him the position of secretary less than two years after founding the association. His legacy on the social and political life of the nation was longer-lived. The GAA played a vital role in the resurgence of nationalist Ireland, both as an instrument of nation building and as a recruiting ground for the Irish Republican Brotherhood (IRB). Its role in the social life of Ireland was even more profound. Without the GAA it is likely that hurling would have died out entirely, while Gaelic football in its current form might never have existed at all. While the ban on foreign games was lifted in 1971, it was only at a special congress in 2001 that the GAA amended its rules to allow members of the security forces in Britain and Northern Ireland to play hurling and Gaelic football.

BRETHREN, John Augustus O'Shea says that the Archbishop's letter, which is here printed, ought to be read, as an order of the day, at every annual meeting of the Athletic Clubs in Ireland. He says 'it is as Irish as an open smile and as stirring as brass music'. I agree with Mr J.A. O'Shea.

'Guard the game well.'

The enemies of the Gaelic Athletic Association have complete control over the so-called Sporting Press of Ireland; and until the beginning of this year they would seem to have exercised a like control over the Sporting departments of the Daily Press of this city. I mention these facts to give you some idea of the great obligation under which we have been placed by William O'Brien, MP, who placed a considerable portion of the *United Ireland* at our disposal at a time when every influential paper in the metropolis was bitterly hostile to the Gaelic Athletic Association.

I believe that the Irish People laid aside a powerful weapon for the cultivation of the intellect when they gave up the free use of their National Language; and I very much fear that the profound depth of religious feeling which so generally prevailed among our Irish-speaking ancestors could scarcely be paralleled among those who habitually speak English at the present day. But whether it is granted or not that with the decline of the Irish language came a decline of religion, of morals, and of intellect, I am sure no sensible person will deny that, as a nation, we have very considerably declined physically since we gave up our national game of HURLING.

The game is called *baire*, in Irish, and the hurley is called *caman*. The goalkeeper is *cul-baire*. The game is probably the oldest game extant. There is not a shadow of doubt that it was played in Ireland two thousand years ago. It was the training of the hurling field that made the men and boys of the Irish Brigade. Guard the game well. But in doing so it will be necessary to play without anger or passion. Irishmen have endured many agonies for the sake of their country without going mad. Why, then, should we gratify our enemies by getting up an unseemly row because one of us get an accidental crack of a stick from a fellow-workman?

HURLING RULES

1. The ground shall, when convenient, be at least 200 yards long by 150 yards broad, or as near to that size as can be got.

2. There shall be boundary lines all around the ground, at a distance of at least five yards from the fences.

3. The goal shall be two upright posts, twenty feet apart, with a cross-bar ten feet from the ground. A goal is won when the ball is driven between the posts and under the cross-bar.

4. The ball is not to be lifted off the ground with the hand, when in play.

5. There shall not be less than fourteen or more than twenty-one players at the side in regular matches.

6. There shall be an umpire for each side and a referee who will decide in cases where the umpires disagree. The referee keeps the time and throws up the ball at the commencement of each goal.

7. The time of play shall be one hour and twenty minutes. Sides to be changed at half-time.

8. Before commencing play hurlers shall draw up in two lines in the centre of the field opposite to each other and catch hands or hurleys across, then separate. The referee then throws the ball along the ground between the players or up high over their heads.

9. No player to catch, trip or push from behind. Penalty, disqualification to the offender and free puck to the opposite side.

10. No player to bring his hurley intentionally in contact with the person of another player. Penalty same as in Rule 9.

11. If the ball is driven over the side-line it shall be thrown in towards the middle of the ground by the referee or one of the umpires; but if it rebounds into the ground it shall be considered in play.

12. If the ball is driven over the end-lines and not through the goal, the player who is defending the goal shall have a free puck from the goal. No player of the opposite side to approach nearer than twenty yards until the ball is struck. The other players to stand on the goal-line. But if the ball is driven over the goal-line by a player whose goal it is, the opposite side shall have a free puck on the ground twenty yards out from the goalposts. Players whose goal it is to stand on the goal-line until the ball is struck. NB: Hitting both right and left is allowable.

A *light* ball, about 4 inches in diameter, made of corks and woollen thread, and covered with leather is best. The hurley may be of any pattern fancied by the player.

FOOTBALL RULES

1. There shall not be less than fourteen or more than twenty-one players a side.

2. There shall be two umpires and a referee. Where the umpires disagree, the referee's decision shall be final.

3. The ground shall be at least 120 yards long by 80 in breadth and properly marked by boundary lines. Boundary lines to be at least five yards from the fences.

4. Goal-posts shall stand at each end in the centre of the goal-line. They shall be 15 feet apart, with cross-bar 8 feet from the ground.

5. The captains of each team shall toss for choice of sides before commencing play and the players shall stand in two ranks opposite each other, until the ball is thrown up, each man holding the hand of one of the other side.

6. Pushing or tripping from behind, holding from behind, or butting with the head shall be deemed foul and players so offending shall be asked to stand aside and may not afterwards take any part in the match, nor can his side substitute another man.

7. The time of actual play shall be one hour. Sides to be changed at half-time.

8. The match shall be decided by the greater number of goals. If no goal be kicked, the match shall be deemed a draw. A goal is scored when the ball is kicked through the goalposts under the cross-bar.

9. When the ball is kicked over the side-line it shall be thrown back in any direction by a player of the other side. If kicked over the goal-line by a player of the other side, the goal-keeper whose line it crosses shall have a free kick. No player on the other side to approach nearer than 25 yards of him till the ball is kicked.

10. The umpires and referee shall have, during the match, full power to disqualify any player or order him to stand aside and discontinue play for any act which they may consider unfair as set out in Rule 6.

No nails or irontips allowed on the boots (strips of leather fastened on the soles will prevent slipping).

The dress for hurling and football to be knee breeches and stockings and boots or shoes.

Poster for the Opening Night of the Abbey Theatre

Ireland's National Theatre opens its doors for the first time, 27 December 1904

The cultural nationalism of the founders of the GAA was also present in the arts. For many, including Douglas Hyde and his colleagues in the Gaelic League, Ireland had become 'West British' and needed to be 'de-Anglicized' with a return to its Gaelic roots in language and culture. For others, language was less important than Ireland's ancient heritage. Poets, playwrights and writers began to look to Irish antiquities, legends and rural life for inspiration. That interest would inform the Anglo-Irish literary revival.

One group to emerge from this set was the Irish Literary Theatre Society established in 1899 by W.B. Yeats, Lady Gregory and Edward Martyn. Its first production, *The Countess Cathleen* by Yeats, opened on 8 May 1899. Over the next six years it put on 24 productions in halls around Dublin. Some, like Yeats's great patriotic play *Cathleen Ni Houlihan*, met with rapturous acclaim. Others, such as J.M. Synge's *In the Shadow of the Glen*, did not.

Back in London, Yeats met the independently wealthy Annie Fredericka Horniman. Attracted by mysticism and the theatre, she soon developed a romantic obsession with him. Her ardour was not reciprocated, but Yeats allowed her to act as his unpaid personal assistant, which involved secretarial work and domestic duties. In 1903 he convinced her to move to Dublin, where she offered to buy him a theatre. Yeats had long wished for his own stage. Indeed, he had already identified a suitable property: two disused buildings on Lower Abbey Street, which had once housed the Mechanics Institute and the city morgue. Horniman enthusiastically leased the buildings, financed the renovations and guaranteed those subsidies necessary in the running of the theatre. Her relationships, however, with the Abbey directors – Yeats, and again Lady Gregory and Synge – quickly soured. When the patent to run the theatre was granted in Lady Gregory's name – it had to be made out to an Irish resident – Horniman was vocal in emphasizing to all and sundry that she, not Gregory, owned the Abbey. Such was the level of animosity between them that she left Dublin before the opening night. She continued to fund the Abbey until 1910, when she broke away in protest at its nationalist productions.

Rehearsals for the Abbey's first programme began at the end of October 1904 in a theatre that would remain something of a building site right up until the first night. On 27 December the Abbey's curtain went up for the first time to a full house of 562 patrons. The audience included members of Dublin's political and literary elite, including 'AE' (George Russell), Edward Martyn, Hugh Lane and Yeats, as well as John Redmond and John Dillon. Lady Gregory (not without irony given her tussle over status with Horniman) was unable to attend.

The first run was five nights and consisted of four one-act plays by the three Abbey directors. Two were new plays: *Spreading the News*, a farce by Lady Gregory; and *On Baile's Strand*, a dramatic piece by Yeats about Cuchullain. The other two plays were revivals of *Cathleen Ni Houlihan* and *In the Shadow of the Glen*. Synge's play had

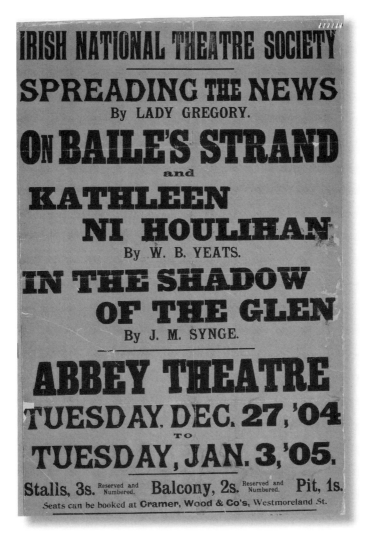

previously earned scathing reviews, but Yeats, who rejoiced in anti-populism, put it into
production anyway. In fact, he seemed a little giddy at the idea of a subsidized theatre.
Addressing the audience on the first night, he noted that in the past, when choosing
plays, the Irish Literary Theatre Society had had to ask if they would please a paying
audience. Now the new theatre meant that the directors would no longer be bound
to give the audience what it wanted. Instead, its motto would be one of 'Be bold, be
bold for evermore, yet be not too bold.' Yeats and his theatre stayed true to the first
part of this axiom, presenting for the most part unpopular and controversial plays to
small audiences.

In 1925 the Abbey became the first theatre in the English-speaking world to be
granted a state subsidy. After a fire in July 1951 left the Mechanics building badly
burned, the Abbey moved southside to the Queens Theatre on Pearse Street. It
returned to a new building, designed by the modernist architect Michael Scott, on
an enlarged site on Abbey Street in 1966.

Ulster Solemn League and Covenant

Ulstermen pledge to resist Home Rule, 1912

THOMAS SINCLAIR (1838–1914) AND OTHERS

Although northern Presbyterians had been responsible for founding the Society of United Irishmen in 1791, their dalliance with Irish nationalism proved short-lived. Following the Act of Union, Protestants of the northeast were among the union's staunchest supporters. The project to unite 'Catholic, protestant and dissenter under the common name of Irishman' had failed. Henceforth northern Protestants generally found little reason to make common cause with Roman Catholic Ireland. Moreover, in terms of its economy, the union seemed to be paying off in the north, where the linen and shipbuilding industries prospered throughout the 19th century.

Catholic nationalists who worked to end the union made few attempts to persuade their northern compatriots towards their point of view. Those rare occasions when they did make the effort usually ended in failure. A report of a visit to Belfast by Daniel O'Connell during his campaign to repeal the Act of Union rejoiced in the headline: 'Repealer repulsed!'

Anti-repeal feeling, though deeply held, was disorganized until the introduction of the first and second Home Rule bills in 1886 and 1893. These woke up northern Protestants to the risk of economic decline outside the union and 'Rome Rule' from Dublin. Opposition to the bills mixed political organization and threats of military resistance. 'Ulster will fight, and Ulster will be right' became the slogan of the time. Serious sectarian violence broke out in Belfast. In the short term, the fear of Home Rule was unfounded since each bill failed at Westminster. The issue became a threat again in 1911 when the Liberal government removed the legislative veto of the House of Lords (a vigorous protector of the union). Home Rule returned to the parliamentary agenda, only this time with the likelihood of success.

On 11 April 1912, the day that the *Titanic* left Queenstown for New York, the Asquith government introduced a third Home Rule bill in the House of Commons. Two days beforehand, some 200,000 unionists had marched in protest from Balmoral showgrounds near Belfast to the city centre. Speaking to the crowd that day, unionist leader Sir Edward Carson made a bold affirmation:

> I now enter into a compact with you, and every one of you, and with the help of God you and I joined together, I giving you the best I can, and you giving me all your strength behind me, we will yet defeat the most nefarious conspiracy that has ever been hatched against a free people. You realize the gravity of the situation that is before us … You are here in this fight to the finish. We ask for nothing more; we will take nothing less. It is our inalienable right as citizens of the United Kingdom, and heaven help the men who try to take it from us.

Until then, many unionists had worked to keep the whole of Ireland tied to Britain. From this point onwards they would be more pragmatic. If they could not keep all Ireland in the United Kingdom, they would settle for keeping Ulster. After the

Belfast protest, James Craig, a brilliant strategist and later the first prime minister of Northern Ireland, began planning for an oath to be taken by *Ulster* unionists, loosely based on the 1643 Scottish Solemn League and Covenant.

The covenanting tradition among Scottish Presbyterians drew its inspiration from the Old Testament. When 17th-century Scottish Presbyterians were at odds with Charles I, they had sworn to uphold their faith and professed only qualified loyalty to the monarch. If the king were faithful to God, they would be faithful to him. Charles ignored this at his peril. The result was a struggle between the crown and the covenanters that culminated in the Bishops Wars of 1639 and 1640, which were followed in turn by the English Civil War.

Thomas Sinclair, a Liberal Unionist, drafted the Ulster Solemn League and Covenant. Compared to its Scottish predecessors, the final document was less trenchant than it might have been. On the advice of the Presbyterian church, the covenant was altered so that it would be binding only during the 'present crisis' rather than for eternity. Even if the final text of the covenant seemed a little subdued, the conscious echoing of the old Scots covenant, not least in the title, invoked a dangerous precedent. After all, on that earlier occasion when the monarch had ignored the covenanters, he had gone on to lose a war, the kingdom and his head.

That summer it was announced that 28 September would be 'Ulster Day', when unionists across the province should dedicate themselves to the covenant. Massive publicity followed. By 28 September the atmosphere had been whipped up into one of genuine zeal. Belfast was the seat of the campaign, but elsewhere throughout Ulster some 500 local premises were made available for men to sign the covenant. Women were not allowed to add their names. Instead, in almost equal numbers, they signed a declaration affirming they would 'associate with the men of Ulster in their uncompromising opposition to the Home Rule Bill now before Parliament'. The day was a triumph of logistics. Belfast City Hall accommodated some 540 signatories at a single time. Edward Carson (and honorary Ulsterman for the day) was the first to sign – doing so, it was claimed, standing before a banner carried at the Battle of the Boyne. By the time the doors to City Hall closed at 11 p.m., Carson's signature had been joined by almost half a million others (including the women's oath). The Public Record Office of Northern Ireland, which now holds the covenant, notes that, contrary to legend, only one person – Frederick Hugh Crawford – seems to have signed in blood.

Ulster Day was hugely significant for the unionists. But its place in unionist and loyalist folk memory was not merely one of taking a stand. Neither was it just a grand day out. This was an explicit threat that Home Rule, even if passed by parliament and supported by a majority of Irish voters, would be resisted by any means necessary. The nature of that resistance became clear quickly afterwards when the Ulster Volunteer Force (UVF) was established. It soon had some 100,000 men in its ranks. So began the militarization, not just of Ulster but also of the whole island. The foundation of the UVF begat a nationalist counterpart, the Irish Volunteers. As Patrick Pearse noted at the time, 'I think the Orangeman with a rifle a much less ridiculous figure than the nationalist without a rifle.'

❦

Being convinced in our consciences that Home Rule would be disastrous to the material well-being of Ulster as well as the whole of Ireland, subversive of our civil and religious freedom, destructive of our citizenship and perilous to the unity of the Empire, we, whose names are under-written, men of Ulster, loyal subjects of His Gracious Majesty King George V., humbly relying on the God whom our fathers in days of stress and trial confidently trusted, do hereby pledge ourselves in solemn Covenant throughout this our time of threatened calamity to stand by one another in defending for ourselves and our children our cherished possession of equal citizenship in the United Kingdom and in using all means which may be found necessary to defeat the present conspiracy to set up a Home Rule Parliament in Ireland. And in the event of such a Parliament being forced upon us we further solemnly and mutually pledge ourselves to refuse to recognise its authority. In sure confidence that God will defend the right we hereto subscribe our names.

And further, we individually declare that we have not already signed this Covenant.

Report on Dublin Housing Conditions

Appraisal of the Dublin tenements, 1914

Stories of exploitative landlords and abused tenants are an important thread running through much of modern Irish history. The Land War, the Land League and Parnell's judicious use of the land question dominated and shaped the course of Irish politics throughout the 19th century. But when it came to rack-renting and maltreatment, this was only half the story. Ignored by politicians at the time, and by many historians since, are the slum landlords, who rented crumbling tenement houses to the Dublin poor. Families with nowhere else to go were condemned to a life of squalor.

The land question was useful to nationalists as a weapon to attack the British government and Anglo-Irish property-owners; the housing question seemed less clear-cut. It was rooted in social inequality at home, often involving middle-class Irish Catholic landlords and working-class Irish Catholic tenants. There was little political capital to be gained by taking up the cause of slum dwellers. In fact, the opposite was true. Giving attention to this might prove politically damaging, since many of the buildings were actually owned by politicians. The 1914 report on working-class housing found that five aldermen and eleven city councillors between them owned 89 tenements and sundry second-class housing in Dublin.

Tenements had existed in Dublin since the late 18th century, but the numbers had mushroomed after the Act of Union. With the parliament gone and Dublin in decline, the well-heeled residents of its Georgian squares had deserted the city. Naturally the value of property collapsed: a Georgian house worth £8,000 in 1790 could be bought for just £500 by 1840. Canny speculators bought up these properties, renting them out by the room. Little or nothing was done to make these quarters habitable. They made for insanitary, cramped and inappropriate residences. As time went on, their condition became worse, as did the overcrowding. During the famine years, there was an influx of people from the country into the capital. Most of these ended up in the tenements. Houses were not designed for the use they were being put to, and over time the buildings became structurally unsound and prone to collapse. It was no surprise that contemporaries described them as 'fever nests and death traps'. Mortality rates from tuberculosis were twice that of London by 1898.

The local authority was well aware of conditions in the tenements and their impact on residents. The 1914 report featured here is only one of a series on the problems of Dublin housing. It provides a vivid illustration of how ordinary people lived. If local politicians and officials were aware of the abomination of the slums, they displayed little or no inclination to remedy the situation. Help when it occurred tended to come from private philanthropists, such as Lord Iveagh, who gave around £1 million towards slum clearance and housing projects. For the most part, though, despite their vast numbers, the unorganized mass of slum dwellers were a forgotten people.

That started to change following the arrival of Jim Larkin in Dublin. The mobilization of unskilled workers in 1909 into the Irish Transport and General Workers' Union gave many of these people a voice for the first time. Efforts by workers to stand up for themselves were often met with resistance by employers. While the report on housing conditions was being written, bosses had locked out thousands of Dublin workers from their jobs. Speaking to a tribunal of inquiry into the lockout, Larkin had lambasted the existence of the 'putrid Dublin slums' and expressed a determination that something must be done to raise the condition of ordinary working people. Condemning the employers and slum landlords, he warned: 'Christ will not be crucified in Dublin by these men.'

In fact, it took another two decades before any effort was made to clear the Dublin slums. Significant numbers would continue living in tenement housing well into the 1940s and 1950s.

About 45 per cent of the working population of Dublin live in tenement houses, and about 50 per cent either in tenement houses or second and third class small houses. It is perhaps well that we should here explain the term 'tenement house' as used in Dublin.

The tenement houses of the present day are for the most part houses that were originally built to accommodate and provide for one family, and as a rule they face a thoroughfare of the City, though some are to be found in Courts and Alleys. The tenement houses as a whole are exceedingly old structures, and are more or less in an advanced state of decay.

Mr Travers' evidence would indicate that the tenement house system was in existence in the year 1840. He stated that there were in that year 353 tenement houses in the City, and that at the time of the famine there were 1,682. By 1850 the number had increased to 5,995; some of which are still in use as tenement houses. The evidence given before the Royal Commission, 1880, would show that by that time the number had still further increased, as it was then stated that there were 9,760 such houses.

'These tenement houses are to be found all over the City.'

The tenement house system is due to many causes which we are not called upon to analyse, but the result is that houses which were built to accommodate one family have been taken over by landlords who farm them out, without in any way making them suitable for the purpose, in one, two, or three roomed dwellings. We had evidence given before us that showed that there are sometimes five owners interested in one tenement house. These tenement houses are to be found all over the City, and quite close to the most fashionable parts, but some areas such as Railway Street, Corporation Street, Cumberland Street, Francis Street, The Coombe, Chamber Street,

Cork Street, portion of Gardiner Street, Dominick Street, and many others, may be said to be entirely devoted to them.

The Sanitary Staff of the Corporation have submitted Returns dividing tenement houses into three classes:

a. 'Houses which appear to be structurally sound; they may not be in good repair, but are capable of being put in good repair, called first class'.

b. 'Houses which are so decayed or so badly constructed as to be on or fast approaching the border-line of being unfit for human habitation, called second class'.

c. 'Houses unfit for human habitation and incapable of being rendered fit for human habitation, called third class.'

The Corporation Returns will be found in the Appendix, and an examination of them discloses that there are 1,516 tenements of class (a) found to be occupied by 8,295 families and by 27,052 persons; 2,228 of class (b) found to be occupied by 10,698 families and 37,552 persons and 1,518 of class (c) found to be occupied by 6,831 families and 22,701 persons. Of the 25,822 families living in tenement houses, the figures supplied would show that 20,108 live in one room, and we might point out that this figure very nearly approaches the corresponding figure given in the Census return of 1911 for the whole City, viz. 21,113 families.

'Dublin has by far the largest percentage of one-roomed tenements of principal cities.'

The 5,322 tenement houses in the City contain 35,227 rooms, and 4,331 cellars or kitchens and of the rooms, 32,851 are occupied and 1,560 of the cellars are occupied. There are 20,108 families occupying one roomed dwellings … It will thus be seen that 78 per cent of the lettings are one room lettings. In a special report to the Board of Trade made in the year 1908 describing the conditions of the working classes in the principal industrial Towns in the United Kingdom, Dublin is singled out as a City of one room tenements … Dublin has by far the largest percentage of one-roomed tenements of principal cities, viz. 33.9, and we have ascertained that the highest percentage in England occurs in Finsbury, viz. 27.7.

… These figures, perhaps, speak for themselves as regards the density of population in these houses, but in order to appreciate their full significance, it will not be out of place to give shortly the condition of life in tenement houses.

There are many tenement houses with seven or eight rooms that house a family in each room, and contain a population of between forty and fifty souls. We have visited one house that we found to be occupied by 98 persons, another by 74, and a third by 73.

REPORT

OF THE

DEPARTMENTAL COMMITTEE

APPOINTED BY THE

LOCAL GOVERNMENT BOARD FOR IRELAND

TO INQUIRE INTO THE

HOUSING CONDITIONS

OF THE

WORKING CLASSES IN THE CITY OF DUBLIN.

Presented to Parliament by Command of His Majesty.

LONDON:

PRINTED UNDER THE AUTHORITY OF HIS MAJESTY'S STATIONERY OFFICE
BY ALEX. THOM & Co., LIMITED, ABBEY STREET, DUBLIN.

To be purchased, either directly or through any Bookseller, from
E. PONSONBY, LIMITED, 116, GRAFTON STREET, DUBLIN; or
WYMAN AND SONS, LIMITED, 29, BREAMS BUILDINGS, FETTER LANE, E.C., and
28, ABINGDON STREET, S.W., and 54, ST. MARY STREET, CARDIFF; or
H.M. STATIONERY OFFICE (SCOTTISH BRANCH), 23, FORTH STREET, EDINBURGH;
or from the Agencies in the British Colonies and Dependencies,
the United States of America, the Continent of Europe and Abroad of
T. FISHER UNWIN, LONDON, W.C.

1914.

'The backs of the houses are very dilapidated and almost ruinous.'

The entrance to all tenement houses is a common door off either a street, lane or alley, and in most cases the door is never shut day or night. The passages and stairs are common, and the rooms all open directly either off the passages or landings. Most of these houses have yards at the back, some of which are of fair size, while others are very small, and some few houses have no yards at all. Generally the only water supply of the house is furnished by a single water tap which is in the yard. The yard is common, and the closet accommodation is to be found there, except in some few cases in which there is no yard, when it is to be found in the basement where there is little light or ventilation. The closet accommodation is common, as the evidence shows, not only to the occupants of the house, but to anyone who likes to come in off the street, and is, of course, common to both sexes. The roofs of these tenement houses are as a rule bad. In some cases the structure of the house appears to be in fairly good repair, and in others it appears to be fairly good in front but the backs of the houses are very dilapidated and almost ruinous. The passages, landings and stairs, are, in many cases, cramped and narrow, and the woodwork defective. The floors of the rooms are often out of repair, and the window frames and sashes in poor condition, those in the landing windows being not infrequently absent. The fireplaces in the room are small open ones, unsuited for general use.

Having visited a large number of these houses in all parts of the city, we have no hesitation in saying that it is no uncommon thing to find halls and landings, yards and closets of the houses in a filthy condition, and in nearly every case human excreta is to be found scattered about the yards and on the floors of the closets and in some cases even in the passages of the house itself. At the same time it is gratifying to find in a number of instances that in spite of the many drawbacks, an effort is made by the occupants to keep their rooms tidy and the walls are often decorated with pictures and when making some of our inspections after Christmas we frequently noticed an attempt to decorate for the season of the year. Of the many closets we inspected, it was the rare exception to find one that could be described as even approaching a clean condition, and in no single case did there seem to be any special accommodation provided for children, but in some isolated cases, notably at Vance's Buildings in Bishop Street, an effort was apparently made to provide special accommodation for males and females, while in 3 and 4 Brown Street, belonging to a Mr Kerlin, and in some of the houses belonging to the Jervis White estate, separate accommodation was provided for each letting.

Having regard to the above conditions, we are quite prepared to accept Sir Charles Cameron's evidence, that the female inhabitants of the tenement houses seldom use the closets; indeed it would be hard to believe otherwise, as we cannot conceive how any self-respecting male or female could be expected to use accommodation such as we have seen.

It was stated in evidence before us, by several witnesses, some of whom were clergymen whose duties bring them into close touch with tenement houses, and who are, therefore, well qualified to speak, that the constantly open doors and the want of lighting in the hall, passages and landings at night, are responsible for much immorality. We fully endorse the evidence given by many witnesses that the surroundings of a tenement house in which there can be no privacy, and in which the children scarcely realise the meaning of the word 'home', form the worst possible atmosphere for the up-bringing of the younger generation who, as one of the witnesses stated, acquire a precocious knowledge of evil from early childhood.

'The surroundings … form the worst possible atmosphere for the up-bringing of the younger generation.'

… In the year 1879, and again in the year 1900, Commissions were appointed to consider the cause of the high death-rate in the City of Dublin, and in 1905 Surgeon-Colonel Flinn, your Medical Inspector for the time, was also asked to report on the subject. In each of the reports it is stated that one of the principal causes contributing to the high death-rate is the bad housing of the working classes in the City … The death rate for the year 1911 … was higher than in any of the large centres of population in England, Wales, or Scotland, and we fear that until the housing problem is adequately dealt with, no substantial reduction in the death-rate may be hoped for.

SIGNATORIES of the Irish Republican Proclamation.

Proclamation of the Irish Republic

The Irish Republic is declared by the leaders of the Easter Rising, 24 April 1916

PATRICK PEARSE (1879–1916) AND OTHERS

On Easter Monday, 24 April 1916, Patrick Pearse proclaimed the Irish Republic from the front step of the General Post Office in Dublin to a bemused crowd of onlookers. The schoolteacher-poet was commander-in-chief of the insurgents drawn from the Irish Volunteers and the Irish Citizen Army (ICA). Decades earlier the Irish Republican Brotherhood (IRB) had adopted the maxim that 'England's difficulty is Ireland's opportunity'. For many, although not all, of the IRB leadership, the outbreak of the Great War in August 1914 was just such a chance.

By 1915, with the war dragging on, the IRB Military Council was formed to plan an insurrection. It would ultimately comprise seven members: Pearse, Thomas Clarke, Sean MacDermott, Eamonn Ceannt, Joseph Plunkett, James Connolly and Thomas MacDonagh. The rising was planned for Easter, with its main focus on Dublin. The strategy, devised primarily by Plunkett, involved occupying key buildings and locations across the city. The rebels would be armed with ammunition from Germany, their 'gallant allies in Europe'. In fact this cache of arms was intercepted before it was landed. Naturally these plans had to be undertaken with the utmost secrecy, but the fact that senior members of the IRB and the Volunteers were not aware of them meant discretion was at a premium even among comrades. This was made doubly true by the fact that the Military Council knew central figures within their own movement would oppose the rebellion. Indeed, the Volunteers' chief of staff, Eoin MacNeill, would ultimately try to abort the rising on its eve.

This discretion meant that the 1916 leaders took most of the details of planning the rising to the grave with them. Among the more hazy aspects of the rebellion is the writing of the Proclamation of the Irish Republic. Kathleen Clarke, wife of Tom, recalled in her autobiography how her husband returned home from a meeting of the Military Council on Holy Tuesday saying that Pearse had been asked to draft a proclamation. Some changes were made to that rough copy, although Kathleen did not say what they were or who had made them. One of these amendments, following an objection by an (unnamed) leader, may have related to a clause on equality between the sexes.

Kathleen Clarke's account backs up the generally accepted belief, based on little more than educated guesswork, that the Proclamation was written by Pearse, with redrafting from Connolly and possibly MacDonagh. The styles were characteristic of each and it is fairly easy to see the joins. Pearse invoked God along with those dead generations that had asserted Ireland's right to national freedom and sovereignty in arms. Connolly affirmed guarantees of religious and civil liberty, equal rights and opportunities for all citizens, along with a promise that the Republic would cherish all the children of the nation in the same way. The manuscript of the Proclamation was written on two pages and entrusted to MacDonagh. The men who went on to print it recalled that it was written in a legible and upright script with hardly any corrections, one concluding at the time that it looked as if it were written by Pearse.

Much more is known about the printing of the Proclamation than its writing. Over Holy Thursday and Good Friday, James Connolly spoke to Christopher Brady, Michael J. Molloy and Liam O'Brien at the Irish Transport and General Workers' Union head-quarters in Liberty Hall. The three worked for the union as printers and compositors. Molloy and O'Brien were also members of the Volunteers. Individually, Connolly asked each man if he would be willing to come to Liberty Hall on Easter Sunday between 10 and 11 a.m. to print some bills. Only Molloy was given an indication of their nature. He was then dispatched to borrow some type from another printer since the press at Liberty Hall did not have enough for the job. After approaching two firms unsuc-cessfully, Molloy got what he needed in West's on Capel Street (after explaining to the proprietor that if he would not lend him the type, it would be taken anyway). Borrowed type notwithstanding, when the three men arrived at the press in Liberty Hall, they found they did not have enough letters for the whole Proclamation. The bill had to be printed in two halves. Even then, they had to improvise by fashioning letters out of sealing wax and using other types where necessary. That process, combined with the old printing press, meant that the work was time-consuming and laborious. Their task was only completed at 1 a.m. on Easter Monday. Exhausted, they went home, forgetting to remove the printing block from the press. When British soldiers came upon the works some days later, the block was smashed to pieces, along with the press itself.

Once the bills were printed, they were entrusted to members of the Citizen Army to take to the GPO. After Pearse made his oration, a future president of Ireland Seán T. O'Kelly, then staff captain in the GPO, was sent out with a bucket of adhesive to post the bills. Whoever sent him out was either desperate or had a wicked sense of humour, for O'Kelly must have been the shortest volunteer available for the job. He pasted the Proclamation along the length of Sackville (now O'Connell) Street and up to the gates of Trinity College, before returning to the GPO.

On the 90th anniversary of the rising, the then taoiseach, Bertie Ahern, described the rising as 'one of the four cornerstones of independent Ireland'. Certainly the Proclamation of the Irish Republic is among the best known Irish documents. Ironically, while Pearse – the 'ideologue and draftsman of the rebellion,' says Alvin Jackson – wrote most of the text, it is the injunction of Connolly to 'cherish all the children of the nation equally' that has endured across the generations.

IRISHMEN AND IRISHWOMEN: In the name of God and of the dead generations from which she receives her old tradition of nationhood, Ireland, through us, summons her children to her flag and strikes for her freedom.

Having organised and trained her manhood through her secret revolutionary organisation, the Irish Republican Brotherhood, and through her open military

POBLACHT NA H EIREANN.

THE PROVISIONAL GOVERNMENT
OF THE
IRISH REPUBLIC
TO THE PEOPLE OF IRELAND.

IRISHMEN AND IRISHWOMEN : In the name of God and of the dead generations
from which she receives her old tradition of nationhood, Ireland, through us, summons
her children to her flag and strikes for her freedom.

Having organised and trained her manhood through her secret revolutionary
organisation, the Irish Republican Brotherhood, and through her open military
organisations, the Irish Volunteers and the Irish Citizen Army, having patiently
perfected her discipline, having resolutely waited for the right moment to reveal
itself, she now seizes that moment, and, supported by her exiled children in America
and by gallant allies in Europe, but relying in the first on her own strength, she
strikes in full confidence of victory.

We declare the right of the people of Ireland to the ownership of Ireland, and to
the unfettered control of Irish destinies, to be sovereign and indefeasible.   The long
usurpation of that right by a foreign people and government has not extinguished the
right, nor can it ever be extinguished except by the destruction of the Irish people.   In
every generation the Irish people have asserted their right to national freedom and
sovereignty ; six times during the past three hundred years they have asserted it in
arms. Standing on that fundamental right and again asserting it in arms in the face
of the world, we hereby proclaim the Irish Republic as a Sovereign Independent State,
and we pledge our lives and the lives of our comrades-in-arms to the cause of its freedom,
of its welfare, and of its exaltation among the nations.

The Irish Republic is entitled to, and hereby claims, the allegiance of every
Irishman and Irishwoman.   The Republic guarantees religious and civil liberty, equal
rights and equal opportunities to all its citizens, and declares its resolve to pursue
the happiness and prosperity of the whole nation and of all its parts, cherishing all
the children of the nation equally, and oblivious of the differences carefully fostered
by an alien government, which have divided a minority from the majority in the past.

Until our arms have brought the opportune moment for the establishment of a
permanent National Government, representative of the whole people of Ireland and
elected by the suffrages of all her men and women, the Provisional Government, hereby
constituted, will administer the civil and military affairs of the Republic in trust for
the people.

We place the cause of the Irish Republic under the protection of the Most High God,
Whose blessing we invoke upon our arms, and we pray that no one who serves that
cause will dishonour it by cowardice, inhumanity, or rapine.   In this supreme hour
the Irish nation must, by its valour and discipline and by the readiness of its children
to sacrifice themselves for the common good, prove itself worthy of the august destiny
to which it is called.

Signed on Behalf of the Provisional Government,
THOMAS J. CLARKE,
SEAN Mac DIARMADA,   THOMAS MacDONAGH,
P. H. PEARSE,   EAMONN CEANNT,
JAMES CONNOLLY.   JOSEPH PLUNKETT.

organisations, the Irish Volunteers and the Irish Citizen Army, having patiently
perfected her discipline, having resolutely waited for the right moment to reveal
itself, she now seizes that moment, and supported by her exiled children in America
and by gallant allies in Europe, but relying in the first on her own strength, she
strikes in full confidence of victory.

We declare the right of the people of Ireland to the ownership of Ireland and to the unfettered control of Irish destinies, to be sovereign and indefeasible. The long usurpation of that right by a foreign people and government has not extinguished the right, nor can it ever be extinguished except by the destruction of the Irish people. In every generation the Irish people have asserted their right to national freedom and sovereignty; six times during the past three hundred years they have asserted it in arms. Standing on that fundamental right and again asserting it in arms in the face of the world, we hereby proclaim the Irish Republic as a Sovereign Independent State, and we pledge our lives and the lives of our comrades in arms to the cause of its freedom, of its welfare, and of its exaltation among the nations.

The Irish Republic is entitled to, and hereby claims, the allegiance of every Irishman and Irishwoman. The Republic guarantees religious and civil liberty, equal rights and equal opportunities to all its citizens, and declares its resolve to pursue the happiness and prosperity of the whole nation and of all its parts, cherishing all of the children of the nation equally, and oblivious of the differences carefully fostered by an alien Government, which have divided a minority from the majority in the past.

Until our arms have brought the opportune moment for the establishment of a permanent National Government, representative of the whole people of Ireland and elected by the suffrages of all her men and women, the Provisional Government, hereby constituted, will administer the civil and military affairs of the Republic in trust for the people.

We place the cause of the Irish Republic under the protection of the Most High God, Whose blessing we invoke upon our arms, and we pray that no one who serves that cause will dishonour it by cowardice, inhumanity, or rapine. In this supreme hour the Irish nation must, by its valour and discipline, and by the readiness of its children to sacrifice themselves for the common good, prove itself worthy of the august destiny to which it is called.

Signed on behalf of the Provisional Government:

THOMAS J. CLARKE,
SEAN MAC DIARMADA, THOMAS MACDONAGH,
P. H. PEARSE, EAMONN CEANNT,
JAMES CONNOLLY, JOSEPH PLUNKETT

Battle of the Somme War Diary

War diary, 2nd Battalion, Royal Irish Regiment, covering operations at Mametz Wood and Bazentin le Petit on the Somme, 1–14 July 1916

The frenzied efforts to enact Home Rule, and by unionists to prevent it, were brought to an abrupt halt when Britain declared war on Germany in August 1914. It was agreed that constitutional matters would be shelved for the duration of the conflict. Unionist and nationalist representatives at Westminster pledged their support for the war effort, yet even in this time of international conflict the national question was destined to become an issue.

For unionists it was a logical step to stand shoulder to shoulder with Britain. For the nationalist leader, John Redmond, it seemed dangerous to offer less than the unionists. Believing that nationalist Ireland's loyalty would be repaid in the long run, Redmond made a controversial speech at Woodenbridge, Co. Wicklow in September, instructing the Irish Volunteers to enlist. Many followed Redmond's call to arms. Some, appalled by news of German massacres in Belgium, enlisted to help secure the freedom of small nations. Others fought for economic reasons. Those such as the future Irish Republican Army man Tom Barry found the lure of military adventure irresistible.

At the outbreak of war, there were already some 20,000 Irishmen in the British army, with another 30,000 in the first line of reserves. In that opening year of the conflict, around 80,000 Irishmen enlisted, of whom half were Ulster Catholics and Protestants. In all, an estimated 206,000 Irishmen served during the Great War, with some 30,000 losing their lives. All were volunteers: the political situation in Ireland was such that, when conscription was introduced in Britain in January 1916, Ireland was exempted.

Among the most significant engagements for the Irish divisions in terms of loss of life was the landing at Suvla Bay in Gallipoli in 1915, when almost 3500 Irish soldiers died. Better remembered is the Battle of the Somme, described as the 'bloodiest battle in history'. This was a major offensive by British troops to relieve Allied forces in Verdun and to break the deadlock of trench warfare. In the short term, the move was a catastrophe. On the first day of the battle, 1 July 1916, some 100,000 soldiers went 'over the top'. Around 60,000 were wounded; 21,000 died (most during the first 45 minutes). Several Irish regiments fought from the outset, but the largest was the 36th (Ulster) Division. On the first two days of the battle, the division, numbering 15,000, suffered 5000 casualties, of which 2069 died.

By the time of the next British offensive, the 16th (Irish) Division had joined the Ulster Division. Both would remain on the Western Front in France for the rest of the war. The 16th suffered significant losses at Guillemont and Guinchy in September 1916 (including the poet and lecturer Tom Kettle MP), at Ypres in August 1917 and during the German Spring Offensive in 1918. As the historian Keith Jeffrey puts it, the Somme was 'a "blood sacrifice" which came to represent for unionists a conclusive demonstration of Ulster's unshakable loyalty to the union'.

In the south, the culture of remembrance that died out after independence has been revived in recent years. Commemoration of the Great War, once a divisive issue, has now become a means of reconciliation. The Somme has also come to symbolize the futility of war. Although most historians agree the battle was an important strategic success for the Allies, it came at a human cost: more than 310,000 men lost their lives in just over a hundred days of fighting.

⤛⤜

The Battalion assembled at 1am in a position in rear of the 20th and 91st Brigades who were in position to attack at zero hour, 7:30am. Orders were received that a new position was to be taken up in close support of the 91st Brigade at 7:30am, which were carried out, the battalion moved into trenches vacated by 22nd Battalion Manchester Regiment under a heavy fire. As the 91st Brigade had reached its final objective for the day the Battalion was not used in the attack, but at 10pm A Company was sent to Mametz to consolidate a position for the 21st Manchester Regiment, and D Company reinforced the 22nd Manchester Regiment with the object of repelling counter attacks. Both these companies withdrew at dawn the following morning and rejoined the Battalion, which was still in Divisional Reserve. On this day our casualties were 50 in all.

… 4th July 1916. In the evening about 7:30pm the battalion received orders to march via Mametz and consolidate the line Quadrangle Trench–Wood Trench–Strip Trench and to make a reconnaissance of Mametz Wood. The three trenches were stated to be in our hands and it was also mentioned that probably no resistance would be encountered in Mametz Wood. The Battalion was heavily encumbered with materials for consolidating and was halted on the road just south of Strip Trench for a rest. Lieutenant Tod and the Battalion scouts were sent out to reconnoitre Strip Trench and one of the scouts returned almost immediately with a prisoner, who informed us that there were a considerable number of Germans in the Wood. As the CO understood that the 1st Royal Welsh Fusiliers were in position on our right he ordered an immediate attack at Mametz Wood before the approach of daylight would reveal to the enemy [the fact that] a Battalion was halted in fours along a road within 100 yards of their position, so the Grenade Company was ordered to attack Strip Trench with B Company in support, while A and C Companies formed a defensive flank facing towards Quadrangle and Wood Trenches, both of which contrary to our information were discovered to be very strongly held by Germans.

'Enemy machine gun fire of great intensity was coming from the east of Mametz Wood.'

The Grenade Company almost immediately got a touch with the enemy and succeeded in bombing along Strip Trench almost as far as its junction with Wood Trench. The enemy was at this point strongly reinforced from the Wood which was very dense and impenetrable and the Grenade Company were gradually bombed back again and forced to fall back on their supports, which were also heavily engaged by the enemy. Enemy machine gun fire of great intensity was coming from the east of Mametz Wood and heavy crossfire from Quadrangle Trench which made our whole position untenable.

'Lieutenant Usher … had been wounded but refused to leave his platoon.'

The CO ordered a retirement to be made to a position about 300 yards back which afforded some cover, and applied for artillery support so that he could effect a retirement to Mametz. This retirement was eventually accomplished and the Battalion mustered again at Mansel Copse. The retirement was made reluctantly as many casualties had been inflicted on the enemy and on one occasion a footing had been effected in the wood and two field guns captured. But the failure of the 1st Royal Welsh Fusiliers to get into position on our right and the strength of the enemy who was being rapidly reinforced made it imperative to retire.

Our casualties were 75 all ranks. Lieutenant Usher and Second Lieutenant Kerr were killed leading attacks on Strip Trench. The former had been wounded but refused to leave his platoon. Second Lieutenant Perrin was wounded by a bomb in the leg which killed the German who threw it – this officer killed two Germans with bombs after being wounded. CSM Hayes was wounded in a gallant attempt to save Lieutenant Usher's life.

5th–6th July 1916. The 2nd Royal Irish and 1st Royal Welsh Fusiliers were ordered to attack Quadrangle Trench–Wood Trench and south corner of Mametz Wood with the 1st Royal Warwicks in support at Bottom Wood. Our objective was Wood Trench and Mametz Wood. This attack was commenced at 10:15pm under a heavy barrage from our guns. C Company under Captain Bell was ordered to attack Wood Trench with A Company in support. The Grenade Company under Captain Gordon-Ralph was again ordered to attack Strip Trench with B Company on their right to form a defensive flank. D Company was kept in Battalion reserve. The Royal Welsh Fusiliers attacked on our left, their objective being Quadrangle Trench.

A rapid and dashing attack was made by all the Companies concerned. C Company reached the wire in front of Wood Trench in less than 10 minutes, while the Grenade Company again entered Strip Trench. The wire in front of Wood Trench was found by C Company to be uncut and being extremely thick could not be penetrated. This Company was exposed to a very heavy close range fire and suffered severely, Captain Bell being killed in the German wire and two of his officers wounded. C Company was ordered to retire about 50 yards under cover of a fold in the ground and await reinforcements from A Company which were brought up rapidly by Captain O'Reilly

as regarding War Diaries and Intelligence
aries are contained in F. S. Regs., Part II.
he Staff Manual respectively. Title pages
e prepared in manuscript.

July 1916

INTELLIGENCE SUMMARY. *or* *The Royal Irish Regt*
(Erase heading not required.)

Date	Hour	Summary of Events and Information
July	14	(Continued).

During these counter attacks the enemy shelled the village and WOOD very heavily and B and D Coys suffered very heavily. Lieuts Tod, Hodges, Ryan, Pike, Pollack, Moran and Grant were wounded. At about 5 p.m the 3/Gordon Highlanders arrived and reinforced the Northern end of the village and gained complete touch with the WOOD on the left. At about 7 p.m the 3/Royal Warwickshire Regt took over the strong points in the village and the Royal Irish assembled on road SOUTH of village whence we marched to bivouack in MAMETZ WOOD). Our total casualties on this day were 334 all ranks. To understand the importance of this operation order appendix III together with reference map MARTINPUICH should be studied. At 8 p.m on this day the first cavalry went through the position held by us, the first cavalry used in this campaign for a period of over 18 months.

2353 Wt. W2544/1454 700,000 5/15 D. D.& L. A.D.S.S./Form/C. 2118.

who took command of both Companies. Three times between midnight and dawn Captain O'Reilly attacked Wood Trench in the most gallant manner, each time being only held up by the German wire which proved an insurmountable obstacle. The enemy's fire was intense and their trenches were very strongly held.

'Attack after attack was made but progress was impossible.'

At dawn the Commanding Officer ordered Captain O'Reilly to give it up and return which he was most reluctant to do although severely wounded in the hand. On our left the Royal Welsh Fusiliers entered the German trenches but were unable to bomb along to our assistance as the Quadrangle Trench did not join up with Wood Trench. Meanwhile the Grenade Company covered by B Company were hammering away at Strip Trench and here fighting was almost entirely of hand to hand nature. Captain Gordon-Ralph was wounded in the neck but carried on until carried away unconscious. Lieutenant Pike who took command of the Grenade Company led two attacks on Strip Trench and once again entered Mametz Wood only to be driven out by fierce bombing counter attacks. Captain Moore-Brabazon was wounded in the foot by an enemy bayonet and handed over command of the company to Lieutenant Blake who was blown up by a shell and carried away shortly after.

Attack after attack was made but progress was impossible and after about 3:30am the battalion was ordered by the BGC 22nd Brigade to retire and return to Mansel Copse.

Our casualties in this attack were 125 all ranks. Captain Bell and Lieutenant White were killed, both inside the German wire; Captain Moore-Brabazon, Captain O'Reilly, Lieutenant Blake, Captain Gordon-Ralph, Lieutenant Price and CSM Burns were wounded. The Chaplain, the Reverend Father Fitzmaurice distinguished himself by rescuing wounded under heavy fire and RSM Carew did very good work getting up ammunition under fire.

… 14th July 1916. Attack started at 4:30am. First stage swiftly successful, Circus Trench taken and held by 1st Royal Warwickshire Regiment without much opposition. Village of Bazentin le Petit captured by the 2nd Royal Irish at 6:30am. 150 prisoners taken in village including a battalion commander. Consolidation of positions laid down in order commenced with assistance of RE. In this attack the village was captured by C Company commanded by Captain Tighe. The Grenade Company cleared all cellars and dugouts closely following C Company's attack. A Company commanded by Lieutenant Hegarty attacked the cemetery and established a defensive line running from X Roads S8a.8.7 to the cemetery including a strong post at the windmill. The Company formed a defensive flank on the left of village and obtained connection with 21st Division … D Company was in Battalion Reserve.

At about 11:45am the enemy counter attacked the Wood on our left and in response to an urgent appeal for reinforcements two Platoons of B Company and two Platoons of D Company were sent to their assistance. This reinforcement almost immediately encountered the enemy in large numbers and was driven back into the village with severe casualties. Lieutenant Finlay was killed in his counter-attack, C Company in process of consolidating strong point northern end of the village was attacked from the Wood on the left hand and outflanked. RE working on the strong points were ordered to retire by their own officers, which retirement was successfully carried out. At this juncture Captain Tighe in command of C Company was killed by an enemy machine gun firing from his left flank in the Wood, and Lieutenant Stuttaford and CSM Smith seriously wounded together with practically all the NCOs of this Company. The enemy at this juncture gained the northern extremity of the village but they vacated it on being counter attacked by heavy fire from D Company and A Company from our right flank.

At 12:45pm the enemy again counter attacked the east side of the village, assembling apparently in High Wood. This attack gained the windmill which was being held by A Company and almost reached the village. Lieutenant Deane and three men were killed at close quarters in the windmill. A counter attack was organised and commanded by the Adjutant which succeeded in driving off the attack. Afterwards the same officer worked through Bazentin Le Petit Wood and re-established the line there previously held by the 21st Division. During these counter attacks the enemy shelled the village and wood very heavily, and B and D companies suffered very heavily. Lieutenants Tod, Hodges, Ryan, Pike, Pollack, Moran and Grant were wounded. At about 5pm the 2nd Gordon Highlanders arrived and reinforced the northern end of the village and gained complete touch with the wood on the left. At about 7pm the 2nd Royal Warwickshire Regiment took over the strong points in the village and the Royal Irish assembled on road south of village, whence we marched to bivouack in Mametz Wood.

Our total casualties on this day were 334 all ranks. At 8pm on this day the first cavalry went through the position held by us, the first cavalry used in this campaign for a period of over 18 months.

Report of the
bour Commission
to Ireland

*uiry into the conduct of British troops
in Ireland, January 1921*

BRITISH LABOUR PARTY

Sinn Féin won a landslide victory in Ireland at the general election held immediately after the Great War in 1918. In accordance with its mandate, the newly elected Sinn Féin MPs refused to take their seats at Westminster and established instead the first Dáil. It met for the first time in Dublin's Mansion House on 21 January 1919. On that same day, the first shots of the war of independence were fired when two members of the Royal Irish Constabulary (RIC) escorting a load of gelignite were killed in an ambush led by Dan Breen and Seán Treacy in Soloheadbeg, Co. Tipperary.

This episode was characteristic of much of the first year of the conflict, which consisted mostly of raids on RIC stations to procure arms and attacks on individual policemen. By the beginning of 1920 the RIC had withdrawn from significant areas of the south and west, with republican forces effectively in control of large areas of the country.

Unwilling to admit that they were fighting a war in Ireland, the British government was left in a bind. If they were not at war, they could not send in the army. But the RIC, as a police force, was not equipped for this kind of scenario. In response Lloyd George's government came up with an unhappy compromise. They began a recruitment drive among demobbed soldiers to augment the RIC. By April 1920, a special training centre for these men was operating in the Curragh. Their uniforms, hastily assembled from RIC and army kit, saw them dubbed the 'Black and Tans'. They were paid 10 shillings a day to 'make appropriate hell' for the rebels. Soon afterwards, in July, a new force was inaugurated. Known as the Auxiliaries, these were demobbed officers, who were supposed to operate independently of – although reporting to – the RIC. In effect, they were subject to neither military nor police control. In fact, they were under no control at all.

Divided into 15 companies of 100 men and dispersed in the most troublesome areas of the country, the Auxiliaries soon earned a reputation as an unruly force capable of great brutality. No matter how excessive their violence or destruction, little effort was made to rein them in. As far as the British government was concerned, the policy of reprisal was working, Lloyd George proclaiming in October 1920, 'we have murder by the throat.' Terror, which included the sack of Balbriggan and of Cork, reached a zenith at the end of that year. Perhaps the most infamous incident was on 21 November, which became known as Bloody Sunday. 'Black and Tans and Auxiliaries' forces opened fire on the crowd during a match at Croke Park, killing 14 apparently in reprisal for the killing that morning of British intelligence officers.

The historian Joe Lee argues that the Black and Tans 'were too few to impose a real reign of terror, but numerous enough to commit sufficient atrocities to provoke nationalist opinion in Ireland and America, and to outrage British liberal opinion, which felt that if Britain could not hold Ireland according to "British" standards then she shouldn't hold Ireland at all'. The British Labour Party – which would form a government for the first time in 1924 – was vocal in condemning the campaign of terror. Arthur Henderson MP, who had been in Lloyd George's war cabinet, slammed the government's 'recourse to methods of violence as a confession of bankruptcy of statesmanship and the desperate expedient of men lost to all sense of humanity'. The Labour Party established a commission chaired by Henderson to investigate events in Ireland. Guided by members of the Irish Labour Party and the Trade Union Congress, they travelled to the areas worst affected by police violence. The report, which was presented to a special conference in January 1921, was temperate in tone, but the sense of shock at the violent behaviour of British forces runs through its pages. It became central to Labour's campaign against violence in Ireland, which included some 500 meetings around Britain. In the short run, the report had little impact on the government, which would refuse to enter unconditional talks with Sinn Féin for almost another year. In the longer term, it was part of the litany of embarrassments that forced Lloyd George to rethink his failed policy in Ireland.

The situation in Ireland today is nothing short of a tragedy, whether from the point of view of the Irish people or from the standpoint of British honour and prestige. British labour is vitally interested in the Irish situation from two points of view. It is concerned with the problem of Irish government and the bestowal upon the people of Ireland of the freedom which they passionately desire. It is concerned also with the degradation which the British people are now suffering in consequence of the policy of repression and coercion which has been carried out in its name.

… [The British Labour Party's] request for an inquiry was refused. The situation in Ireland did not improve. Indeed, it grew worse, and the LP, therefore, decided to set up a Commission under its own auspices to inquire into the whole question of 'reprisals' and violence in Ireland.

THE REIGN OF VIOLENCE: 'Reprisals'

We shall, in this report, deal in some detail with a number of the recent tragic occurrences in Ireland. The government has repeatedly condoned 'reprisals,' and the Chief Secretary has defended the action of the armed forces of the Crown. On numerous occasions in the House of Commons he has given a point blank denial to statements made by members of the House on the basis of information received from non-official Irish sources. He has made assertions … that many of the unhappy events in Ireland of which the British public has heard during the past few months were either figments of the imagination or incidents in which the acts of the Crown forces were justifiable. The results of our investigations will show how much truth there is in this point of view.

'These are the methods of the Inquisition.'

1. General terrorism and provocative behaviour

In every part of Ireland that we visited we were impressed by the atmosphere of terrorism which prevailed. This is due to some extent to uncertainty; people are afraid that their houses might be burned; they fear that they might be arrested or even dragged from their beds and shot.

'The insolent and provocative conduct of certain sections of the Crown forces.'

But terrorism is accentuated by other less direct methods. Lorries of armed men with their rifles 'at the ready' are frequent sights in the towns and even in the country districts. We are aware that the Irish Secretary would have us believe that these 'brave men' might be shot by 'cowardly assassins' in the streets, but we cannot believe that for men to carry rifles 'at the ready' is a means of protection against the possibility of being shot from a window or at a distance. This display of arms assists to spread the feeling of terror. The sight of 'tin hats,' drawn bayonets, and revolvers, and here and there of sandbags, or machine guns, or powerful searchlights, is calculated to terrorise the civilian population.

… The insolent and provocative conduct of certain sections of the Crown forces is even more likely to inspire fear or to incite 'reprisals.' In at least one town to our own knowledge, the RIC often carry 'Black and Tan' flags on their motor lorries, glorying in the title which has spread fear throughout the land. Sometimes, below it will be found a small Sinn Féin flag, or the flag of the Irish Republic will be trailed at the tail of the lorry in the dust or mire of the road. We would submit that no disciplined force would so deliberately encourage bitterness of spirit or inflame feelings of retaliation in this way. We have witnessed with feelings of shame the insolent swagger of individual 'Black and Tans' in the streets of Irish towns … It is unfortunate also that the civilian population should witness – as many have done – members of the Crown forces under the influence of drink. A member of the Commission stated to his colleagues that he had seen in the street an Auxiliary cadet, revolver in hand, distinctly the worse for liquor.

At a railway station, the members of the Commission saw a number of 'Black and Tans' … invade a refreshment room … Some of the uniformed men were the worse for drink, and one … lurched along the platform of the station using his rifle, presumably loaded, as a walking stick … In some places, members of the Crown forces have compelled shopkeepers to obliterate the Irish signs over their doors and windows. This we know has happened at Killarney, Tralee, and Listowel.

Perhaps the most potent method of spreading terror is that which is frequently adopted during raids and searches … as illustration we may quote the case of a local

REPORT OF THE LABOUR COMMISSION TO IRELAND

PART I
INTRODUCTION

THE situation in Ireland to-day is nothing short of a tragedy, whether from the point of view of the Irish people or from the standpoint of British honour and prestige. British labour is vitally interested in the Irish situation from two points of view. It is concerned with the problem of Irish Government and the bestowal upon the people of Ireland of the freedom which they passionately desire. It is concerned also with the degradation which the British people are now suffering in consequence of the policy of repression and coercion which has been carried out in its name. On the general problem of the settlement of the political problem in Ireland, the Labour Party has declared its policy. The manifesto embodying this policy is reprinted as an appendix to this Report. Labour representatives in the House of Commons have protested against the policy of physical force applied to Ireland, as the Labour Party regards recourse to methods of violence as a confession of bankruptcy of statesmanship and the desperate expedient of men lost to all sense of humanity.

On October 25 Mr. Arthur Henderson moved in the House of Commons :

> That this house regrets the present state of lawlessness in Ireland and the lack of discipline in the armed forces of the Crown, resulting in the death or injury of innocent citizens and the destruction of property ; and is of opinion that an independent investigation should at once be instituted into the causes, nature, and extent of reprisals on the part of those whose duty is the maintenance of law and order.

This proposed vote of censure condemned the action of the British Government and its agents in Ireland, and asked for an independent inquiry. The request for an inquiry was refused. The situation in Ireland did not improve. Indeed, it grew worse, and the Labour Party, therefore, decided to set up a Commission under its own auspices to inquire into the whole question of "reprisals" and violence in Ireland.

The Personnel of the Commission

The Parliamentary Labour Party appointed three of its members, the Right Hon. Arthur Henderson, M.P., Mr. J. Lawson, M.P., and Mr. W. Lunn, M.P., to serve on the Commission, whilst the Executive Committee of the Labour Party appointed its chairman (Mr. A. G. Cameron), its vice-chairman (Mr. F. W. Jowett), and Mr. J. Bromley to represent the Executive of the party. At the first meeting of the Commission Mr. Henderson was unanimously elected as chairman. In view of the importance of the delegation's work, and the opportunities which it was thought might arise to assist the establishment of peace in Ireland, the Right Hon. W. Adamson, M.P., joined the Commission. Brigadier-General C. B. Thomson became military adviser, and Captain C. W. Kendall, legal

(1)

trade union official. We do not for one moment believe that the Government can prove anything against him – unless to be a trade union official is a crime – and we are convinced of his veracity. Some months ago he was arrested and imprisoned for five days without any reason being assigned. More recently, he was visited by armed men after he had retired to bed. His wife and children were told to leave the bedroom. The man, whose only garment was his shirt, was told to put up his hands and, with the muzzle of a rifle barrel placed to his bare chest, he was interrogated for a space of twenty five minutes on matters on which he had no knowledge. These are the methods of the Inquisition.

… After Curfew in Dublin we heard on several nights the firing of shots. As civilians out after ten p.m. run the risk of being shot at sight, and as the police and military utilise the curfew hours for raiding purposes, it is a fair assumption that shots during the night are generally fired by them. We have been told that often this firing is not intended for purposes of destruction, in which case we can only conclude that its purpose is terrorism.

2. The burning of property

Generally, as … in the recent great fire at Cork, the Chief Secretary denies the existence of evidence showing that the fires were caused by forces which theoretically are under his control. There is, however, ample evidence … to show that buildings have been deliberately burnt and in many cases utterly destroyed by servants of the Crown. The premises which have been destroyed include creameries, factories, and other large business premises, as well as shops, private houses and farms.

> *'Many small cottages have been destroyed*
> *by the Crown forces.'*

… The Commission made inquiries into the burning of a farm, the tenant of which was an aged and bed-ridden woman of seventy-five years. Members of the Commission found the house and farm buildings in ruins, with the exception of a small fowl-house. This shelter, without windows and lighted only when the door is open, was occupied by the two daughters of the old lady, and a boy of about eight years, their nephew. They are living now under deplorable conditions. The tenant of the farm has been removed to the workhouse. Two policemen and a number of men in civilian dress came to the farm and asked for a son of the tenant. He was not at home. The occupants were told to 'clear out.' The old lady, who was ill, was taken outside, and the two sisters, partly dressed and without boots, together with the small boy in his nightshirt, left the house. The men poured petrol on the beds and furniture, on the outhouses and the pigsty, and even on the pigs and poultry. The buildings were burnt to the ground, and about forty fowls were burnt to death, but the pigs were rescued. The family spent the night in the fields. On the morning after the fire, two full tins of petrol and some empty tins were found in the farmyard.

In Balbriggan many small cottages have been destroyed by the Crown forces. Many citizens of Cork have suffered the loss of their homes. The countryside has not escaped, for in our inquiries we came across hamlets where cottages here and there had been burnt, usually by the Black and Tans or other Crown forces as part of a night's programme. In how many small country towns there are to be seen the charred remains of homes we cannot say, but it is beyond doubt that arson has been committed on a large scale.

> *'The whole of the civilian population*
> *has been in varying degrees under the terror.'*

The atmosphere of Cork prior to the latest acts of incendiarism was beyond description. During the time we were in the city terrorism was at its height. Cork has perhaps suffered longer from the brutal domination of ill-disciplined armed forces than any other town in Ireland, probably because it has been regarded as one of the most important Sinn Fein centres. Within the past twelve months there have been three Lord Mayors of Cork. Lord Mayor McCurtain was murdered in the presence of his wife. Mr Terence MacSwiney died in prison. His present successor is 'on the run' and carrying out his duties as best he can.

The whole of the civilian population has been in varying degrees under the terror. During the month of November alone we were informed by the Cork City Council that over 200 Curfew arrests had been made, four Sinn Fein clubs burnt to the ground, twelve large business premises destroyed by fire (in addition to attempts made to fire others including the City Hall), seven men shot dead, a dozen men dangerously wounded, fifteen trains held up, four publicly placarded threats to the citizens of Cork issued, and over 500 houses of private citizens forcibly entered and searched. This by no means completes the list of incidents which occurred in Cork in the space of a single month. There were, in addition, attempted arrests which were unsuccessful, much indiscriminate shooting, and many minor outrages upon the people of Cork.

… The Commission was impressed by the sense of impending disaster which overhung the city of Cork during the time it was staying there. This uncertainty was ended by the tragic occurrences of Saturday, December 11, when the Regent Street of Cork was destroyed by incendiaries. By this date the Commission had returned to Dublin, but it decided to send two members of the Commission to Cork to make immediate investigations. The newspaper reports of the Cork fires conveyed but a faint impression of the terrible havoc wrought in the city. The most valuable premises in the town were utterly destroyed, large business houses and massively fronted shops were reduced to piles of smouldering debris, charred woodwork, and twisted iron girders.

Shortly after 9pm on Saturday, December 11, Auxiliary Police and Black and Tans appeared in large numbers in the streets of the city, and at the revolver point (before actual firing took place) drove people to their homes earlier than the Curfew regulations required.

This was regarded by the citizens as ominous and increased the nervousness which had been caused by the ambush at Dillon's Cross during the same day and the apprehensions of reprisals that were naturally entertained by the people. The streets were soon entirely deserted and the work of destruction begun.

The first of the burnings took place at Grant's extensive premises in Patrick Street, and during the night new fires broke out. At 4am the City Hall was fired and the efforts of the firemen failed to save it. It was completely gutted … the City Library adjacent to the Hall was also destroyed … eye-witnesses observing the fires from adjacent premises state positively that the incendiaries were agents of the British Government … the fires appear to have been an organised attempt to destroy the most valuable premises in the city.

Balbriggan

The incidents which occurred at Balbriggan on the night of September 20–21 last have been admitted by the British Government to be in the nature of a 'reprisal' for the shooting of two members of the RIC. There is no doubt in our minds after visiting Balbriggan and taking evidence in the Town Hall there that the Crown forces were utterly out of hand and took the law into their own hands to inflict punishment on the population of the town for the death of Inspector Burke and the wounding of another policeman.

'Almost all the houses had been burnt or their windows broken.'

Shops, houses, and inns were set on fire, and in one long street almost all the houses had been burnt or their windows broken. The illustration given in the Report shows a portion of the right side of this street. On the left are a number of houses of a newer type, erected by the local authority, now in ruins. The hosiery factory of Messrs. Deedes, Templer, and Co. Ltd. … is now a mere shell. Messrs. Smith and Co.'s factory was saved from destruction only through the intervention of a man who appealed to the policemen who said they were going to burn it down.

The incendiaries appear to have gloated over their evil works for they waved their caps and cheered. There is evidence to show that they looted drink. A local policeman admitted that the outrages were 'going too far,' but he was sworn at by the invaders for asking them to desist from further damage.

'Balbriggan offers a clear example of a 'reprisal'.'

Two civilians were killed and others injured. We discovered cases of brutal treatment by the police. The people fled in terror to the fields, in very many cases clad only in their night attire. Men, women and children spent the night out of doors and for days afterwards the little town became practically deserted with the approach of nightfall, the population leaving their homes for the night through fear of another attack. In addition to two civilians who were killed, two women died from the effects of exposure, and four babies suffering from measles were taken out to the fields and died as a consequence.

Balbriggan offers a clear example of a 'reprisal' where men wearing the uniform of the British Crown broke out of control and took a savage revenge upon the whole population of the town for an 'outrage' upon members of the Royal Irish Constabulary.

The
Anglo-Irish
Treaty

Articles of agreement for a treaty between
Great Britain and Ireland, 6 December 1921

DAVID LLOYD GEORGE (1863–1945) AND OTHERS

Two and a half years after the war of independence began, a truce between the British and Irish sides was agreed in the summer of 1921. During July, the president, Éamon de Valera, and the British prime minister, David Lloyd George, held four unproductive meetings in an effort to reach consensus. Lloyd George was willing to offer dominion status, which marked a level of political automony far greater than that provided by the 1920 Government of Ireland Act. This was nowhere near the 32-county independent republic demanded by de Valera and Sinn Féin.

Although the discussions failed, an uneasy truce held. Over the next months, de Valera and Lloyd George kept lines of communication open, even if their letters only confirmed that there was no common ground between them. Eventually Lloyd George, determined to bring matters to a head, issued an invitation to the Irish side to enter into further talks in London. De Valera formally accepted on 30 September.

Since Lloyd George had clearly signalled that any British concessions would fall well short of a republic, individual members of the Irish cabinet were reluctant to volunteer for the negotiating team. Five deputies were eventually selected, although none relished their appointment. Arthur Griffith was to be chairman, assisted by Michael Collins (who was particularly unenthusiastic), Robert Barton, George Gavan Duffy and Éamon Duggan. De Valera had refused point blank to head the delegation, despite pleas at cabinet. He declined again when, during the Dáil's ratification of the delegation, the minister for local government, W.T. Cosgrave, moved that de Valera lead the team. Cosgrave noted that president de Valera, 'had an extraordinary experience in negotiations. He also had the advantage of being in touch already. The head of the state in England was Mr. Lloyd George and would be one of the plenipotentiaries on the side of England.' Moreover, as Cosgrave put it, this was a team they were sending over and they were leaving their ablest player in reserve. Nevertheless, de Valera continued his refusal to join the delegation, a decision that has remained the stuff of controversy ever since.

The Irish contingent was ill prepared for the negotiations and the 'reserve team' without de Valera was no match for the likes of Lloyd George, Austen Chamberlain, Lord Birkenhead and Winston Churchill. They were experienced politicians, used to negotiating at the highest level: the prime minister, for one, had played a key role in the Paris Peace Conference at the end of the First World War. The Anglo-Irish negotiations opened on 11 October in London (putting the Irish side at an immediate disadvantage). The mood within the Irish camp was fraught. There was a significant level of distrust between the men, which was made more acute as the group split into smaller sub-committees during the negotiations. The republic remained out of bounds, and while there were some concessions on oaths, Britain's determination to make Ireland retain ties of Empire looked like a deal breaker. The details of partition also remained complicated, although it was agreed that a boundary commission would return to the issue at a later date.

Facing an Irish delegation unwilling to accept a deal, Lloyd George promised 'immediate and terrible war' within three days. The threat worked. On 6 December 1921, the Dáil representatives signed the articles of agreement of the Anglo-Irish Treaty. This provided for an Irish Free State that would be a dominion of the British Empire. Six counties would be partitioned from the new state for the time being. The delegation returned to Dublin to face the wrath of de Valera and others, who believed they had exceeded their authority. No-one thought the agreement ideal, but most, like Michael Collins, took a pragmatic view that it provided 'the freedom to achieve freedom.' In the event, cabinet approved the treaty on 8 December. The Dáil followed one month later. The treaty gave Ireland as much independence as Britain was prepared to concede. 'The republic' had never been on the table. As Collins later put it, the surrender of that republic occurred 'with the acceptance of the invitation' to negotiate rather than with the signing of the treaty itself.

1. Ireland shall have the same constitutional status in the Community of Nations known as the British Empire as the Dominion of Canada, the Commonwealth of Australia, the Dominion of New Zealand and the Union of South Africa, with a Parliament having powers to make laws for the peace, order and good government of Ireland and an Executive responsible to that Parliament, and shall be styled and known as the Irish Free State.

2. Subject to the provisions hereinafter set out the position of the Irish Free State in relation to the Imperial Parliament and Government and otherwise shall be that of the Dominion of Canada, and the law practice and constitutional usage governing the relationship of the Crown or the representative of the Crown and of the Imperial Parliament to the Dominion of Canada shall govern their relationship to the Irish Free State.

3. The representative of the Crown in Ireland shall be appointed in like manner as the Governor-General of Canada and in accordance with the practice observed in the making of such appointments.

4. The oath to be taken by Members of the Parliament of the Irish Free State shall be in the following form:

I ...... do solemnly swear true faith and allegiance to the Constitution of the Irish Free State as by law established and that I will be faithful to H.M. King George V, his heirs and successors by law, in virtue of the common citizenship of Ireland with Great Britain and her adherence to and membership of the group of nations forming the British Commonwealth of Nations.

5. The Irish Free State shall assume liability for the service of the Public Debt of the United Kingdom as existing at the date hereof and towards the payment of war

~~PROPOSED~~ ARTICLES OF AGREEMENT.

—

1.   Ireland shall have the same constitutional status in the Community of Nations known as the British Empire as the Dominion of Canada, the Commonwealth of Australia, the Dominion of New Zealand, and the Union of South Africa, with a Parliament having powers to make laws for the peace order and good government of Ireland and an Executive responsible to that Parliament, and shall be styled and known as the Irish Free State.

2.   Subject to the provisions hereinafter set out the position of the Irish Free State in relation to the Imperial Parliament and Government and otherwise shall be that of the Dominion of Canada, and the law, practice and constitutional usage governing the relationship of the Crown or the representative of the Crown and of the Imperial Parliament to the Dominion of Canada shall govern their relationship to the Irish Free State.

3.   The representative of the Crown in Ireland shall be appointed in like manner as the Governor-General of Canada and in accordance with the practice observed in the making of such appointments.

4.   The oath to be taken by Members of the Parliament of the Irish Free State shall be in the following form:-

I.......do solemnly swear true faith and allegiance to the Constitution of the Irish Free State as by law established and that I will be faithful to H.M.King George V., his heirs and successors by law, in virtue of the common citizenship of Ireland with Great Britain and her adherence to and membership of the group of nations forming the British Commonwealth of Nations.

1.

passing of the Government of
constituting   a provisional Government shall take the steps nec-
provisional Government the powers
the discharge of its duties, pro-
such provisional Government shall
his or her acceptance of this in-
gement shall not continue in force
twelve months from the date hereof.

all be submitted forthwith by His
the approval of Parliament and by
to a meeting summoned for the purpose
to sit in the House of Commons of
if approved shall be ratified by the

On behalf of the Irish
Delegation

Art ó Gríobhtha (Arthur Griffith)
Mícheál ó Coileáin
Riobárd Bartún
Eudmonn S. ó Dúgáin
Seórsa Gabháin uí Dhubhthaigh

On behalf of the British
Delegation

D Lloyd George
Austen Chamberlain
Birkenhead
Winston S. Churchill

December   , 1921.

pensions as existing at that date in such proportion as may be fair and equitable, having regard to any just claims on the part of Ireland by way of set-off or counter-claim, the amount of such sums being determined in default of agreement by the arbitration of one or more independent persons being citizens of the British Empire.

'I do solemnly swear true faith and allegiance to the Constitution of the Irish Free State.'

6. Until an arrangement has been made between the British and Irish Governments whereby the Irish Free State undertakes her own coastal defence, the defence by sea of Great Britain and Ireland shall be undertaken by His Majesty's Imperial Forces. But this shall not prevent the construction or maintenance by the Government of the Irish Free State of such vessels as are necessary for the protection of the Revenue or the Fisheries.

The foregoing provisions of this Article shall be reviewed at a Conference of Representatives of the British and Irish Governments to be held at the expiration of five years from the date hereof with a view to a share in her own coastal defence.

7. The Government of the Irish Free State shall afford to His Majesty's Imperial Forces:

    (a) In time of peace such harbour and other facilities as are indicated in the Annex hereto, or such other facilities as may from time to time be agreed between the British Government and the Government of the Irish Free State; and

    (b) In time of war or of strained relations with a Foreign Power such harbour and other facilities as the British Government may require for the purposes of such defence as aforesaid.

8. With a view to securing the observance of the principle of international limitation of armaments, if the Government of the Irish Free State establishes and maintains a military defence force, the establishments thereof shall not exceed in size such proportion of the military establishments maintained in Great Britain as that which the population of Ireland bears to the population of Great Britain.

9. The ports of Great Britain and the Irish Free State shall be freely open to the ships of the other country on payment of the customary port and other dues.

10. The Government of the Irish Free State agrees to pay fair compensation on terms not less favourable than those accorded by the Act of 1920 to judges, officials, members of Police Forces and other Public Servants who are discharged by it or who retire in consequence of the change of Government effected in pursuance hereof.

[It is] provided that this agreement shall not apply to members of the Auxiliary Police Force or to persons recruited in Great Britain for the Royal Irish Constabulary during the two years next preceding the date hereof. The British Government will assume responsibility for such compensation or pensions as may be payable to any of these excepted persons.

11. Until the expiration of one month from the passing of the Act of Parliament for the ratification of this instrument, the powers of the Parliament and the Government of the Irish Free State shall not be exercisable as respects Northern Ireland and the provisions of the Government of Ireland Act, 1920, shall so far as they relate to Northern Ireland remain of full force and effect, and no election shall be held for the return of members to serve in the Parliament of the Irish Free State for constituencies in Northern Ireland, unless a resolution is passed by both Houses of the Parliament of Northern Ireland in favour of the holding of such election before the end of the said month.

'The powers of the Parliament and Government of the Irish Free State shall no longer extend to Northern Ireland.'

12. If before the expiration of the said month, an address is presented to His Majesty by both Houses of the Parliament of Northern Ireland to that effect, the powers of the Parliament and Government of the Irish Free State shall no longer extend to Northern Ireland, and the provisions of the Government of Ireland Act, 1920 (including those relating to the Council of Ireland) shall, so far as they relate to Northern Ireland, continue to be of full force and effect, and this instrument shall have effect subject to the necessary modifications.

Provided that if such an address is so presented a Commission consisting of three Persons, one to be appointed by the Government of the Irish Free State, one to be appointed by the Government of Northern Ireland and one who shall be Chairman to be appointed by the British Government shall determine in accordance with the wishes of the inhabitants, so far as may be compatible with economic and geographic conditions, the boundaries between Northern Ireland and the rest of Ireland, and for the purposes of the Government of Ireland Act, 1920, and of this instrument, the boundary of Northern Ireland shall be such as may be determined by such Commission.

13. For the purpose of the last foregoing article, the powers of the Parliament of Southern Ireland under the Government of Ireland Act, 1920, to elect members of the Council of Ireland shall after the Parliament of the Irish Free State is constituted be exercised by that Parliament.

14. After the expiration of the said month, if no such address as is mentioned in Article 12 hereof is presented, the Parliament and Government of Northern Ireland shall continue to exercise as respects Northern Ireland the powers conferred on them by the Government of Ireland Act, 1920, but the Parliament and Government of the Irish Free State shall in Northern Ireland have in relation to matters in respect of which the Parliament of Northern Ireland has not power to make laws under that Act (including matters which under the said Act are within the jurisdiction of the Council of Ireland) the same powers as in the rest of Ireland, subject to such other provisions as may be agreed in manner hereinafter appearing.

15. At any time after the date hereof the Government of Northern Ireland and the provisional Government of Southern Ireland hereinafter constituted may meet for the purpose of discussing the provisions subject to which the last foregoing article is to operate in the event of no such address as is therein mentioned being presented and those provisions may include:

    (a) Safeguards with regard to patronage in Northern Ireland:

    (b) Safeguards with regard to the collection of revenue in Northern Ireland:

    (c) Safeguards with regard to import and export duties affecting the trade or industry of Northern Ireland:

    (d) Safeguards for minorities in Northern Ireland:

    (e) The settlement of the financial relations between Northern Ireland and the Irish Free State:

    (f) The establishment and powers of a local militia in Northern Ireland and the relation of the Defence Forces of the Irish Free State and of Northern Ireland respectively:

and if at any such meeting provisions are agreed to, the same shall have effect as if they were included amongst the provisions subject to which the Powers of the Parliament and Government of the Irish Free State are to be exercisable in Northern Ireland under Article 14 hereof.

'Neither the Parliament of the Irish Free State nor the Parliament of Northern Ireland shall make any law so as ... to ... restrict the free exercise ... of religious belief.'

16. Neither the Parliament of the Irish Free State nor the Parliament of Northern Ireland shall make any law so as either directly or indirectly to endow any religion or prohibit or restrict the free exercise thereof or give any preference or impose any disability on account of religious belief or religious status or affect prejudicially the right of any child to attend a school receiving public money without attending religious instruction at the school or make any discrimination as respects state aid between schools under the management of different religious denominations or divert from any religious denomination or any educational institution any of its property except for public utility purposes and on payment of compensation.

17. By way of provisional arrangement for the administration of Southern Ireland during the interval which must elapse between the date hereof and the constitution of a Parliament and Government of the Irish Free State in accordance therewith, steps shall be taken forthwith for summoning a meeting of members of Parliament elected for constituencies in Southern Ireland since the passing of the Government of Ireland Act, 1920, and for constituting a provisional Government, and the British Government shall take the steps necessary to transfer to such provisional Government the powers and machinery requisite for the discharge of its duties, provided that every member of such provisional Government shall have signified in writing his or her acceptance of this instrument. But this arrangement shall not continue in force beyond the expiration of twelve months from the date hereof.

18. This instrument shall be submitted forthwith by His Majesty's Government for the approval of Parliament and by the Irish signatories to a meeting summoned for the purpose of the members elected to sit in the House of Commons of Southern Ireland, and if approved shall be ratified by the necessary legislation.

On behalf of the Irish Delegation.   On behalf of the British Delegation.

Signed   *Signed*

ART Ó GRÍOBHTHA.   D. LLOYD GEORGE.

MICHEAL Ó COILÉAIN.   AUSTEN CHAMBERLAIN.
RIOBÁRD BARTÚN.   BIRKENHEAD.
EUDHMONN S. Ó DÚGÁIN.   WINSTON S. CHURCHILL.
SEÓRSA GHABHÁIN UÍ DHUBHTHAIGH.   L. WORTHINGTON-EVANS.
                                               HAMAR GREENWOOD.
                                               GORDON HEWART.

December 6th, 1921

ANNEX

1. The following are the specific facilities required:

   Dockyard Port at Berehaven
   (a) Admiralty property and rights to be retained as at the rate hereof.
        Harbour defences to remain in charge of British care and maintenance parties.

Queenstown

(b) Harbour defences to remain in charge of British care and maintenance parties. Certain mooring buoys to be retained for use of His Majesty's ships.

Belfast Lough

(c) Harbour defences to remain in charge of British care and maintenance parties.

Lough Swilly

(d) Harbour defences to remain in charge of British care and maintenance parties.

Aviation

(e) Facilities in the neighbourhood of the above Ports for coastal defence by air.

Oil Fuel Storage

(f) Haulbowline, Rathmullen – To be offered for sale to commercial companies under guarantee that purchasers shall maintain a certain minimum stock for Admiralty purposes.

2. A Convention shall be made between the British Government and the Government of the Irish Free State to give effect to the following conditions:

(a) That submarine cables shall not be landed or wireless stations for communications with places outside Ireland be established, except by agreement with the British Government; that the existing cable landing rights and wireless concessions shall not be withdrawn except by agreement with the British Government; and that the British Government shall be entitled to land additional submarine cables or establish additional wireless stations for communication with places outside Ireland.

(b) That lighthouses, buoys, beacons, and any navigational marks or navigational aids shall be maintained by the Government of the Irish Free State as at the date hereof and shall not be removed or added to except by agreement with the British Government.

(c) That war signal stations shall be closed down and left in charge of care and maintenance parties, the Government of the Irish Free State being offered the option of taking them over and working them for commercial purposes subject to Admiralty inspection, and guaranteeing the upkeep of existing telegraphic communication therewith.

3. A Convention shall be made between the same Governments for the regulation of Civil Communication by Air.

Pastoral Letter

The Catholic hierarchy condemns the anti-Treaty forces in the Civil War, 11 October 1922

THE CATHOLIC BISHOPS OF IRELAND

Dáil Éireann's ratification of the Anglo-Irish Treaty had led to ruptures within both the Sinn Féin party and the Irish Republican Army (IRA). On 16 January 1922, there was a formal transfer of power from Britain to the Provisional Government, but those who had rejected the Treaty refused to recognize its legitimacy. In April, units of the IRA's Dublin Brigade led by Liam Mellows and Rory O'Connor took over the Four Courts. There followed a stand-off between the IRA and the National Army, as moderates on both sides tried to prevent the political hostilities boiling over into military conflict.

In the end, the IRA's assassination in London of Sir Henry Wilson, Conservative and Unionist MP for North Down, on 22 June brought matters to a head. The British government issued an ultimatum that the IRA men should be rooted out of their positions at the Four Courts. On 28 June, National Army soldiers began to shell the building with ammunition supplied by the British government. It marked the beginning of the civil war.

After three days of bombardment the garrison surrendered. The fighting in Dublin continued for several days with further shelling and pitched street battles. Some 65 people were killed and 281 wounded. The devastation to property was immense. This included the destruction of centuries' worth of documents held at the Public Record Office of Ireland at the Four Courts. By 5 July, Free State forces had effectively taken the capital. Fighting moved to the country. At the end of the month, Waterford and Limerick, two of the strongest anti-Treaty heartlands in 'the Munster Republic', were largely under National Army control; republicans remained in control of Cork.

Now that former comrades were fighting against each other, the bitterness between the sides was intense. The guerrilla tactics, ambushes and reprisals echoed fighting in the war of independence. As Seán Lemass, who fought on the anti-Treaty side, later remarked, 'terrible things were done on both sides'. The Provisional Government's position was stronger, but the republicans proved tenacious and difficult to wear down.

In August the government suffered important setbacks. The president, Arthur Griffith, died from a brain haemorrhage. Michael Collins, head of the Provisional Government and commander-in-chief of the national army, was shot dead in an ambush at Béal na mBláth, Co. Cork. The death of the latter made the Provisonal Government more resolved than ever to end the conflict by whatever means necessary. In September they offered insurgents an amnesty to be taken up by 15 October. Anyone failing to take the amnesty would face a special military tribunal and possible execution.

The majority of Catholic clergy opposed the anti-Treatyites and often did so vocally. In the wake of Collins's death, the government looked to the church to sanction its new strategy. In early October, the bishops drew up a pastoral letter, which, after approval by the Provisional Government, was issued in Maynooth and published in the national press. As the historian Patrick Murray observed, 'the Provisional Government could scarcely have expected more enthusiastic or more powerful support'. The letter denied the sacraments in life and a Christian burial in death to those who died on active service or by hunger strike for the anti-Treatyites. In the eyes of republicans it did much more than that. Between November 1922 and March 1923, 81 republicans (rather than the 77 of popular lore) were subjected to judicial execution. Others were killed in unofficial reprisals. For many, the pastoral letter not only gave the state moral sanction to conduct these killings, but they were its logical outcome. The hierarchy's public silence throughout the executions appeared to confirm that view.

The civil war continued until 24 May 1923, when Frank Aiken, who had recently succeeded Liam Lynch as chief of staff of the IRA, issued an order to cease fire and dump arms.

⁂

The present state of Ireland is a sorrow and humiliation to its friends all over the world. To us, Irish Bishops, it is, because of the moral and religious issues at stake, a source of the most painful anxiety. Our country that but yesterday was so glorious is now a bye-word before the nations for domestic strife, as disgraceful as it is criminal and suicidal. A section of the community, refusing to acknowledge the Government set up by the nation have chosen to attack their own country as if she were a foreign Power. Forgetting, apparently, that a dead nation cannot be free, they have deliberately set out to make our Motherland, as far as they could, a heap of ruins.

They have wrecked Ireland from end to end, burning and destroying national property of enormous value, breaking roads, bridges and railways, seeking by this insensate blockade to starve the people, or bury them in social stagnation. They have caused more damage to Ireland in three months than could be laid to the charge of British rule in so many decades.

> ## 'Killing in an unjust war is as much murder before God as if there were no war.'

They carry on what they call a war, but which, in the absence of any legitimate authority to justify it, is morally only a system of murder and assassination of the National forces – for it must not be forgotten that killing in an unjust war is as much murder before God as if there were no war. They ambush military lorries in the crowded streets thereby killing and wounding not only the soldiers of the Nation, but peaceful citizens. They have, to our horror, shot bands of these troops on their way to Mass on Sunday; and set mine traps in the public roads and blown to fragments some of the bravest Irishmen that ever lived.

Side by side with this woeful destruction of life and property there is running a campaign of plunder, raiding banks and private houses, seizing the lands and property of others, burning mansions and country houses, destroying demesnes and slaying cattle.

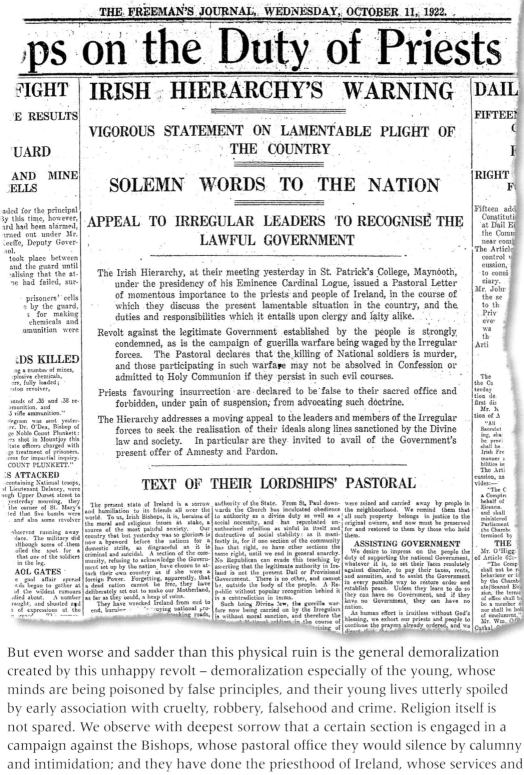

ps on the Duty of Priests

IRISH HIERARCHY'S WARNING

VIGOROUS STATEMENT ON LAMENTABLE PLIGHT OF THE COUNTRY

SOLEMN WORDS TO THE NATION

APPEAL TO IRREGULAR LEADERS TO RECOGNISE THE LAWFUL GOVERNMENT

The Irish Hierarchy, at their meeting yesterday in St. Patrick's College, Maynooth, under the presidency of his Eminence Cardinal Logue, issued a Pastoral Letter of momentous importance to the priests and people of Ireland, in the course of which they discuss the present lamentable situation in the country, and the duties and responsibilities which it entails upon clergy and laity alike.

Revolt against the legitimate Government established by the people is strongly condemned, as is the campaign of guerilla warfare being waged by the Irregular forces. The Pastoral declares that the killing of National soldiers is murder, and those participating in such warfare may not be absolved in Confession or admitted to Holy Communion if they persist in such evil courses.

Priests favouring insurrection are declared to be false to their sacred office and forbidden, under pain of suspension, from advocating such doctrine.

The Hierarchy addresses a moving appeal to the leaders and members of the Irregular forces to seek the realisation of their ideals along lines sanctioned by the Divine law and society. In particular are they invited to avail of the Government's present offer of Amnesty and Pardon.

TEXT OF THEIR LORDSHIPS' PASTORAL

The present state of Ireland is a sorrow and humiliation to its friends all over the world. To us, Irish Bishops, it is, because of the moral and religious issues at stake, a source of the most painful anxiety. Our country that but yesterday was so glorious is now a byword before the nations for a domestic strife, as disgraceful as it is criminal and suicidal. A section of the community, refusing to acknowledge the Government set up by the nation, have chosen to attack their own country as if she were a foreign Power. Forgetting, apparently, that a dead nation cannot be free, they have deliberately set out to make our Motherland, as far as they could, a heap of ruins. They have wrecked Ireland from end to end, burning ... ... roying national pro- ... ... king roads,

authority of the State. From St. Paul downwards the Church has inculcated obedience to authority as a divine duty as well as a social necessity, and has reprobated unauthorised rebellion as sinful in itself and destructive of social stability: as it manifestly is, for if one section of the community has that right, so have other sections the same right, until we end in general anarchy. No Republican can evade this teaching by asserting that the legitimate authority in Ireland is not the present Dail or Provisional Government. There is no other, and cannot be, outside the body of the people. A Republic without popular recognition behind it is a contradiction in terms.

Such being Divine law, the guerilla warfare now being carried on by the Irregulars is without moral sanction, and therefore the ... of National soldiers in the course of ... izing of

were seized and carried away by people in the neighbourhood. We remind them that all such property belongs in justice to the original owners, and now must be preserved for and restored to them by those who hold them.

ASSISTING GOVERNMENT

We desire to impress on the people the duty of supporting the national Government, whatever it is, to set their faces resolutely against disorder, to pay their taxes, rents, and annuities, and to assist the Government in every possible way to restore order and establish peace. Unless they learn to do so they can have no Government, and if they have no Government, they can have no nation.

As human effort is fruitless without God's blessing, we exhort our priests and people to continue the prayers already ordered, and we direct ...

FIGHT

E RESULTS

UARD

AND MINE ELLS

...aded for the principal By this time, however, ...rd had been alarmed, ...rned out under Mr. ...eeffe, Deputy Governol.

...took place between and the guard until ...alising that the at... ...ne had failed, sur-

prisoners' cells ...e by the guard, ...s for making chemicals and ...munition were

DS KILLED

...ng a number of mines, ...plosive chemicals, ...rs, fully loaded; ...ston revolver;

...unds of .35 and .38 re... ...mmunition. and ...3 rifle ammunition." ...elegram was sent yester... ...v. Dr. O'Dea, Bishop of ...ge Noble Count Plunkett: ...rs shot in Mountjoy this ...tate officers charged with ...ge treatment of prisoners. ...ress for impartial inquiry. COUNT PLUNKETT."

S ATTACKED

...containing National troops, ...f Lieutenant Delaney, were ...ough Upper Dorset street to ...yesterday morning, they ...the corner of St. Mary's ...ted that five bombs were ... and also some revolver

...observed running away ...place. The military did ...although some of them ...olled the spot for a ...that one of the soldiers in the leg.

AOL GATES

...e gaol affair spread ...wds began to gather at ...d the wildest rumours ...died about. A number ...raught, and shouted and ...s of expressions at the ...

DAIL

FIFTEEN

RIGHT F

Fifteen add Constituti ...at Dail Ei the Commu near comp The Article control v cussion, v to consi ciary. Mr. John the se to th Priv ever wa th Arti

The the Co terday tion de first di Mr. K tion of A "All Saorstat ing, shal be provi shall be Irish Fre manner bilities n The Arti cussion, as vides:— "The C a Comptr behalf of Eireann. and shall ministered Parliament the Chambe termined by

THE Mr. O'Higg of Article 62:— "The Comp shall not be r behaviour or i by the Chambe ate/Seanad Eire sion, the term of office shall be be a member o nor shall be hol of emolument." Mr. Wm. O'Cathal ...

But even worse and sadder than this physical ruin is the general demoralization created by this unhappy revolt – demoralization especially of the young, whose minds are being poisoned by false principles, and their young lives utterly spoiled by early association with cruelty, robbery, falsehood and crime. Religion itself is not spared. We observe with deepest sorrow that a certain section is engaged in a campaign against the Bishops, whose pastoral office they would silence by calumny and intimidation; and they have done the priesthood of Ireland, whose services and sacrifices for their country will be historic, the insult of suggesting a cabal amongst them to browbeat their bishops and revolt against their authority. And, in spite of all this sin and crime, they claim to be good Catholics and demand at the hands of the Church her most sacred privileges like the Sacraments reserved for her worthy members. When we think of what these young men were only a few months ago, so many of them generous, kind-hearted and good, and see them now involved in this network of crime, our hearts are filled with bitterest anguish.

It is almost inconceivable how decent Irish boys could degenerate as tragically, and reconcile such a mass of criminality with their duties to God and to Ireland. The strain on our country for the last few years will account for much of it. Vanity, perhaps self-conceit, may have blinded some who think that they, and not the nation, must dictate the national policy. Greed for land, love of loot and anarchy have affected others, and they, we regret to say, are not a few; but the main cause of this demoralization is to be found in false notions of social morality.

'No nation can live where ... obedience to authority and law is not firmly and religiously maintained.'

The long struggle of centuries against foreign rule and misrule has weakened respect for civil authority in the national conscience. This is a great misfortune, a great drawback and a great peril to our young Government. For no nation can live where the civic sense of obedience to authority and law is not firmly and religiously maintained. And if Ireland is ever to realise anything but a miserable destiny of anarchy all classes of her citizens must cultivate respect for and obedience to the Government set up by the nation in whatever shape it takes while acting within the law of God. This difficulty is now being cruelly exploited for the ruin, as we see, of Ireland. The claim is now made that a minority are entitled, when they think it right, to take arms and destroy the National Government. Last April, foreseeing the danger, we raised Our voices in the most solemn manner against the disruptive and immoral principle. We pointed out to our young men the conscientious difficulties in which it would involve them, and warned them against it. Disregard for the Divine Law then laid down by the Bishops is the chief cause of all our present sorrows and calamities.

We now again authoritatively renew that teaching and warn our Catholic people that they are conscientiously bound to abide by it, subject of course to an appeal to the Holy See.

'No one is justified in rebelling against the legitimate Government.'

No one is justified in rebelling against the legitimate Government, whatever it is, set up by the nation and acting within its rights.

The opposite doctrine is false, contrary to Christian morals and opposed to the constant teaching of the Church. 'Let every soul', says St Paul, 'be subject to the higher powers' – that is to the legitimate authority of the State. From St Paul downwards the Church has inculcated obedience to authority as a divine duty as well as a social necessity; and has reprobated unauthorised rebellion as sinful in itself and destructive of social stability: as it manifestly is, for if one section of the community has the right, so have the other sections the same right, until we end in general anarchy. No Republican can evade this teaching by asserting that the legitimate authority in Ireland is not the present Dáil or Provisional Government. There is no other, and cannot be, outside the body of the people. A Republic without popular recognition behind it is a contradiction in terms.

Such being Divine Law, the guerrilla warfare now being carried on by the Irregulars is without moral sanction, and therefore the killing of National soldiers in the course of it is murder before God. The seizing of public and private property is robbery. The breaking of roads, bridges and railways is criminal destruction, the invasion of homes and the molestation of citizens is a grievous crime. All those who in contravention of the teaching participate in such crimes, are guilty of grievous sins, and may not be absolved in Confession, nor admitted to Holy Communion, if they persist in such evil courses.

… With all earnestness we appeal to the leaders in this saddest revolt to rise above their own feelings, to remember the claim of God and the sufferings of the people in their conscience, and to abandon methods which they now know beyond the shadow of a doubt are un-Catholic and immoral, and look to the realisation of their ideals along lines sanctioned by Divine Law and society.

Let them not think we are insensible to their feelings – we think of them with compassion, carrying as they do on their shoulders a heavy responsibility for what is now happening in Ireland. Once more we wish to appeal to the young men in this movement in the Name of God to return to their innocent homes and make, if necessary, the big sacrifice of their feelings for the common good. And surely it is no humiliation, having done their best to abide by the verdict of Ireland.

We know that some of them are troubled and held back by the oath they took. A lawful oath is indeed a sacred bond between God and man; but no oath can bind any man to carry on a warfare against his own country in circumstances forbidden by the law of God. It would be an offence to God and to the very nature of an oath to say so.

We, therefore, hope and pray that they will take advantage of the Government's present offer and make peace with their own country, a peace which will bring both happiness and honour to themselves and joy to Ireland generally and to the friends of Ireland all over the world.

'No oath can bind any man to carry on a warfare …
in circumstances forbidden by the law of God.'

Bunreacht na hÉireann

Constitution of Ireland, 1937

ÉAMON DE VALERA (1882–1975)
AND OTHERS

Bunreacht na hÉireann, the constitution of Ireland, was adopted by the people in a referendum on 1 July 1937 and came into force on 29 December. It was at the time – and remains – a controversial document. Formulated under the close guidance of the taoiseach, Éamon de Valera, it was never seen as just a legal framework for the working of the state. Instead it was 'de Valera's constitution', a partisan document that his opponents at the time regarded as a flawed manifestation in its author's image.

Some criticisms of the constitution are reasonable; many more are misguided and anachronistic. As the senior counsel and legal historian Gerard Hogan points out, much analysis has overstated the Catholic influences on the document and neglected to recognize it as an improvement on its predecessor, which had ended in 'almost total failure'. Whatever the controversies within Ireland, it was well regarded outside the state: India adopted many of its principles when enacting its own constitution in 1950.

Bunreacht na hÉireann replaced the Free State constitution of 1922. This latter had been part of the Treaty settlement and thus, many republicans felt, lacked moral authority. The document had been a fairly typical liberal democratic constitution, drawn up by a committee of jurists and others in early 1922. After its various refer-ences to Irish sovereignty were removed at the behest of the British government, it came into force on 6 December 1922 (a year after the signing of the Treaty). Cumann na nGaedheal governments often amended the constitution. Most significant was the 1931 Constitution (Amendment No.17) Act that included a Public Safety Act, which in effect set aside guarantees of civil liberty. Even when the letter of the constitution did not change, its spirit was often ignored. Typical of this was the state's disregard for religious liberties, as shown for example by the banning of divorce.

By the time Fianna Fáil came to power in 1932, the constitution was already consider-ably altered. More radical changes were to come. De Valera spent a considerable proportion of his first years in office expunging clauses. In 1933 he removed the oath to the king and abolished the right of appeal to the Privy Council. Three years later, the crisis surrounding the abdication of Edward VIII provided the opportunity to introduce the Constitutional Amendment Act, which removed the role of the crown in domestic matters and further whittled down the role of the governor general to virtually nothing. By 1936, Brian Farrell notes, 'virtually every page [of the constitution] was cluttered with deletions, additions and amendments'. Forty-one of its eighty-three articles had been altered. What remained bore the indelible hallmark of British law. In May 1936 de Valera announced that a new authentically Irish constitution was needed.

While de Valera provided the political will for the project, John Hearne, legal adviser to the Department of External Affairs, did much of the drafting. His role has often been overlooked by historians, who have tended to focus instead on those who exerted informal influence. De Valera consulted with several churchmen on the draft, most notably Cardinal Joseph MacRory and John Charles McQuaid, then the president of de Valera's alma mater, Blackrock College. The hierarchy had been consulted on the

1922 draft too, so there was nothing unusual about this, but the tone of the 1937 constitution appeared to be more explicitly Catholic than its predecessor. Most notorious was the article enshrining the 'special position' of the Catholic church as 'the guardian of the Faith professed by the great majority of the citizens'. This fell far short of what many Catholic churchmen and lay groups such as Maria Duce demanded, namely, that Catholicism would be identified as the established state religion. The recognition in Article 44.13 of 'the Church of Ireland, the Presbyterian Church in Ireland, the Methodist Church in Ireland, the Religious Society of Friends in Ireland, as well as the Jewish Congregations and the other religious denominations existing in Ireland at the date of the coming into operation of this Constitution' was regarded by many as tantamount to heresy. This vital protection of religious and civil liberties (specifically among Jewish people) was no means a given when the document was being drafted. Also significant was the provision for equality of opportunity among people of all faiths – unlike the British constitution, for instance, which obliges the monarch, his or her spouse and heirs to be members of the Established Church.

Nevertheless, the 'special position' became a *cause célèbre*, first among Protestants in Northern Ireland, who regarded it as yet another manifestation of the southern state's thrall to Rome, and second to liberals, who thought it sectarian. It was amended following a referendum in 1972; reference to any particular religion was replaced by a guarantee that every citizen had 'freedom of conscience and the free profession and practice of religion … subject to public order and morality'.

To date, there have been 27 amendments to the 1937 constitution dealing with issues from Irish sovereignty to morality. Many of the more contentious clauses have been removed or amended, while other controversial changes have been added. Perhaps most famously, Articles 2 and 3 – which unionists interpreted as a hostile claim to a united Ireland – were amended on 2 December 1999 as part of the Belfast Agreement.

Of the issues that caused most controversy at the time of enactment in 1937, only those clauses dealing with the position of women in Irish society remain unchanged.

In the Name of the Most Holy Trinity, from Whom is all authority and to Whom, as our final end, all actions both of men and States must be referred,

We, the people of Éire

Humbly acknowledging all our obligations to our Divine Lord, Jesus Christ, Who sustained our fathers through centuries of trial,

Gratefully remembering their heroic and unremitting struggle to regain the rightful independence of our Nation,

And seeking to promote the common good, with due observance of Prudence, Justice and Charity, so that the dignity and freedom of the individual may be assured, true social order attained, the unity of our country restored, and concord established with other nations,

Do hereby adopt, enact, and give to ourselves this Constitution.

THE NATION

Article 1
The Irish nation hereby affirms its inalienable, indefeasible, and sovereign right to choose its own form of Government, to determine its relations with other nations, and to develop its life, political, economic and cultural, in accordance with its own genius and traditions.

Article 2
The national territory consists of the whole island of Ireland, its islands and the territorial seas.

Article 3
Pending the re-integration of the national territory, and without prejudice to the right of the Parliament and Government established by this Constitution to exercise jurisdiction over the whole of that territory, the laws enacted by that Parliament shall have the like area and extent of application as the laws of Saorstát Éireann and the like extra-territorial effect.

THE STATE

Article 4
The name of the State is Éire, or in the English language, *Ireland.*

Article 5
Ireland is a sovereign, independent, democratic state.

Article 6
1. All powers of government, legislative, executive and judicial, derive, under God, from the people, whose right it is to designate the rulers of the State and, in final appeal, to decide all questions of national policy, according to the public good.
2. These powers of government are exercisable only by or on the authority of the organs of State established by this Constitution.

Article 7
The national flag is the tricolour of green, white and orange.

Article 8
1. The Irish language as the national language is the first official language.
2. The English language is recognised as a second official language.

3. Provision may, however, be made by law for the exclusive use of either of the said languages for any one or more official purposes, either throughout the State or in any part thereof.

Article 9

1   On the coming into operation of this Constitution any person who was a citizen of Saorstát Éireann immediately before the coming into operation of this Constitution shall become and be a citizen of Ireland.

2   The future acquisition and loss of Irish nationality and citizenship shall be determined in accordance with law.

3   No person may be excluded from Irish nationality and citizenship by reason of the sex of such person.

2. Fidelity to the nation and loyalty to the State are fundamental political duties of all citizens … .

THE GOVERNMENT

Article 28

1. The Government shall consist of not less than seven and not more than fifteen members who shall be appointed by the President in accordance with the provisions of this Constitution.

2. The executive power of the State shall, subject to the provisions of this Constitution, be exercised by or on the authority of the Government.

3. 1   War shall not be declared and the State shall not participate in any war save with the assent of Dáil Éireann … .

3   Nothing in this Constitution other than Article 15.5.2 shall be invoked to invalidate any law enacted by the Oireachtas which is expressed to be for the purpose of securing the public safety and the preservation of the State in time of war or armed rebellion … 'Time of war' includes a time when there is taking place an armed conflict in which the State is not a participant but in respect of which each of the Houses of the Oireachtas shall have resolved that, arising out of such armed conflict, a national emergency exists affecting the vital interests of the State and 'time of war or armed rebellion' includes such time after the termination of any war … or armed conflict … until each of the Houses of the Oireachtas shall have resolved that the national emergency … has ceased to exist … .

FUNDAMENTAL RIGHTS

PERSONAL RIGHTS

Article 40

1. All citizens shall, as human persons, be held equal before the law.
    This shall not be held to mean that the State shall not in its enactments have due regard to differences of capacity, physical and moral, and of social function.

2. 1   Titles of nobility shall not be conferred by the State.

    2   No title of nobility or of honour may be accepted by any citizen except with the prior approval of the Government.

3. 1   The State guarantees in its laws to respect, and, as far as practicable, by its laws to defend and vindicate the personal rights of the citizen.

    2   The State shall, in particular, by its laws protect as best it may from unjust attack and, in the case of injustice done, vindicate the life, person, good name, and property rights of every citizen … .

5. The dwelling of every citizen is inviolable and shall not be forcibly entered save in accordance with law.

6. 1   The State guarantees liberty for the exercise of the following rights, subject to public order and morality: –

    i.   The right of citizens to express freely their convictions and opinions. The education of public opinion being, however, a matter of such grave import to the common good, the state shall endeavour to ensure that organs of public opinion, such as the radio, the press, the cinema, while preserving their rightful liberty of expression, including criticism of Government policy, shall not be used to undermine public order or morality or the authority of the State.
    The publication or utterance of blasphemous, seditious, or indecent matter is an offence which shall be punishable in accordance with law.

    ii. The right of the citizens to assemble peaceably and without arms. Provision may be made by law to prevent or control meetings which are determined in accordance with law to be calculated to cause a breach of the peace or to be a danger or nuisance to the general public and to prevent or control meetings in the vicinity of either House of the Oireachtas.

    iii. The right of the citizens to form associations and unions. Laws, however, may be enacted for the regulation and control in the public interest of the exercise of the foregoing right.

    2   Laws regulating the manner in which the right of forming associations and unions and the right of free assembly may be exercised shall contain no political, religious or class discrimination.

THE FAMILY

Article 41

1. 1   The State recognises the Family as the natural primary and fundamental unit group of Society, and as a moral institution possessing inalienable and imprescriptible rights, antecedent and superior to all positive law.

    2   The State, therefore, guarantees to protect the Family in its constitution and authority, as the necessary basis of social order and as indispensable to the

welfare of the Nation and the State.

2. 1   In particular, the State recognises that by her life within the home, woman gives to the State a support without which the common good cannot be achieved.

    2   The State shall, therefore, endeavour to ensure that mothers shall not be obliged by economic necessity to engage in labour to the neglect of their duties in the home.

3. 1   The State pledges itself to guard with special care the institution of Marriage, on which the Family is founded, and to protect it against attack.

    2   No law shall be enacted providing for the grant of a dissolution of marriage.

    3   No person whose marriage has been dissolved under the civil law of any other State but is a subsisting valid marriage under the law for the time being in force within the jurisdiction of the Government and Parliament established by this Constitution shall be capable of contracting a valid marriage within that jurisdiction during the lifetime of the other party to the marriage so dissolved … .

RELIGION

Article 44

1. 1   The State acknowledges that the homage of public worship is due to Almighty God. It shall hold His Name in reverence, and shall respect and honour religion.

    2   The State recognises the special position of the Holy Catholic Apostolic and Roman Church as the guardian of the Faith professed by the great majority of the citizens.

    3   The State also recognises the Church of Ireland, the Presbyterian Church in Ireland, the Methodist Church in Ireland, the Religious Society of Friends in Ireland, as well as the Jewish Congregations and the other religious denominations existing in Ireland at the date of the coming into operation of this Constitution.

2. 1   Freedom of conscience and the free profession and practice of religion are, subject to public order and morality, guaranteed to every citizen.

    2   The State guarantees not to endow any religion.

    3   The State shall not impose any disabilities or make any discrimination on the ground of religious profession, belief or status … .

DIRECTIVE PRINCIPLES OF SOCIAL POLICY

Article 45

The principles of social policy set forth in this Article are intended for the general guidance of the Oireachtas. The application of those principles in the making of laws shall be the care of the Oireachtas exclusively, and shall not be cognisable by any Court under any of the provisions of this Constitution.

1. The State shall strive to promote the welfare of the whole people by securing and protecting as effectively as it may a social order in which justice and charity shall inform all the institutions of the national life.

2. The State shall, in particular, direct its policy towards securing
   i. That the citizens (all of whom, men and women equally, have the right to an adequate means of livelihood) may through their occupations find the means of making reasonable provision for their domestic needs.
   ii. That the ownership and control of the material resources of the community may be so distributed amongst private individuals and the various classes as best to subserve the common good.
   iii. That, especially, the operation of free competition shall not be allowed so to develop as to result in the concentration of the ownership or control of essential commodities in a few individuals to the common detriment.
   iv. That in what pertains to the control of credit the constant and predominant aim shall be the welfare of the people as a whole.
   v. That there may be established on the land in economic security as many families as in the circumstances shall be practicable.

3. 1 The State shall favour and, where necessary, supplement private initiative in industry and commerce.
   2 The State shall endeavour to secure that private enterprise shall be so conducted as to ensure reasonable efficiency in the production and distribution of goods and as to protect the public against unjust exploitation.

4. 1 The State pledges itself to safeguard with especial care the economic interests of the weaker sections of the community, and, where necessary, to contribute to the support of the infirm, the widow, the orphan, and the aged.
   2 The State shall endeavour to ensure that the strength and health of workers, men and women, and the tender age of children shall not be abused and that citizens shall not be forced by economic necessity to enter vocations unsuited to their age, sex or strength.

AMENDMENT TO THE CONSTITUTION

Article 46

1. Any provision of the Constitution may be amended, whether by way of variation, addition, or repeal, in the manner provided by this Article.

2. Every proposal for an amendment of this Constitution shall be initiated in Dáil Éireann as a Bill, and shall upon having been passed or deemed to have been passed by both Houses of the Oireachtas, be submitted by Referendum to the decision of the people in accordance with the law for the time being in force relating to the Referendum.

TAR ASTEAĊ INS NA h-ÓſLAIſ

The American Note

*US criticism of Irish neutrality during the
Second World War, and de Valera's response,
February–March 1944*

CORDELL HULL (1871–1955) AND
ÉAMON DE VALERA (1882–1975)

A declaration of war is the ultimate assertion of sovereignty. So too is a declaration of neutrality. For as long as British forces remained on Irish territory, neutrality was an impossibility for independent Ireland. This changed in 1938 after Prime Minister Neville Chamberlain decided to give up Britain's claims on the Treaty ports of Lough Swilly, Berehaven and Cobh. When the Second World War broke out the following year, Ireland declared that it would remain neutral in the conflict.

That decision was universally popular, enjoying cross-party support in the Dáil, with only a single deputy, James Dillon of Fine Gael, voting for Ireland's participation in the war. Great care was taken with the appearance of neutrality, not least in the maintenance of diplomatic relations with belligerents on both sides. That move was deeply resented by many Allied leaders and diplomats. When Winston Churchill became British prime minister in May 1940, he applied persistent pressure on Ireland to enter the conflict, to no avail. In practice, however, Irish neutrality was not applied equally and in many ways Ireland was more useful to the Allies outside the war than in it. Most obviously, there was military and intelligence cooperation, as well a blind eye turned to Allied operations in Ireland. A lack of travel restrictions meant that some 60,000 Irish people from the 26 Counties were able to enlist in the British forces, with around 200,000 others contributing on the home front by working in British factories. Still, while British diplomats admitted that the Irish government's 'friendly interpretation of neutrality' had helped the Allies, they struggled to forgive the refusal to hand back the Treaty ports.

America entered the war in December 1941 after the bombing of its fleet at Pearl Harbor. The US representative in Ireland since May 1940 had been David Gray, who had no background in diplomacy. He would become a bitter opponent of Irish neutrality. His most important qualification for the position was that he was married to the younger sister of Eleanor Roosevelt. Often considered 'gauche and assertive', he managed to turn the already tense relations between the Dublin and Washington governments into a serious quarrel. He was ignorant about both the security situation in Ireland and the extent of cooperation between Irish and British intelligence services. As Eunan O'Halpin notes, while Gray was fixated on espionage, he was both uninformed and misinformed on intelligence matters, often taken in by 'reports and rumours, nearly all of them without foundation'. His obsession with spies became more acute as planning advanced for the Anglo-American invasion of France – Operation Overlord.

At one level Gray had a point. As a neutral country, Ireland was home to legations from Axis and Allied countries, but Dublin also had a reputation for being a haven to all sorts of spies. While it was true that the Germans and Japanese were sending information from Dublin, this did little or nothing to damage the Allies: the traffic in espionage was of little consequence and, more importantly, British intelligence was monitoring transmissions. Nevertheless, by 1944, with the Allies ready to re-take

France, the question of legations and radios became particularly awkward. Panicky about spies and the Axis presence in Dublin, Gray encouraged Washington to take a firm stand. On 21 February 1944, he presented the taoiseach with a formal note from US Secretary of State Cordell Hull demanding that Ireland expel the Axis diplomats operating in Dublin. The note was more measured than Gray had originally advised – he wanted Washington to demand use of the Treaty ports – but it still went too far for de Valera, who flew into a rage. Before he had finished reading it, he told Gray, 'Of course the answer will be no; as long as I am here it will be no.'

De Valera drafted a response to the note with Joseph Walshe, the secretary of the Department of External Affairs. On 7 March the government issued a statement and published the full text of the correspondence in the press a few days later. Public opinion united behind the taoiseach. Even usually unsympathetic sources, such as the *Irish Times*, applauded the defence of neutrality against US intimidation. According to Professor Terrence Brown, people respected the way de Valera 'kept his nerve, when the fate of the country was an uncertain one and when he had the great powers lined up against him'.

The American demand, had the government caved in, would have been as unhelpful as it was impolitic since British intelligence was monitoring the German legation's communications. Expelling the legation would have cut off a useful source of Axis information. That it was better for Allied interests in the long run did nothing to diminish the tension created by the crisis. At home though, de Valera's response to the note only bolstered his reputation. Defeated in a Dáil division two months later, he called a snap election. He romped home, thanks in no small part to his stand against the world's greatest power.

*F*rom *Cordell Hull, 21 February 1944*

Your Excellency will recall that in your speech at Cork, delivered on December 14th, 1941, you expressed sentiments of special friendship for the American people on the occasion of their entry into the present war and closed by saying, 'The policy of the state remains unchanged. We can only be a friendly neutral.'

'The Irish Government … continues to operate … in favour of the Axis Powers.'

As you will also recall, extracts of this speech were transmitted to the President by the Minister at Washington. The President, while conveying his appreciation for this expression of friendship, stated his confidence that the Irish Government and the Irish people whose freedom is at stake no less than ours would know how to meet their responsibilities in this situation.

It has become increasingly apparent that, in spite of the declared desire of the Irish Government that its neutrality should not operate in favour of either of the belligerents, it has, in fact, operated, and continues to operate, in favour of the Axis Powers and against the United Nations, on whom your security and the maintenance of your national economy depend.

One of the gravest and most inequitable results of this situation is the opportunity for highly organised espionage which the geographical position of Ireland affords to the Axis and denies to the United Nations.

Situated, as you are, in close proximity to Britain and divided only by an intangible boundary from Northern Ireland, where are situated important American bases, with a continuous traffic to and from both countries, Axis agents enjoy an almost unrestricted opportunity for bringing military information of vital importance from Great Britain and Northern Ireland into Ireland, and, from there, transmitting it by various routes and methods to Germany.

No opportunity corresponding to this is open to the United Nations, for the Axis has no military dispositions which may be observed from Ireland.

'We do not question the good faith of the Irish Government.'

We do not question the good faith of the Irish Government in its efforts to suppress Axis espionage.

Whether, or to what extent it has succeeded in preventing acts of espionage against American shipping and American forces in Great Britain and Northern Ireland is, of course, impossible to determine with certainty. Nevertheless, it is a fact that the German and Japanese Diplomatic and Consular representatives still continue to reside in Dublin and enjoy the special privileges and immunities customarily accorded such officials.

That Axis representatives in neutral countries use those special privileges and immunities as a cloak for espionage activities against the United Nations has been demonstrated over and over again.

It would be naive to assume that Axis agencies did not exploit the conditions in Ireland, as they have in other countries. It is our understanding that the German Legation in Dublin, until recently, at least, has had in its possession a radio-sending set. This is evidence of the intention of the German Government to use this means of communication.

Supporting evidence was furnished by two parachutists, equipped with radio-sending sets, dropped on your territory by German planes.

As you know from common report, United Nations' military operations are in preparation in both Britain and Northern Ireland. It is vital that information from which may be deduced their nature and direction should not reach the enemy.

'The lives of thousands of United Nations' soldiers are at stake.'

Not only the success of the operations, but the lives of thousands of United Nations' soldiers are at stake.

We request, therefore, that the Irish Government take appropriate steps for the recall of the German and Japanese representatives in Ireland. We would be lacking in candour if we did not state our hope that this action will take the form of severance of all diplomatic relations between Ireland and these two countries.

You will, of course, readily understand the compelling reasons why we ask as an absolute minimum the removal of these Axis representatives, whose presence in Ireland must inevitably be regarded as constituting a danger to the lives of American soldiers and the success of Allied military operations. It is hardly necessary to point out that time is of extreme importance, and that, we trust, Your Excellency will favour us with your reply at your earliest convenience.

From Éamon de Valera, 10 March 1944

The Note of the American Government was handed to me by the American Minster on February 21st. I informed him at once that the request it contained was one with which it was impossible for the Irish Government to comply. The Irish Government have since given the matter careful consideration, and I now confirm the reply which I then gave verbally.

The Irish Government have also received the assurance of the American Government conveyed to the Irish Minister at Washington and later confirmed by the American Minister here in an interview with me on February 29th, to the effect that the American Government did not contemplate proceeding to military or other measures because of the reply which had been given. The American Minister quoted in particular the President's personal message to me of February 26th, 1942, that 'there is not now, nor was there then, the first thought or intention of invading the territory of Ireland or of threatening the security of the Irish,' and added that this attitude was unchanged.

The Irish Government wish to express their appreciation of this assurance. They were indeed surprised that so grave a Note as that of February 21st should have been addressed to them. The terms of the Note seemed to them altogether out of harmony with the facts and with the traditional relations of friendship between the Irish and American peoples.

RICE 3D.   DUBLIN, SATURDAY, MARCH 11, 1944   NO.

Miners Still On Strike

Ministry of Fuel and Power Wales said yesterday that he strike was "just a little A few more anthracite pits lle, but some steam coal pits till partially operating.

asford (Wrexham) strikers de to resume to-morrow night. urham, 1,200 men and boys at ore Colliery decided to remain pending satisfactory negotia , but at South Hetton Colliery her thousand, who had been out Thursday, resumed yesterday. he 90,000 Welsh miners went to the pits yesterday, but not ork. It was a "collar and tie de" to the colliery offices to their pay for last week, plus first pay under the Porter ard. A week's pay in hand was to them. The men will thus not short of money this week. Even they go back to work on Monday and this can be put no higher n a strong possibility—300,000 s of vital coal production will e been lost since last Monday, the strike will have meant a s in wages by to-day of £400,000. in Scotland, where the strike fects 7,300 men and 16 pits, the oppage spread from Ayrshire to ifeshire. The miners' executive and M.P.s are to appeal for the strike to be called off, so that negotiations for a settlement of outstanding grievances may proceed. Mean while, in London, a move has been made to get a full debate on coal, if the situation has not eased, at he next sitting of the Commons. A conference is to take place at rexham to-day between the North ales Coal-Owners' Association and presentatives of the North Wales ners' Association.

The Minister of Fuel and Power given a special direction restric the supply of coal to domestic ther controlled premises in counties of the Welsh coal

Allied Attacks In Beachhead

EIRE REJECTS REQUEST FROM U.S.A. TO RECALL AXIS REPRESENTATIVES

THE Government has rejected a request from the United States Government that German and Japanese representatives shall be recalled from this country.

The American Government in a Note alleges that Eire's neutrality is operating in favour of the Axis Powers; that Axis espionage exists in this country, and that "not only the success of forthcoming Allied military operations but the lives of thousands of United Nations' soldiers are at stake."

AMERICAN ASSURANCE

The reply of the Government of Eire, released last night, was signed by Mr. de Valera, and stated: "The Irish Government could not entertain the American proposal without complete betrayal of their democratic trust." Irish neutrality was the logical consequence of the country's history and the forced partition of national territory.

Mr. de Valera's Note stated that the United States Government had given an assurance that America did not contemplate any military or other action against Eire in consequence of her reply.

The United States Note, deli vered to Mr. de Valera by the U.S.A. Minister in Dublin, stated : "Your Excellency will recall that in your speech at Cork, delivered on December 14th, 1941, you expressed sentiments of special friendship for the American people on the occasion of their entry into the present war and closed by saying, 'The policy of the State remains unchanged. We can only be a friendly neutral.'

"As you will also recall, extracts of this speech were transmitted to the President by your Minister at Washington. The President, while conveying his appreciation for this xpression of friendship, stated his that the Irish Government

"No opportunity corresponding to this is open to the United Nations, for the Axis has no military disposi tions which may be observed from Ireland.

"We do not question the good faith of the Irish Government in its efforts to suppress Axis espionage. Whether, or to what extent it has succeeded in preventing acts of

for espionage activities against the United Nations has been demon strated over and over again.

"It would be naïve to asumes that Axis agencies did not exploit the conditions to the full in Ireland, as they have in other countries. It is our understanding that the German Legation in Dublin, until recently, at least, has had in its possession a radio-sending set. This is evidence of the intention of the German Government to use this means of communication.

"PARACHUTISTS"

"Supporting evidence was fur nished by two parachutists, equipped th radio-sending

Fuel This

"INDICATION serious develop and we have no ing it except by more turf," Minister for In merce, said in night. The ma present domestic pended on greater ever before.

Declaring that curtailment of co very real and that could not maintai services for more period, Mr. Le townspeople livin provide their o and all indu should arrange duction of the

It was nec maintain eve would minimi economic dis curtailment effect, that m prevent the u pose or in which an alte used.

SMALL R

Up to the Minister, they had in preventing undu domestic fuel consun taining a ration of national turf supply. reserves were now e quantity of turf dra national pool this double that drawn las result was that at th present season their r in the turf dumps wou to 60 per cent. of the twelve months ago.

While the organisati the County Surveyors producing counties Development Board, camps, would spare n out the last sod of t tributions would no To managers of indu the Minister said supplies should cont quantities available tained for the es services. Most facto producing areas

They doubted that such a Note could have been presented had the American Government been fully aware of the uniformly friendly character of Irish neutrality in relation to the United States and of the measures which had been taken by the Irish Government, within the limits of their power, to safeguard American interests.

They felt, moreover, that the American Government should have realised that the removal of the representatives of a foreign State or the demand of the Government to which they are accredited is universally recognised as a first step towards war, and that the Irish Government could not entertain the American proposal without a complete betrayal of their democratic trust.

'Irish neutrality represents the united will of people and Parliament.'

Irish neutrality represents the united will of people and Parliament. It is the logical consequence of Irish history and of the forced partition of the national territory.

Already, before America's entry into the war, the policy of the Irish Government towards Britain, America's ally, had been directed towards carrying out the intention indicated in a statement of policy made by me in Dáil Éireann on May 29th, 1935 – namely, that 'our territory would never be permitted to be used as a base for attack upon Britain'. That policy has during the war been faithfully pursued.

From the beginning, by the establishment of strong observation and defence forces, by a wide and rigorous censorship of the Press and of communications, by an expansive anti-espionage organisation, and by every other means within our power, we have endeavoured to prevent the leakage through Ireland of any information which might in any way endanger British lives or the safety of Great Britain.

Since the United States entered the war the same spirit of scrupulous regard for American interests has been shown. American officials have had an opportunity of seeing the measures which have been taken – they have, indeed, made favourable comments on their effectiveness – and it is satisfactory to observe that in the Note itself not a single instance of neglect is alleged and no proof of injury to American interests adduced. Should American lives be lost, it will not be through any indifference or neglect of its duty on the part of this State.

As was known to the American officials, it is true that the German Minister had a wireless transmitter. But he had been for a long time debarred from using it, and it has been in the custody of the Irish Government for some months. As regards the two parachutists dropped in Ireland last December, they were apprehended within a few hours. Two other agents dropped here since the war began met with a similar fate. The fifth, who arrived during the first year of the war, remained at large until December 3rd, 1941, but the police were aware of his presence here almost from the first moment of landing, and successful activities on his part were rendered impossible.

The total number of persons, inclusive of those parachutists, suspected of intention to engage in espionage, and now held in Irish prisons is ten foreign and two Irish nationals. Those are the facts, and it is doubtful if any other country can show such a record of care and successful vigilance.

The British Government have informed the Irish Government that they welcomed the initiative of the American Government in sending the Note, and that they attached the utmost importance to it. The Irish Government do not wish to comment upon this, except to remark that it is perhaps not known to the American Government that the feelings of the Irish people towards Britain have, during the war, undergone a considerable change, precisely because Britain has not attempted to violate our neutrality. The Irish Government would agree that it would be regrettable if any incidents now should alter that happy result.

'The Irish Government … must, in all circumstances, protect the neutrality of the Irish State.'

The Irish Government are, therefore, safeguarding, and will continue to safeguard, the interests of the United States, but they must, in all circumstances, protect the neutrality of the Irish State and the democratic way of life of the Irish people. Their attitude will continue to be determined, not by fear of any measures which could be employed against them, but by goodwill and the fundamental friendship existing between the two peoples.

The Republic of Ireland Act

*Ireland declares itself
a Republic and leaves the
British Commonwealth, 1948*

JOHN A. COSTELLO (1891–1976)
AND OTHERS

In December 1936, during the crisis surrounding the abdication of Edward VIII, the taoiseach, Éamon de Valera, had pushed through two pieces of legislation to modify the constitutional role of the crown. One bill removed the monarch's remaining legislative, executive and constitutional functions in the domestic affairs of the state; a second, the External Relations Act, confirmed the monarch's role as head of the Commonwealth, in which Ireland retained its membership.

The External Relations Act proved an unhappy compromise, not least when Bunreacht na hÉireann was enacted the following year. This left Ireland with two heads of state: the president in domestic matters and the king in foreign affairs. The External Relations Act also hampered Irish governments in making diplomatic appointments and entering into international agreements, which had to be authorized first in London. In 1947, ten years after the introduction of Bunreacht na hÉireann, de Valera moved to repeal the External Relations Act but a general election in February 1948 saw him lose office after 16 years in power.

The new government was a coalition united only in a wish to 'put them [Fianna Fáil] out'. It comprised parties across the left–right and nationalist spectrums, led by Fine Gael's John A. Costello. Repeal of the External Relations Act was half-heartedly raised during the early months of the new government, but while it was clear that such a move enjoyed support across the board, nothing suggested this was a priority. It came as something of a surprise therefore when the Irish press reported that the taoiseach had announced during a visit to Canada that Ireland was going to leave the Commonwealth.

Costello was a reserved man, who was often ill at ease at official and social functions. As one senior diplomat observed, he had 'as much notion of diplomacy as I have of astrology'. During his visit to Canada, the taoiseach's discomfort had been heightened by the behaviour of Canada's governor general, Lord Alexander, an ardent imperialist who boasted of his planter roots in Derry. When the Canadians refused to toast the Irish president at a formal dinner, Costello became furious at the slight. When he complained of the omission to the Canadian prime minister, Mackenzie King, he was told bluntly that the toast to the king covered Ireland. For Costello, this rebuff was a vivid illustration of the unsustainable tensions inherent in the External Relations Act. It also seemed a calculated insult to himself, the office and the Irish nation. To add rudeness to injury he found himself seated in front of a replica of 'Roaring Meg', one of the cannons used in the siege of Derry in 1689.

It was all too much for Costello. Two days later he told a press conference that Ireland would be leaving the Commonwealth to become a republic. It was haphazard diplomacy certainly, and the incident at dinner lent an element of farce to events. The affronted Costello appeared to have declared a republic in a fit of pique in (as he himself put it) 'Ottawa, of all places'. In fact, the issue had been discussed at cabinet before Costello's departure.

On 17 November 1948 a bill to repeal the External Relations Act was put before the Dáil. It declared that 'the description of the state shall be the Republic of Ireland'. The president was given the authority to 'exercise the executive power or any executive function of the state in or in connection with its external relations'. The bill was signed into law by the president on 21 December, although it did not come into force until Easter Monday 1949.

The choice of date – 33 years after the Easter Rising – was no accident, although Lord Rugby had hoped for a more 'inoffensive anniversary', such as that marking the meeting of the first Dáil. Still, it seemed as though the time for symbolism had already passed. 'Republic Day' was marked by a military parade past the GPO in Dublin and a mass at the Pro-Cathedral, but the celebrations fell a little flat. Most of the relics of British rule – partition apart – had already been removed. Some even argued that the declaration of the republic had actually copper-fastened partition, if not by the act itself, then in the British government's response. The Ireland Act, passed at Westminster in 1949, provided special citizenship status for Irish people living in Britain and maintained trade preferences between the two states. Yet its declaration that 'in no event will Northern Ireland or any part thereof cease to be part ... of the United Kingdom without the consent of the Parliament of Northern Ireland' was the first and most significant guarantee given to unionists by a British government.

***

No. 22/1948:

AN ACT TO REPEAL THE EXECUTIVE AUTHORITY (EXTERNAL RELATIONS) ACT, 1936, TO DECLARE THAT THE DESCRIPTION OF THE STATE SHALL BE THE REPUBLIC OF IRELAND, AND TO ENABLE THE PRESIDENT TO EXERCISE THE EXECUTIVE POWER OR ANY EXECUTIVE FUNCTION OF THE STATE IN OR IN CONNECTION WITH ITS EXTERNAL RELATIONS.

[21*st December*, 1948.]

BE IT ENACTED BY THE OIREACHTAS AS FOLLOWS:—
1.—The Executive Authority (External Relations) Act, 1936 (No. 58 of 1936), is hereby repealed.
2.—It is hereby declared that the description of the State shall be the Republic of Ireland.
3.—The President, on the authority and on the advice of the Government, may exercise the executive power or any executive function of the State in or in connection with its external relations.
4.—This Act shall come into operation on such day as the Government may by order appoint.
5.—This Act may be cited as The Republic of Ireland Act, 1948.

An Irish Navvy:
Diary of an Exile

*Account by Donall MacAmhlaigh
on his experiences as a labourer
in England in the 1950s*

DONALL MACAMHLAIGH (1926–89)

Eight million people emigrated from Ireland in the years between the Act of Union of 1800 and the foundation of the new independent state in 1922. In 1841 Ireland's population made up around one third of the population of the United Kingdom; by 1911 it was less than one tenth of the total. Between the eve of the famine and the eve of independence, Ireland's population halved.

If many pre-independence nationalists regarded this exodus as the result of British misrule, it became more difficult after 1922 to blame foreign perfidy or maladministration for a decline in population that showed no sign of ending. Every census showed a fall in population figures from the previous one. A low birth rate was partly to blame, but ultimately the simple explanation was that people were leaving the country in droves. Where they went depended on the opportunities available in destination countries at different times. Places where family and friends had already settled were obviously popular. During the Emergency (1939–45), large numbers of Irish people emigrated to take advantage of Britain's need for labour on the home front. Irish civil servants had been afraid of what would happen when these emigrants, used to higher wages and better benefits, returned home *en masse*. They need not have worried: most Irish workers stayed put. As the war ended, bombed-out Britain needed to rebuild, creating jobs for thousands of Irish men. For women, there were opportunities to work in factories, in the service industries and particularly as nurses in the new National Health Service. Between 1946 and 1951 the number of Irish arriving annually in the UK alone was some 25,000.

During the 1948 general election, emigration became one of the key issues of the campaign. One party, Clann na Poblachta, went so far as to say it would place legal prohibitions on emigration. That never happened, but the new coalition government, which included Clann na Poblachta, did establish a commission to examine Ireland's demographic slump. Not surprisingly, its *Report on Emigration and Other Population Problems* (submitted to the government five years after the commission was appointed) found that economic factors were paramount in people's decision to leave. In many cases it was the lack of stable employment and the consequent inability to plan for the future that caused many to go. Yet while economic factors were most important, the report recognized that other social, political, cultural and psychological issues also played their part. For women especially, life overseas seemed to offer more prospects and the possibility of improved social status. Moreover, 'to the young mind' urban life abroad appeared infinitely preferable to the 'dull, drab, monotonous, backward and lonely' existence of rural Ireland. By the time the commission reported, the numbers leaving Ireland each year had reached 40,000. In June 1956 the Central Statistics Office published figures that showed Ireland's population had reached its lowest recorded level. The only remaining question was at what stage would the country's politicians and administrators admit that Ireland's 'population problem' had turned into a calamitous crisis.

Donall MacAmhlaigh was one of those tens of thousands who took the boat to Holyhead during the 1950s. Born outside Galway in 1926, he worked in a series of jobs after leaving school aged 15, before joining the army in 1948. Unable to find work after three years in the army, he decided to emigrate to Britain, as so many of his friends and neighbours had done before him. He secured employment as a live-in stoker in a hospital in Northampton until low pay tempted him to swap security for the higher wages of life as a navvy. Work as a labourer on the construction sites of post-war Britain was difficult and casual. Like other navvies, he had to follow the work, so he never put down roots in any one city, setting up temporary home in a succession of digs and camps. The navvy's life contrasted with that of most Irish emigrants to Britain, who lived a more sedentary existence working in factories and hospitals. What both groups shared though was an inability to settle down. Many of the Irish who emigrated to England and lived there for decades could never abandon the belief that it was a temporary arrangement before eventually returning home.

The life of a navvy was tough, but the wages were decent and the camaraderie among the Irish ex-pats was one of the things that kept the men going. So too was the social life around the Irish bars of various cities and towns. MacAmhlaigh kept a record of his time as a navvy in England, which was first published as *Dialann Deoraí* in 1960 and was translated into English four years later. It is a vivid, engagingly written and often moving account of the experience of being Irish in Britain.

In an addendum to the *Report on Emigration*, the famed statistician Roy Geary noted that 'statistics can measure only economic and demographic entities. They cannot measure welfare or happiness.' MacAmhlaigh did not try to measure welfare or happiness, but he did manage to convey something of what it felt like to be that most ubiquitous of global citizens: the Irishman abroad.

I got up early and caught the 8.08 am from Callow for London. I didn't bring my bag with me for I was really hopeful of getting a job from Higgs & Hill but I'm sorry to say that I didn't succeed. The clerk told me that they wouldn't be sending anyone out to the country for a while yet. I moved over to Acton, then, to Lowery's office, to see what was going there. His big Scots secretary was in the room but he told me that there was nothing doing just now. I was on the point of leaving when in came Peteen himself. He greeted me in Irish and I mentioned that I was looking for work. The Scot didn't know from God what we were talking about and I'm damn sure he wasn't a bit pleased. In the end, Lowery told me to go out to Raynes Park tonight where they would be pulling cables.

'They're all Connemara people … here and it would go hard with you to find a word of English.'

… I then went over to the dance in the Shamrock and met plenty there. They're all Connemara people that come here and it would go hard with you to find a word of English there … I left the dance a bit early as I had to go and find a night's lodging for myself. I made my way down Harrow Road until at last I found a place to stay. I felt like going down to Ward's in Maida Vale but at the same time I was a bit reluctant to do so as his wife Maire had thrown me out the year before for taking Packy out drinking. Up I went to the bedroom that the landlady offered me. But I found a man in the bed already and damned if I knew what on earth to do. Anyway, he told me to get in beside him which I did as I didn't think I could get anywhere else at that time of night.

A bloody big fellow he was and I nearly fell out of the bed as soon as I got into it. Talkative, too, he was and he told me that he had spent most of his life over in Boston. He lost his wife a long time ago and had one daughter. This girl was responsible for his leaving America. She had been bad with asthma ever since she was born and he had spent years taking her from place to place hoping that the poor creature would improve. He had spent everything he earned doing this; and isn't it strange that, in the end, she didn't get her health until they ended up here in this foggy city. So they've been here ever since – the daughter working in a hospital and the old man out navvying.

After I had got his life story – a Murphy from Cork he was – he started giving out the Rosary and I answered him. I must say that this amazed me for long as I have been in this country this is the first time that I have come across two strangers in the same bed saying the Rosary together.

'The devil has seized hold of enough Irishmen here in London.'

We got a great breakfast next morning and I must say I liked the company I found below at it. They were all from West Cork and I could hardly understand the half of what they were saying. At first, I thought they were speaking Irish but, indeed, no! Murphy and I went off to Mass together. I was astonished at the sermon that was preached – all about the lads fighting in the pubs and dancehalls. The priest came out very strongly against them, saying they were nothing but ignorant beasts that let down their country and their faith. There's no denying that this sort of thing is necessary for the devil has seized hold of enough Irishmen here in London.

I was never so unwilling to get along to work as I was the next morning getting down to that damned foundry. And to make the whole damned thing worse, I was put working indoors, hauling huge casks of molten iron around and pouring them into the moulds. On overhead rails, there are wheels that carry the casks (or skips, as they are called) around with the skips hanging by chains from the wheels. For myself, I was terrified in case some of the red-hot metal would spill over on me but the crowd here are so used to it that they can do what they like with the skips without any danger of roasting themselves alive. The air was thick with smoke and smuts and I would have given anything to have been able to get out of the hell-hole into the fresh air.

I caught a few glimpses of the furnaces that melt the iron and it filled me with terror just to look at them. Had there been the screeching and wailing of the souls of the damned, it would have been Hell itself. For the life of me, I can't understand how a man can spend his days in such places when there is work to be had out under the health-giving blue sky. But, of course, habit is what does it. If you were born and brought up in a hold like a rabbit, you'd never know that there was any life other than the darkness and the crampedness.

'I never saw the likes of this lodging for hardship and hunger.'

… I never saw the likes of this lodging for hardship and hunger and I've seen a few. It's getting worse, too. The dinner wasn't too bad once even if the other meals were awful but now the dinner itself is dreadful. I'll be in some other house by next week or I'll know the reason why. The lodgers here are all too easy-going with her and I'm certain that if she laid a plate of grass down in front of Mike Ned, he wouldn't say boo to her. I've heard that the Connemara boys have good digs down in Royal Terrace and I'll give them a chance as soon as I have a bit of money.

We knocked off at twelve on Saturday and I can tell you I felt well-satisfied when we did so. I spent the morning inside the foundry going around with the skip and I was getting right used to it. It's a miserable life these foundry-workers have compared with navvies, as I well know myself. The navvy spends his time out in the open air and he doesn't stay too long in the one place. One time he's out working in the country while another he's in the big town. Wherever he is, there's a variety of people and things to be seen by him throughout the day whereas in the foundry or the factory, a man only sees the same crowd, day in day out all the year round, and you'd know it by looking at him. He leads a very constricted life and I don't hanker after it at all.

Economic

Development

DUBLIN:
PUBLISHED BY THE STATIONERY OFFIC

To be purchased from the
GOVERNMENT PUBLICATIONS SALE OFFICE, G.P.O. A
or through any Bookseller.

Price seven shillings and sixpenc

(Pr. 4803.)

ECONOMIC   DEVELOPMEN

This study of national development problems and opportuni
was prepared by the Secretary of the Department of Finance, with
cooperation of others in, or connected with, the public service. T
views and recommendations it contains were considered by t
Government in the formulation of its recently-issued Programme f
Economic Expansion.   The study is being published to make availab
the information assembled and coordinated in it and to stimulate intere
in the subject of national development.

The study was completed in May, 1958, but in some instances i
has been found possible to take into account developments subsequen
to that date.

Department of Finance,
November, 1958.

Economic
Development

Proposals to open the Irish economy
to international trade, November 1958

T.K. WHITAKER (B.1916)

The idea that Ireland was a land without a future was widely held in the 1950s. The country's standard of living was low – a fact underlined in letters home from emigrants, who continued to leave Ireland in tens of thousands every year. The failure of successive governments to find solutions made the situation even worse.

For some time individual politicians, public servants and trade union leaders had been vocal about the need for a new approach to the Irish economy, but there had been resistance to change within successive governments and the Department of Finance. As one commentator noted, it would take a 'severe jolt' to focus minds on change. That jolt came in 1956. The economy was badly hit by the oil shocks that resulted from the Suez Crisis. This exacerbated the austerity measures designed to correct a balance of payments deficit. With constant bad news on the economic front backed up by abysmal emigration figures from the census, it was clear that something had to be done before the Irish in Ireland simply haemorrhaged away.

Events in 1956 coincided with the appointment of a new secretary to run the Department of Finance. T.K. Whitaker was then the youngest-ever secretary of a government department, whose obvious talent had led to his appointment 'out of turn'. The historian J.J. Lee notes that at this stage Whitaker appeared 'outstanding more for his energy and intellectual power than for imagination'. Once in the post, however, he quickly showed a capacity to develop and embrace big ideas on economic reform. By the end of 1957 his team at the department were putting together a plan to save the Irish economy, which was eventually published as *Economic Development* and became known popularly as the 'Grey Book'.

There were two core ideas in *Economic Development*. The first was that the government would have to take a more systematic, planned approach to the economy. The second and most significant was the removal of the tariff barriers erected around Ireland's industry by Seán Lemass and Fianna Fáil in the 1930s. This would open up the Irish economy to international trade and competition. As the report noted: 'The possibility of freer trade in Europe carries disquieting implications for some Irish industries and raises special problems of adaptation and adjustment ... it seems clear that, sooner or later, protection will have to go and the challenge of free trade be accepted.' This allowed for foreign companies to invest in Ireland and ultimately paved the way for Ireland's membership of the European Economic Community in 1973.

Economic Development offered a radical approach to Ireland's economic woes that would require broad political support. It was largely with this in mind that the report was issued under the name of its primary architect. This was unprecedented, but it helped stop it from being seen as a Fianna Fáil – and therefore political – plan. *Economic Development* was not a policy document as such, rather a suggested approach to change. It provided much of the blueprint for Seán Lemass's 'Programme for Economic Expansion' and those that followed during the 1960s. Lemass had followed John Maynard Keynes's dictum that 'When facts change, I change my mind'. The Irish economy blossomed during the 1960s; not all benefited equally, especially since cuts in social spending hurt the poorer sections of society, but employment grew and emigration dropped dramatically. For a rather dry policy document, *Economic Development* has now taken on an iconic status. Although some historians and economists have questioned just how much of it was implemented and how great an impact it had, the effect on morale was beyond doubt. The 'Grey Book' brought a much-needed air of confidence to a country that had been paralysed by despair. Whitaker gave Ireland back its self-respect.

It is apparent that we have come to a critical and decisive point in our economic affairs. The policies hitherto followed, though given a fair trial, have not resulted in a viable economy. We have power, transport facilities, public services, houses, hospitals and a general 'infrastructure' on a scale which is reasonable by western European standards, yet large-scale emigration and unemployment still persist. The population is falling, the national income rising more slowly than the rest of Europe. A great and sustained effort to increase production, employment and living standards is necessary to avert economic decadence.

> *'There is, therefore, a real need … to buttress confidence in the country's future and to stimulate the interest and enthusiasm of the young.'*

… There is also a sound psychological reason for having an integrated development programme. The absence of such a programme tends to deepen the all-too-prevalent mood of despondency about the country's future. A sense of anxiety is, indeed, justified. But it can too easily degenerate into feelings of frustration and despair. After 35 years of native government people are asking whether we can achieve an acceptable degree of economic progress. The common talk amongst parents in towns, as in rural Ireland, is of their children having to emigrate as soon as their education is completed in order to be sure of a reasonable livelihood. To the children themselves and to many already in employment the jobs available at home look unattractive by comparison with those obtainable in such variety and so readily elsewhere. All this seems to be setting up a vicious circle – of increasing emigration, resulting in a smaller domestic market depleted of initiatives and skill, and a reduced incentive, whether for Irishmen or foreigners, to undertake and organise the productive enterprises which alone can provide increased employment opportunities and higher living standards. There is, therefore, a real need at present to buttress confidence in the country's future and to stimulate the interest and enthusiasm of the young in particular.

'Success or failure will depend primarily on the individual reactions of the Irish people.'

… No programme of development can be effective unless it generates increased effort, enterprise and saving on the part of a multitude of individuals. Its eventual success or failure will depend primarily on the individual reactions of the Irish people. If they have not the will to develop, even the best possible programme is useless.

A concerted and comprehensive programme aimed at a steady progress in material welfare, even though supported by the Churches and other leaders of opinion, could only be successful if the individual members of the community were realistic and patriotic enough to accept the standard of living produced by their own exertions here, even if it should continue for some time to be lower than the standard available abroad. Otherwise the possibility of economic progress scarcely exists.

For all these reasons the importance of the next five to ten years for the economic and political future of Ireland cannot be over-stressed. Policies should be re-examined without regard to past views or commitments. It is desirable to remind ourselves that at all times in a nation's history decisions have to be taken; that there is no guarantee when they are taken that they will prove right; and that the greatest fault lies in pursing a policy after it has proved to be unsuitable or ineffective. What matters above all is to understand the present position and find the best and quickest ways of improving it.

In pressing on with this study, despite the claims of ordinary office work, it has been an inspiration to turn to the following words of the Bishop of Clonfert, Most Rev. Dr. Philbin:

> Our version of history has tended to make us think of freedom as an end in itself and of independent government – like marriage in a fairy story – as the solution of all ills. Freedom is useful in proportion to the use we make of it. We seem to have relaxed our patriotic energies just at the time when there was most need to mobilise them. Although our enterprise in purely spiritual fields has never been greater, we have shown little initiative or organisational ability in agriculture and industry and commerce. There is here the widest and most varied field for the play of the vital force that our religion contains.

This study is a contribution, in the spirit advocated by the Bishop of Clonfert, towards the working out of the national good in the economic sphere. It is hoped that, supplemented by productive ideas from other sources, it will help to dispel despondency about the country's future. We can afford our present standard of living, which is so much higher than most of the inhabitants of this world enjoy. Possibilities of improvement are there, if we wish to realise them. It would be well to shut the door on the past and to move forward, energetically, intelligently and with the will to succeed, but without expecting miracles of progress in a short time.

Demands of the Northern Ireland Civil Rights Association

Call to end civic inequalities, June 1969

The Northern Ireland state was one characterized by inequality almost from the beginning. Most of the legal safeguards for the Catholic minority were stripped away early on. Active discrimination, along with the general unwillingness of Catholics to recognize the state, left them as second-class citizens. The boast by the prime minister of Northern Ireland, James Craig, in 1933 that he led a 'Protestant Parliament and a Protestant State' was hardly one likely to engender Catholic loyalty to the Stormont regime.

For the first four decades of Northern Ireland's existence, most Catholics looked towards ending partition and the establishing of a united Ireland as the means by which they might secure political and economic equality. Nationalists worked towards this through political action, republicans through violence. Neither enjoyed much success.

In the 1960s the Catholic community began to change its approach. A new educated Catholic middle class demanded opportunities to match their training but discrimination was as overt as ever. Terence O'Neill, prime minister of Northern Ireland from 1963, was more liberal than his predecessors, but his government continued to favour Protestants. New factories were located in Protestant areas. A new university was built in the Protestant town of Coleraine rather than in the city of Derry. Local government sectarianism and corruption continued, with Catholics often denied social housing by councils elected through gerrymandering.

Rather than concentrating on partition, Catholics began to campaign for equal status and reform of the Stormont regime. In January 1967 the Northern Ireland Civil Rights Association (NICRA) was established. It included members of the republican clubs, the Northern Ireland Labour Party, the Irish Trade Union Congress, the Campaign for Social Justice and the Communist Party of Ireland. In any other liberal democracy their demands would have looked benign. In Northern Ireland they seemed almost revolutionary. For the first year of its existence, NICRA's demands and methods differed little from those of its predecessors. Its real impact came after a decision made in mid-1968 to take the campaign onto the streets. It was not the first or the only organization to do so, notes historian Bob Purdie, but it was 'the most important group within the civil rights movement and it initiated the events that led to the creation of a mass movement'.

Protestant extremists and members of the Royal Ulster Constabulary and the B Specials auxiliary force countered the marches with violence. This prompted the government in London to force O'Neill's hand in initiating reform. The package he put forward in November 1968 turned out to be too little, too late. With tensions running extremely high, he gave his famous warning that Ulster stood at the crossroads. A narrow decision to introduce one man, one vote at local elections ultimately led to the collapse of O'Neill's administration at the end of April 1969. James Chichester-Clarke, one of the opponents of reform, became prime minister. The fact that the demands published by NICRA in June 1969 replicated its original list was an indictment of Stormont, but also demonstrated the impotence of London in asserting its will. Even more damning was the fact that demands for basic civil liberties provoked such a strong response, a vivid illustration of what W.B. Yeats described as 'great hatred, little room.'

SUPPORT THE DEMANDS OF THE CIVIL RIGHTS MOVEMENT

ONE MAN ONE VOTE
We demand the British franchise. That means votes at 18 for all in both Stormont and local government elections.

FAIR BOUNDARIES
We demand an end to gerrymandering by the Unionist Government. We want an Impartial Commission set up by Westminister to draw the electoral boundaries of the proposed new local authorities.

HOUSES ON NEED
We demand a compulsory points scheme for the allocation of houses. A credible scheme has been published, but many local authorities refuse to operate it. There should also be provision for appeal in the scheme to control abuses by local authorities.

ANTI - DISCRIMINATION LAWS
We demand that the law control religious discrimination which is rife in all areas of life in Northern Ireland. Such a law should also outlaw the incitment of religious hatred, and include control of public authorities, local and central alike.

CIVIL LIBERTIES
We demand an end to the repressive laws of the Stormont Government. That means the repeal of the Special Powers Act, the withdrawal of the Public Order Bill, the repeal or amendment of the Public Order Act, 1951.

Chains or Change

Manifesto, 6 March 1971

IRISH WOMEN'S LIBERATION MOVEMENT

Following the general election in 1918, Countess Markievicz became the first woman MP elected to Westminster and the first female elected as a government minister in Dáil Éireann. It would be 60 years before another woman, Máire Geoghegan-Quinn, held a seat in cabinet. Irish women had been active in the nationalist movement and in the campaign for female suffrage in the early 20th century. After independence, however, it became clear early on that they would not be on a par with men in the new state.

During the 1920s, Cumann na nGaedheal governments whittled away rights for women by prohibiting them from serving on juries, discriminating against them in the civil service and banning the importation and sale of contraceptives. When Fianna Fáil came to power in 1932, they followed on from where Cumann na nGaedheal had left off by introducing a marriage bar for women teachers and civil servants, and imposing other legal barriers to equality and employment. Ireland was by no means alone in discriminating against women in this way. Marriage bars and sex discrimination in the workplace existed across Western Europe and in the United States. In fact, during the 1930s, women in Germany, Spain and Poland actually lost the vote. The idea that Irish women were not alone in their inferior status was immaterial to the small but vocal women's movement.

The 1937 constitution appeared to reinforce this second-class status with its references to 'women's life within the home'. Some have suggested that de Valera's attitude to women was more paternal than patriarchal, and in this regard he was by no means unique. Noël Browne was widely regarded as the great progressive and liberal of his time. When he clashed with the Catholic hierarchy in his efforts to introduce free health care for mothers and children in 1951, he won the loyalty of many women who saw him as a politician – perhaps the *only* politician – who was on their side. Still, while Browne was concerned with women's interests and was a vocal supporter of legalizing contraceptives, he too was quite traditional. As late as 1971, Browne wrote that women who wished to have careers should not have children since 'motherhood is necessarily a full-time occupation'. If Browne was as radical as elected politicians got, clearly the limits of liberalism in Ireland were very narrow indeed.

Some important legislation had been passed during the 1960s. The most significant was the Succession Act which came into law in 1965, which entitled widows to a share of their husband's estate even if, as around half of Irish men did at the time, he died intestate. It had an immeasurably positive effect on the lives of Irish widows and was arguably the greatest advance in women's rights since 1922. Later, in 1970, a new deserted wives allowance was established. Otherwise things legally were as bad as ever. Wives had subservient standing to their husbands. And single or married, women were refused equal pay.

The 1960s saw an increased interest in left-wing politics in Ireland, with people taking to the streets against US policy in Vietnam and on civil rights. Women's issues were strangely absent. The calls for equal pay had become louder during the decade, particularly among women trade unionists. In 1969 a Commission on the Status of Women was established by the government, but Irish feminism, such as it was, appeared very measured. As Maeve Binchy noted at the time, the biggest problem for Irish women's movements was that they were too afraid of what people thought. Not for them the bra-burning protests adopted by some American feminists. It was not until the winter of 1970 that the second wave of feminism that had begun in the United States finally crashed on Irish shores. In October, the *Irish Times* quoted the observation of a visiting women's libber that it was 'very odd that in this country of all places, you don't find a strong women's liberation movement.' That same month, the Irish Women's Liberation Movement (IWLM) was founded in Dublin by around a dozen women, mostly *Irish Times* journalists. It was not the first organization to push for women's rights, but it was by far the most radical.

In terms of numbers and duration, the IWLM never grew far beyond its small beginnings. Nevertheless, its impact belied its size or longevity. The movement did not influence public policy directly, but it never really tried to. Its aim was to get women to think about their circumstances and position in society. The goal, said Mary Maher of the *Irish Times*, was for women to get 'narked'. Piecemeal reforms, including the vote, she said, were not good enough. Women had to reject the stereotypes that society had pushed on them.

On 6 March 1971 the IWLM published its manifesto, *Chains or Change*, documenting the 'civil wrongs of Irishwomen'. That night, IWLM founder members Máirín Johnson and Nell McCafferty, and independent speakers, including future president Mary Robinson, appeared on a panel discussion on the Telefís Éireann programme *The Late Late Show*. The programme was reasonably sedate until the panel had finished and the debate was opened to the floor. The IWLM members seated in the audience were less restrained than their colleagues had been. A remark from journalist Mary Kenny that male legislators in Dáil Éireann did not 'give a damn' about women prompted deputy Garret FitzGerald (who lived nearby) to hurry to the studio to tell the women that inequality was their fault. They had not pushed hard enough for it. His remarks, and perhaps more importantly his attempt to upstage the women, infuriated the IWLM members, but it made for compelling viewing. Not surprisingly, the pamphlet in question, retailing at 10 new pence, sold out almost overnight. Although described as a manifesto, it was less a prescription for change than a list of grievances. They may appear almost mundane today, but that makes them all the more telling as a description of 1970s reality.

The IWLM, with its pamphlet, television appearances and clever publicity stunts, such as the contraceptive train to Belfast and forays into the Forty Foot male-only bathing spot, brought the question of women's inequality to the forefront of the social agenda. As far as politics was concerned, its achievements were modest. Mary Kenny was probably right when she said that men in Leinster House cared little for the stature of women. Men in Brussels, however, were more enlightened. Ireland joined the European Economic Community in 1973, an act that would quickly challenge the unequal status of women in Irish society.

The Legal inequities of Irishwomen.

Article 40 of the Irish constitution promises equal rights before the law to all citizens of the Republic of Ireland.

One million, four hundred and thirty-four thousand, nine hundred and seventy Irish citizens (at the last count) are not accorded such equal rights. These are the women of Ireland.

'Ireland is one of the last countries …
where women are considered to be unfit for jury service.'

Possibly the most visible inequity before the law which Irishwomen suffer is the fact that they are not called upon for jury service. Ireland is one of the last countries of the Western World where women are considered to be unfit for jury service.

It is, of course, true that a woman (providing she is a householder) may apply to serve on a jury. Lawyers will recall that one woman even succeeded in being accepted some years ago. But not only is this so rare an occurrence that it is regarded as a phenomenon; even when she does apply, there is, in practice, a snag. Judges and lawyers are often suspicious of an ulterior motive in a woman juror – such as a prejudiced interest in particular kinds of cases – and can therefore object to her and have her disqualified.

Women themselves frequently say that they are indifferent to this inequity, since jury service is commonly regarded as tedious; but the fact remains that it is patently unjust to the person being 'tried'. Twelve male householders are not a representative balanced social group. A woman on trial is not being judged by her peers – an elementary principle of Justice pre-dating even Common Law. It may be said that some so-called primitive tribal societies – with their democratic selection of male and female village elders – are actually in advance of Ireland on this principle.

What's more, we in Ireland have actually refused to comply with United Nations recommendations on this point.

The UN Charter of the Political Rights of Women was drawn up and signed by member states in 1950. It was ratified by Ireland in 1968, with certain reservations. We refused to sign Article 11 of the Charter on the assumption that jury service not being obligatory for women was not a discriminatory practice. Ireland also maintained that our position in regard to equal pay – it not being statutory in this country – was not discriminatory.

How our representative at the UN could have stood up and made such an illogical claim is unfathomable to any rational female mind. He did.

Legally, this situation could be declared unconstitutional – clearly contravening Article 40 of the Constitution. It remains yet to be challenged in the courts.

'Upon marriage a woman in Ireland enters into a state of civil death.'

Although there has been some piecemeal reform in the legal status of married women in this country, it can still be said that upon marriage a woman in Ireland enters into a state of civil death.

Since 1957, a married woman is allowed to hold and dispose of property, to sue and be sued, to contract. Subsequent legislation has allowed her certain basic rights of inheritance upon her husband's estate.

Nonetheless, a married woman in Ireland has still no real identity or existence in her own right. She is still regarded as the chattel of her husband. Her domicile is automatically her husband's – that is to say, if he happens to be in America, she is also legally speaking in America, no matter where she might 'actually' be. She must have permission from him for all kinds of things – pledging any credit or making almost any kind of private financial arrangements; putting the children on her passport; in certain cases, if she needs to have a gynaecological operation.

A man may desert his wife for as long as he chooses – but return whenever he wishes and automatically resume all his marital and parental rights. A woman immediately forfeits all her rights, including access to the marital home or to the children, if she leaves him.

'He' can change their name without consulting her.

'She' may not.

'He' is not obliged to reveal to her what he earns.

'She' is to him.

If 'she' pays tax on her own income, it is her husband who is entitled to any of her rebates.

'He' is entitled to scrutinise her taxation forms.

'She' is not entitled to see his.

'He' is not obliged to support her above and beyond what he considers she needs. She may only pledge his credit for the bare necessities – over and above he can disclaim all responsibility.

If 'she' spends her earnings running their home, she may not give away, sell or raise money on the contents.

If 'he' improves 'her' property, he may be entitled to be paid, especially if he is a skilled craftsman.

If 'she' saves money out of the housekeeping allowance which he has seen fit to give her, it is still legally 'his' money and she may not spend it as she pleases.

'She' is not entitled to any of his savings, even if it is 'her' household economies which have made these savings possible.

If a wife feels that she is not being adequately provided for (and remember, it is the husband who decides, quite arbitrarily, what constitutes 'provision'), she must challenge him in the courts. She has no other means of redress. Even then, in contrast to other countries (such as, for example, West Germany) there is no statutory ruling about what percentage of his (their) income she is entitled to.

'A woman immediately forfeits all her rights, including access to the marital home or to the children, if she leaves.'

In regard to the children, the situation of the Irish wife is even more anomalous.

Though the Irish Constitution emphasises the *duties* of both parents, the law accords *rights* overwhelmingly to one – the father.

The father is the legal guardian of the children; he has the sole right to decide upon their education, religion and domicile. He can draw from the children's post office savings – she can't. He must give consent to an operation on the children. He can have the children named on his passport without her consent and take them abroad without her permission.

Legally, the Children's Allowance money is his. If he should wish to squander every penny of it, he is perfectly within his rights.

The constitution of this country promises a special place to women in the home. But the law – most of it made by 19th century British legislators – has not fulfilled that promise. Before the law, Irishwomen in the home have noticeably inferior status.

And then, of course, if the woman wishes, or needs, to go out to work, she runs into unequal pay, the marriage bar, no amenities and penalising taxation.

A personal summing-up by a working mother:
Five good reasons why it is better to live in sin.

NUMBER ONE:

You can keep your job. If you're in the Civil Service or in semi-state body employment, working for the trade unions or the banks, you'll go without further debate. This is not to say you won't necessarily be re-hired. In some places, you will be on a temporary week-to-week or day-to-day basis as the company needs you. This is true in many semi-state bodies. You'll also probably be re-hired for less pay and in a lower grade than what you enjoy – if that's the word – now. If you're in the civil service, you and the man you decided not to marry can have two children and you'll still be able to keep your job; you will have a maternity leave of several months. We make the point not to criticise the civil Service for its responsible treatment of unmarried mothers, only to ask why they feel less responsible toward married women even before they have children? To marry is to accept compulsory retirement until an age when your children are old enough so that you can try to find part-time work. So that 15 years from now, you'll find yourself back in the labour force, probably not in a Trade Union, and therefore unable to fight dismissal, low pay, poor conditions. Many of the skills you may have acquired by this time will be lost by then and you'll probably have to take unskilled work or less pay. Unless the Unions are more organised at part-time level than they now are, you'll be without any strength in negotiations. If your husband has died or deserted you or become an invalid, you'll have to work in these conditions.

'Before the law, Irishwomen in the home have noticeably inferior status.'

NUMBER TWO:

If you decide not to marry, you won't have to pay more income tax on your earnings than you pay now. As a single woman, you are allowed only £7.10 of what you earn tax free; the rest is taxed at 26p in the £. A married woman is allowed only £2.10 tax free. … The situation is that two single people with a combined income of £41 a week pay roughly £7.22½ in tax. As soon as they're married they'll pay about £9.72½.

NUMBER THREE:

The reason is that by staying single you'll keep whatever business identity you now have. Once you marry, you will be unable to open a charge account without your husband's signature, even if you have a job or a checking account. Most hire-purchase arrangements will be closed to you without your husband's approval.

Many motor insurance companies insist on your husband's signature, even if the car is yours. You will have difficulty transacting any business arrangement which is one reason why a good number of housewives have to resort to illegal money-lenders. A married woman cannot even apply for the children's allowance, which is legally her husband's. And her husband's signature is also required in certain hospitals for gynaecological operations. If her friends or children get in trouble with the law, a married woman will be denied the right to stand bail unless her home is owned in her own name. Even then, she has to go through detailed scrutinisation.

Just to make sure your status as a married woman is that of a total dependent [sic] the law sees to it that the wife has no statutory right to force her husband to give her any money at all, no matter how much he earns or how many he feeds.

'If you live in sin you don't submit to the insult that society offers women who marry – the status of property.'

The first three reasons for living in sin sound practical ones. Anyone on the brink of marriage isn't likely to consider reasons four and five too closely, because she doesn't think too deeply about the possibility of the relationship going sour. Marriages have turned out badly for many people, though. A woman who is only living in sin can remember reason Number Four: you can leave when things have finally become unbearable, merely by walking out the door. A married woman who leaves her husband is presumed to have deserted him, and has no right to his house, furniture or income.

Which brings us to Number five: if you live in sin you don't submit to the insult that society offers women who marry – the status of property. An adult and equal relationship is something two people forge together. The institution of marriage is something invented to preserve male superiority and a system of female chattels.

Widgery Report on Bloody Sunday

Report of the tribunal appointed to inquire into the events on Sunday 30 January 1972

LORD WIDGERY (1911–81)

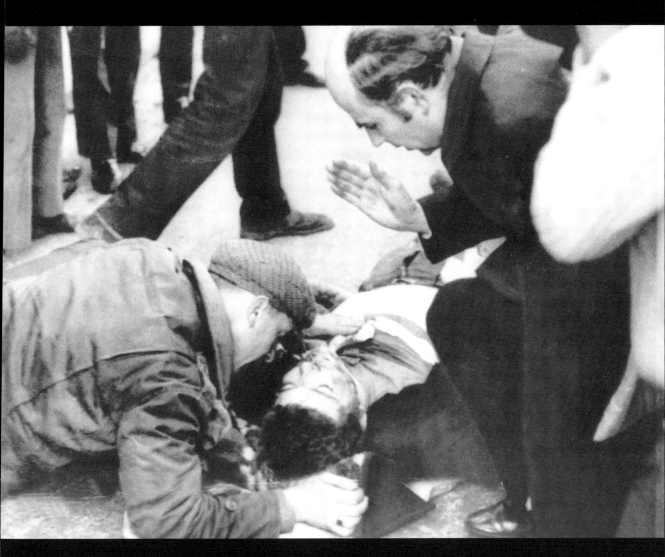

The Stormont government introduced internment without trial in Northern Ireland on 9 August 1971. The move was controversial and unpopular in the Catholic community, which condemned the government's decision as an assault on civil liberties. Nonetheless, in the face of continued vociferous protests, between 9 August 1971 and 5 December 1975, a total of 1981 people were detained; 1874 of the internees were Catholic/republican, while just 107 were Protestant/loyalist.

On Sunday 30 January 1972 some 6000 people joined an anti-internment march in Derry organized by the Northern Ireland Civil Rights Association. The previous weekend a similar march to Magilligan Prison Camp, Co. Derry, had seen members of the Parachute Regiment fire rubber bullets and use their batons against protesters. This action had led to the Paras being forcibly pacified by their superiors. They were present again a week later in Derry. As the marchers made their way to 'Free Derry corner', they came up against army barricades. Some protesters began to throw stones, which in turn led to rioting. 'In other contexts this might be counted as a violent confrontation,' recalls Eamonn McCann, 'but in William Street in Derry it was very much par for the course.' Initially the army responded with tear gas, rubber bullets and water cannon. Soon afterwards, soldiers opened fire with live rounds. According to later British army evidence, 21 soldiers fired their weapons, shooting 108 rounds between them. Thirteen men died at the scene. There were many other casualties, one of whom subsequently died of his wounds. Afterwards, soldiers claimed that they had acted in response to shots fired against them by a sniper, although no ballistic evidence was ever produced to back this up.

The killing of civilians by the security forces would have been shocking in any circumstances. Television brought the event into people's homes. Most striking of all was footage of a young priest, Father Edward Daly (later bishop of Derry). Using a blood-soaked handkerchief as a white flag, this stooped figure ran the gauntlet to allow the body of a fatally wounded 17-year-old boy, Jackie Duddy, to be removed from the Rossville flats. For many Catholics in Northern Ireland and the Republic, numbed shock at these scenes quickly turned to fury. A crowd in Dublin vented its anger by burning down the British embassy in Merrion Square.

The following day, the British prime minister, Edward Heath, invited the Lord Chief Justice, Lord Widgery, to conduct a tribunal of inquiry into the events. Heath warned him that Britain was 'fighting a war on two fronts, one of them a propaganda war'. The inquiry lasted 11 weeks. The report, published on 18 April 1972, found no fault on the part of those soldiers who fired live rounds on the day and declared a 'strong suspicion' that some of those killed 'had been firing weapons or handling bombs'. Critics immediately branded the report a whitewash. Certainly it seemed to have fulfilled the desire of the secretary to the tribunal to 'pile up the case against the deceased'.

The subsequent case against the Widgery Report is infinitely longer than the document itself. Academics, journalists and witnesses have forensically challenged its key findings. Particular attention has focused on the fact that many eyewitnesses were not called and that the interpretation of forensic evidence was flawed.

Bloody Sunday was a key turning-point in the Troubles. 'What happened in Derry on that January day helped to ensure more than two decades of subsequent IRA violence,' notes Tim Pat Coogan. According to *Lost Lives: the stories of the men, women and children who died as a result of the Northern Ireland troubles*, 502 people were killed in the 12 months following 'Bloody Sunday', more than twice the total number of deaths during the previous six years.

In January 1998 British Prime Minister Tony Blair announced a new inquiry into the events to be presided over by Lord Saville. 'It is in the interests of everyone,' he told the House of Commons, 'that the truth is established and told.'

...

2. The terms of reference of the Inquiry were as stated in the Parliamentary Resolutions and the Warrants of Appointment. At a preliminary hearing on 14 February I explained that my interpretation of those terms was that the Inquiry was essentially a fact-finding exercise, by which I meant that its purpose was to reconstruct, with as much detail as was necessary, the events which led up to the shooting of a number of people in the streets of Londonderry on the afternoon of Sunday 30 January. The Tribunal was not concerned with making moral judgments; its task was to try and form an objective view of the events and the sequence in which they occurred, so that those who were concerned to form judgments would have a firm basis on which to reach their conclusions. The Tribunal would, therefore, listen to witnesses who were present on the occasion and who could assist in reconstructing the events from the evidence of what they saw with their own eyes or heard with their own ears. I wished to hear evidence from people who supported each of the versions of the events of 30 January which had been given currency.

3. I emphasised the narrowness of the confines of the Inquiry, the value of which would largely depend on its being conducted and concluded expeditiously. If considerations not directly relevant to the matters under review were allowed to take up time, the production of the Tribunal's Report would be delayed. The limits of the Inquiry in space were the streets of Londonderry in which the disturbances and the shooting took place; in time, the period beginning with the moment when the march first became involved in violence and ending with the deaths of the deceased and the conclusion of the affair.

4. At the first substantive hearing I explained that the emphasis on the importance of eye witnesses did not exclude evidence such as that of pathologists. Nor did it exclude consideration of the orders given to the Army before the march. The officers who

INQUIRY INTO THE EVENTS ON 30 JANUARY 1972 WHICH LED TO LOSS OF LIFE IN CONNECTION WITH THE PROCESSION IN LONDONDERRY ON THAT DAY

REPORT OF THE TRIBUNAL APPOINTED UNDER THE TRIBUNALS OF INQUIRY (EVIDENCE) ACT 1921

To:

THE RIGHT HONOURABLE REGINALD MAUDLING, MP
Her Majesty's Principal Secretary of State for the Home Department

PART ONE
INTRODUCTION

Appointment of Tribunal

1. On Sunday 30 January 1972 British soldiers opened fire in the streets of Londonderry. Thirteen civilians lost their lives and a like number were injured; their names are listed in Appendix A. On the following day I accepted an invitation from Her Majesty's Government to conduct a Tribunal of Inquiry into these events. Both Houses of Parliament adopted a Resolution in the following terms on 1 February:

> "That it is expedient that a Tribunal be established for inquiring into a definite matter of urgent public importance, namely the events on Sunday 30 January which led to loss of life in connection with the procession in Londonderry on that day."

In order to ensure that the powers vested in the Tribunal would extend to transferred matters under the Government of Ireland Act, 1920, as well as to matters reserved to Westminster, a Resolution in identical terms was adopted in both Houses of the Northern Ireland Parliament. The Home Secretary, The Right Honourable Reginald Maudling, signed a Warrant of Appointment on 2 February. The Warrant declared that the Tribunals of Inquiry (Evidence) Act, 1921 should apply to the Tribunal and that the Tribunal was constituted as a Tribunal within the meaning of that Act. A Warrant of Appointment in identical terms was signed by the Governor of Northern Ireland, Lord Grey, on 4 February. The Secretary to the Tribunal was appointed on 6 February and left at once for Northern Ireland. Meanwhile the Treasury Solicitor's Department had already started taking statements from witnesses in London.

Terms of Reference

2. The terms of reference of the Inquiry were as stated in the Parliamentary Resolutions and the Warrants of Appointment. At a preliminary hearing on 14 February I explained that my interpretation of those terms was that the Inquiry was essentially a fact-finding exercise, by which I meant that its purpose was to reconstruct, with as much detail as was necessary, the events which led up to the shooting of a number of people in the streets of Londonderry on the afternoon of Sunday 30 January. The Tribunal was not concerned with making

1

conceived the orders and made the plans, including those for the employment of the 1st Battalion of the Parachute Regiment, would appear before me … .

'During these 17 sessions 114 witnesses gave evidence and were cross-examined.'

6. The first substantive hearing of the Tribunal was held on 21 February and I continued to sit in Coleraine until 14 March. During these 17 sessions 114 witnesses gave evidence and were cross-examined. The witnesses, who are listed in Appendix B, fell into six main groups: priests; other people from Londonderry; press and television reporters, photographers, cameramen and sound recordists; soldiers, including the relevant officers; police officers; doctors, forensic experts and pathologists. After all the evidence had been taken three further sessions were held in the Royal Courts of Justice in London on 16, 17 and 20 March, at which I heard the closing speeches of Counsel for the relatives of the deceased, for the Army and for the Tribunal … .

8. A large quantity of material had to be examined. As has been mentioned above, the number of witnesses called was 114; but a much larger number of statements, roughly double that number, was taken, all of which were considered in arriving at a decision as to the witnesses to be called. This was in addition to the statements taken from the soldiers by the Royal Military Police on the night of 30 to 31 January. The Northern Ireland Civil Rights Association collected a large number of statements from people in Londonderry said to be willing to give evidence. These statements reached me at an advanced stage in the Inquiry. In so far as they contained new material, not traversing ground already familiar from evidence given before me, I have made use of them. Seven of the wounded appeared before the Tribunal and gave evidence. I did not think it necessary to take evidence from those of the wounded who were still in hospital.

9. … The events with which the Tribunal was primarily concerned took place on the west bank, and indeed wholly within an area about a quarter of a mile square, bounded on the north by Great James Street, on the east by Strand Road, Waterloo Place and the City Wall, on the south by Free Derry Corner and Westland Street and on the west by Fahan Street West and the Little Diamond.

SECURITY BACKGROUND: EVENTS IN LONDONDERRY DURING THE PREVIOUS SIX MONTHS

10. The Bogside and the Creggan, the Republican views of whose people are well known, were the scene of large scale rioting in 1969 and have suffered sporadic rioting by hooligans ever since. In the early summer of 1971 a good deal of progress had been made towards restoring normal life. The Royal Ulster Constabulary was patrolling almost everywhere in the area on foot, the Army was little in evidence, the hooligan element had been isolated and the IRA was quiescent. At the beginning of July, however, gunmen appeared and an IRA campaign began. Wide-spread violence ensued with the inevitable military counter-action. Nevertheless at the end of August it was decided, after consultation with a group of prominent local citizens, to reduce the level of military activity in the hope that moderate opinion would prevail and the IRA gunmen be isolated from the community.

'The law was not effectively enforced in the area.'

11. From the end of August to the end of October an uneasy equilibrium was maintained. In a conscious effort to avoid provocation the Army made itself less obvious. Though parts of the Bogside and Creggan were patrolled, no military initiative was taken except in response to aggression or for specific search or arrest operations. The improvement hoped for did not, however, take place. The residents of the Bogside and Creggan threw up or repaired over 50 barricades, including the one in Rossville Street which figured prominently in the proceedings of the Inquiry; frequent sniping and bombing attacks were made on the security forces; and the IRA tightened its grip on the district. Thus although at the end of October the policy was still one of passive containment, sniping and bombing had become increasingly common in virtually the whole of Londonderry west of the River Foyle. The Royal Ulster Constabulary had not operated in the Bogside and Creggan since June or July … the law was not effectively enforced in the area.

12. At the end of October, 8 Infantry Brigade, within whose area of command the City of Londonderry lay, was given instructions progressively to regain the initiative from the terrorists and reimpose the rule of law on the Creggan and Bogside. Hooligan activity was to be vigorously countered and arrest operations were to be mounted. As a result, a series of operations was carried out in the Bogside and Creggan at battalion strength with the object of clearing barricades, making arrests and searching premises about which intelligence reports had been received. These operations hardened the attitude of the community against the Army, so that the troops were operating in an entirely hostile environment and as time went on were opposed by all elements of the community when they entered the Bogside and Creggan. The Army's static positions and observation posts were fired on and a large number of youths, many of them unemployed, gathered daily at the points of entry into the areas which were guarded by troops in order to attack them with stones and other missiles. Many nail and petrol bombs were thrown during these attacks. Gunmen made full use of the cover offered to them by the gangs of youths, which made it more and more difficult to engage the youths at close quarters and make arrests. The Creggan became almost a fortress. Whenever troops appeared near there at night search-lights were switched on and car horns blazed. The terrorists were still firmly in control … .

14. At the beginning of 1972 Army foot patrols were not able to operate south of William Street by day because of sniper fire, although the Army continued to patrol in the Bogside at night and to enter by day if there was a specific reason for so doing. There were no foot patrols by day during January. The hooligan gangs in Londonderry constituted a special threat to security. Their tactics were to engineer daily breaches of law and order in the face of the security forces, particularly in the William Street area, during which the lives of the soldiers were at risk from attendant snipers and nail bombers. The hooligans could be contained but not dispersed without serious risk to the troops.

15. This was the background against which it was learned that, despite the fact that parades and processions had been prohibited throughout Northern Ireland by law since 9 August 1971, there was to be a protest march in Londonderry on Sunday 30 January, organised by the Northern Ireland Civil Rights Association (NICRA). It was the opinion of the Army commanders that if the march took place, whatever the intentions of NICRA might be, the hooligans backed up by the gunmen would take control. In the light of this view the security forces made their plans to block the march.

THE ARMY PLAN TO CONTAIN THE MARCH

16. The proposed march placed the security forces in a dilemma. An attempt to stop by force a crowd of 5,000 or more, perhaps as many as 20 or 25,000, might result in heavy casualties or even in the overrunning of the troops by sheer weight of numbers. To allow such a well publicised march to take place without opposition however would bring the law into disrepute and make control of future marches impossible.

17. Chief Superintendent Lagan, the head of the Royal Ulster Constabulary in Londonderry, thought that the dangers of interfering with the march were too great and that no action should be taken against it save to photograph the leaders with a view to their being prosecuted later. His opinion was reported to the Chief Constable of Northern Ireland and to the Commander 8 Infantry Brigade (Brigadier MacLellan) who passed it to General Ford, the Commander Land Forces Northern Ireland. The final decision, which was taken by higher authority after General Ford and the Chief Constable had been consulted, was to allow the march to begin but to contain it within the general area of the Bogside and the Creggan Estate so as to prevent rioting in the City centre and damage to commercial premises and shops. On 25 January General Ford put the Commander 8 Infantry Brigade in charge of the operation and ordered him to prepare a detailed plan. The plan is 8 Infantry Brigade Operation Order No 2/72 dated 27 January.

18. The Brigade Commander's plan required the erection of barriers sealing off each of the streets through which the marchers might cross the containment line … .

'There is not a shred of evidence to support these suggestions.'

19. The Operation Order provided that the march should be dealt with in as low a key as possible for as long as possible and indeed that if it took place entirely within the Bogside and Creggan it should go unchallenged. No action was to be taken against the marchers unless they tried to breach the barriers or used violence against the security forces. CS gas was not to be used except as a last resort if troops were about to be overrun and the rioters could no longer be held off with water cannon and riot guns. (These guns, which fire rubber bullets, are also known as baton guns; and the rubber bullets as baton rounds.)

20. Under the heading of 'Hooliganism' the Operation Order provided:

> 'An arrest force is to be held centrally behind the check points and launched in a scoop-up operation to arrest as many hooligans and rioters as possible.'

21. The Operation Order, which was classified 'Secret', thus clearly allotted to 1 Para the task of an arrest operation against hooligans. Under cross-examination, however, the senior Army officers, and particularly General Ford, were severely attacked on the grounds that they did not genuinely intend to use 1 Para in this way. It was suggested that 1 Para had been specially brought to Londonderry because they were known to be the roughest and toughest unit in Northern Ireland and it was intended to use them in one of two ways: either to flush out any IRA gunmen in the Bogside and destroy them by superior training and fire power; or to send a punitive force into the Bogside to give the residents a rough handling and discourage them from making or supporting further attacks on the troops.

22. There is not a shred of evidence to support these suggestions and they have been denied by all the officers concerned. I am satisfied that the Brigade Operation Order accurately expressed the Brigade Commander's intention for the employment of 1 Para and that suggestions to the contrary are unfounded. 1 Para was chosen for the arrest role because it was the only experienced uncommitted battalion in Northern Ireland … .

54. To those who seek to apportion responsibility for the events of 30 January the question 'Who fired first?' is vital. I am entirely satisfied that the first firing in the courtyard was directed at the soldiers. Such a conclusion is not reached by counting heads or by selecting one particular witness as truthful in preference to another. It is a conclusion gradually built up over many days of listening to evidence and watching the demeanour of witnesses under cross-examination. It does not mean that witnesses who spoke in the opposite sense were not doing their best to be truthful. On the contrary I was much impressed by the care with which many of them, particularly the newspaper reporters, television men and photographers, gave evidence … there was no reason why they [the Paras] should have suddenly desisted and begun to shoot unless they had come under fire themselves. If the soldiers are wrong they were parties in a lying conspiracy which must have come to light in the rigorous cross-examination to which they were subjected … .

'Who fired first?'

97. Those accustomed to listening to witnesses could not fail to be impressed by the demeanour of the soldiers of 1 Para. They gave their evidence with confidence and without hesitation or prevarication and withstood a rigorous cross-examination without contradicting themselves or each other. With one or two exceptions I accept that they were telling the truth as they remembered it.

SUMMARY OF CONCLUSIONS

1. There would have been no deaths in Londonderry on 30 January if those who organised the illegal march had not thereby created a highly dangerous situation in which a clash between demonstrators and the security forces was almost inevitable … .

10. None of the deceased or wounded is proved to have been shot whilst handling a firearm or bomb. Some are wholly acquitted of complicity in such action; but there is a strong suspicion that some others had been firing weapons or handling bombs in the course of the afternoon and that yet others had been closely supporting them.

11. There was no general breakdown in discipline. For the most part the soldiers acted as they did because they thought their orders required it. No order and no training can ensure that a soldier will always act wisely, as well as bravely and with initiative. The individual soldier ought not to have to bear the burden of deciding whether to open fire in confusion such as prevailed on 30 January. In the conditions prevailing in Northern Ireland, however, this is often inescapable.

WIDGERY

W.J. Smith, *Secretary*

REPUBLIC OF IRELAND

Poorest of the rich

TAKE a tiny, open ex-peasant economy. Place it next door to a much larger one, from which it broke away with great bitterness barely a lifetime ago. Infuse it with a passionate desire to enjoy the same lifestyle as its former masters, but without the same industrial heritage or natural resources. Inevitable result: extravagance, frustration, debt. Ireland today is bravely facing up to the consequences of a decade of borrowing to pay for better public services than its wealth justified. Its citizens, many of whom have already endured six years of stagnant real incomes, are just beginning to come to terms with the extent to which the country has to change, if long-term growth is to be secured.

Ireland is easily the poorest country in rich north-west Europe. Its gross domestic product is a mere 64% of the European Community average. Yet in the mid-1970s it set out to build a welfare state as generous as Britain's. While world recession and oil shock made other countries curtail social spending, Ireland's hugely expanded. And so, by the end of the 1970s, the country had waded deeper into debt. Large payments of debt interest began to add to the demands on the public purse. To meet them, tax bills increased, putting pressure on pay and driving a growing number of skilled people to emigrate. The unemployment rate rose to 19%: the highest in Europe apart from Spain. In the 1980s Ireland has managed the remarkable combination of falling living standards and deteriorating competitiveness.

By the autumn of 1986 the country was on the skids. In four years its national debt had doubled, to

I£25 billion—I£28,000 for every Irish household, some 40% of it in foreign currency. As a proportion of gross domestic product, Ireland's debt was the biggest in Europe. Servicing costs were gobbling one-third of annual tax revenue and 90% of the revenue from income tax. Real interest rates of 10% were driving business to despair. A panicky flight of capital had begun. The International Monetary Fund expected a call for help.

Then, last March, came the fall of the hamstrung coalition of the Fine Gael and Labour parties, in power since 1982. The man whose party took office, Mr Charles Haughey of Fianna Fail, bears much of the blame for the extravagances of the late 1970s. Yet, to general relief, he set about hacking public spending with brutal determination.

Learning to live modestly again

Ireland is now beginning to accept that a country with two-thirds the national wealth of its neighbours can afford only two-thirds the public services. At the least, three years of grinding retrenchment lie ahead. But once the public finances are back on the straight and narrow, the old struggle to build a competitive Irish industry will re-emerge. The republic's population of 3½m is too small to support a vigorous home market. Besides, it needs current-account surpluses to pay its foreign debt. What should it build on—fashionable high-tech products which may upsticks for Taipei or Atlanta at the drop of a tax allowance? Or its own more pedestrian natural advantages—its grass, its well-educated youngsters, its lovely countryside? In the past, Ireland's indus-

Poor Ireland behaved as though it was rich, writes Frances Cairncross. Now it must pay the price

I£ = £0.89
I£ = $1.68

Poorest of the Rich

Article on Ireland, 16 January 1988

THE ECONOMIST

The Irish economy may have prospered during the 1960s, but the respite from economic gloom was short-lived. In 1972 Ireland began a seemingly inexorable slide towards the abyss of national oblivion. That year George Colley, newly appointed Fianna Fáil minister for finance, ran a deficit in the current budget for the first time. Colley rationalized that unemployment was on the rise and the economy was performing below par. A bit of pump priming seemed exactly what was needed to get things moving again (not least with a general election in the offing).

In fact, apart from increasing the national debt, the effect was to create an inflationary spiral by ramping up prices, which in turn prompted higher wage demands.

Not to be outdone with spending promises at the polls, the Fine Gael–Labour coalition that won in 1973 did so on a platform of matching, and even surpassing, Fianna Fáil. Inflation was endemic internationally following the oil shock that year, but with national pay awards reaching levels of just under 30 percent by the mid-1970s, Ireland was clearly out of control. Under the new coalition, the exchequer's foreign debt increased eight-fold. By 1977, it was time for another election. Once again the politics of expediency won the day, as Fianna Fáil took office under Jack Lynch on the back of a give-away manifesto. Another oil shock in 1979 further pulverized the Irish economy and only exacerbated the wasteful habits of successive governments. By 1981 inflation had topped 20 percent. Unemployment was on the rise, and would hit 17 percent by 1987.

Ireland was stumbling from one helpless government to another, with none apparently able to get a grip on events. Charles Haughey replaced Lynch as taoiseach in 1979. Not long afterwards, he made a television address to inform the nation that Ireland was living beyond its means. Self-sacrifice was needed. It was a famous speech that was followed by infamous procrastination. Spending continued unabated. Next up was a Fine Gael–Labour coalition. It was deeply divided over spending cuts, which Fine Gael favoured and Labour vehemently opposed. By 1987 Labour could take no more and scuttled the government. Fine Gael went to the country on a manifesto of swingeing cutbacks: its vote fell by 12 percent.

Fianna Fáil returned with a minority administration. In opposition it had fought the government's efforts at retrenchment and had contested the 1987 election with the slogan 'health cuts hurt the old, the sick and the handicapped'. If people thought they had voted for a government with deep pockets, they were soon disabused. Haughey appointed Ray McSharry as minister for finance. He immediately – and courageously – introduced savage cuts in spending, earning himself the nickname 'Mac the Knife'. The policy was not popular, but in a welcome instance of political integrity the Fine Gael leader, Alan Dukes, announced that his party would support the minority government so long as it pursued an economic policy in the national interest. Alongside retrenchment, the government opened negotiations with the trade union movement and employers' organizations, which led to the Programme for National Recovery (PNR) –

the first of the modern social partnership arrangements that helped end the cycle of crippling stagflation. Although few realized it, the Celtic Tiger cub was emerging blinking and wobbly-legged from the economic long grass.

In January 1988 the influential *Economist* published a humiliating special report on Ireland. The cover showed a woman and her child begging on a Dublin street. The headline that went with it declared Ireland to be: 'The poorest of the rich'.

The reforms that would lead to the Irish economic miracle were already under way, but surely the magazine's contemptuous tone about the 'ex-peasant' economy 'with a passionate desire to enjoy the same lifestyle as its former masters' would have been enough to steel the resolve of any Irish policy maker. As it was, retrenchment and partnership saw debt fall and the economy stabilize. Low corporate tax rates encouraged huge foreign investment. Almost a decade later *The Economist* returned to take another look, this time at 'Europe's shining light'. The banner headline on this occasion saluted 'The luck of the Irish'.

Luck, of course, had nothing – or not much – to do with it.

Take a tiny, open ex-peasant economy. Place it next door to a much larger one, from which it broke away with great bitterness barely a lifetime ago. Infuse it with a passionate desire to enjoy the same lifestyle as its former masters, but without the same industrial heritage or natural resources. Inevitable result: extravagance, frustration, debt. Ireland today is bravely facing up to the consequences of a decade of borrowing to pay for better public services than its wealth justified. Its citizens, many of whom have already endured six years of stagnant real incomes, are just beginning to come to terms with the extent to which the country has to change, if long-term growth is to be secured.

'Ireland is easily the poorest country in rich north-west Europe.'

Ireland is easily the poorest country in rich north-west Europe. Its gross domestic product is a mere 64% of the European Community average. Yet in the mid-1970s it set out to build a welfare state as generous as Britain's. While world recession and oil shock made other countries curtail social spending, Ireland's hugely expanded. And so, by the end of the 1970s, the country had waded deeper into debt. Large payments of debt interest began to add to the demands on the public purse. To meet them, tax bills increased, putting pressure on pay and driving a growing number of skilled people to emigrate. The unemployment rate rose to 19%: the highest in Europe apart from Spain. In the 1980s Ireland had managed the remarkable combination of falling living standards and deteriorating competitiveness.

By the autumn of 1986 the country was on the skids. In four years its national debt had doubled, to I£25 billion – I£28,000 for every Irish household, some 40% of its foreign currency. As a proportion of gross domestic product, Ireland's debt was the biggest in Europe. Servicing costs were gobbling one-third of annual tax revenue and 90% of the revenue from income tax. Real interest rates of 10% were driving business to despair. A panicky flight of capital had begun. The International Monetary Fund expected a call for help.

'An economy as open as Ireland's
cannot prosper with such burdens.'

Then, last March, came the fall of the hamstrung coalition of the Fine Gael and Labour parties, in power since 1982. The man whose party took office, Mr Charles Haughey of Fianna Fail, bears much of the blame for the extravagances of the late 1970s. Yet, to general relief, he set about hacking public spending with brutal determination.

Learning to live modestly again

Ireland is now beginning to accept that a country with two-thirds the national wealth of its neighbours can afford only two-thirds the public services. At the least, three years of grinding retrenchment lie ahead. But once the public finances are back on the straight and narrow, the old struggle to build a competitive Irish industry will re-emerge. The republic's population of 3.5m is too small to support a vigorous home market. Besides, it needs current-account surpluses to pay its foreign debt. What should it build on – fashionable high-tech products which may upsticks for Taipei or Atlanta at the drop of a tax allowance? Or its own more pedestrian natural advantages – its grass, its well-educated youngsters, its lovely countryside? In the past, Ireland's industrial policy has been one of the most imaginative in the world. It has produced impressive results. But the debate about its future is one which other peripheral countries and regions should watch carefully.

The government is about to turn its attention to tax. Ireland has Western Europe's highest standard value-added tax, its highest income tax on the average worker, almost its highest excise duties and corporation tax. A single man with no allowances faces a marginal rate of tax and other deductions of 65.75%. An economy as open as Ireland's cannot prosper with such burdens. Budgets will be mainly constrained by the need to get borrowing down, fast. But radical reform of taxation is essential for Ireland's future growth.

After years of mismanagement by weak governments, Ireland desperately needs a period of political stability. Mr Haughey does not have a majority in the Dáil (parliament). But Fine Gael, the main opposition party, is in debt and out of favour; its new young leader, Mr Alan Dukes, faces plenty of internal opposition. Mr Dukes knows what needs to be done to the economy, and should be willing to let Fianna Fail get on with it. But Mr Haughey's position was weakened late last year, when the British government pressed him to ratify the European convention on the extradition of terrorists. His attempts to appease his nationalist backbenchers angered the opposition parties. Beleaguered, he was defeated in the Dáil on the important issue of cutting teachers' numbers. To reassert his authority he may have to call yet another general election.

'Desperate measures are needed.'

Almost all the opposition parties agree that desperate measures are needed to right the economy, and none much wants the opprobrium for taking them. Ireland potentially has a de facto National government, with Fine Gael acquiescing in most Fianna Fail policies. That is arguably the most stable arrangement the country can now hope for.

The Belfast ('Good Friday') Agreement

Agreement to establish a multi-party power-sharing executive in Northern Ireland, 10 April 1998

On 31 August 1994 the Irish Republican Army (IRA) announced a 'complete cessation of military operations'. The main loyalist paramilitary organizations followed suit in October. The IRA ceasefire came after several years of behind-the-scenes negotiations, beginning in the late 1980s between the Sinn Féin leader Gerry Adams and the SDLP's John Hume. For some time talks had also been taking place through back channels between the republican leadership and the British government.

Discussions between the British and Irish governments resulted in the Downing Street Declaration in December 1993. This included a recognition by the British government 'that it is for the people of the island of Ireland alone, by agreement between the two parts respectively, to exercise their right of self-determination on the basis of consent, freely and concurrently given, North and South, to bring about a united Ireland, if that is their wish.'

The paramilitary ceasefires opened a window for further and intense negotiations, but the chance for peace was diminished by the political situation in Westminster. John Major's Conservative government held office with a slim majority and often needed unionist support in the House of Commons. Any concessions towards nationalists or republicans would not only be resisted, but might also undermine his administration. The most contentious issue was decommissioning, with unionists and the British government adamant that Sinn Féin could not be admitted to formal talks on Northern Ireland until it had put its weapons beyond use. IRA frustration at the lack of political progress manifested itself on 9 February 1996 in the bombing of Canary Wharf, which killed two people and ended the ceasefire.

In May and June of the following year new governments were elected in Britain and Ireland, giving new impetus to the peace process. When it was announced that Sinn Féin could enter discussions without preconditions, the IRA renewed the ceasefire. Multi-party talks, under the chairmanship of US Senator George Mitchell, began in Belfast on 15 September. These featured representatives from most of the main parties – the Ulster Unionist Party, the SDLP, Sinn Féin, the Alliance Party, and three smaller groups, the Progressive Unionist Party, the Women's Coalition and the Ulster Democratic Party – as well as the British and Irish governments. Ian Paisley's Democratic Unionist Party (at that stage the second largest unionist party) and the smaller UK Unionist Party boycotted the process.

Negotiations carried on for months without much evidence of progress. There were three strands to the discussions (internal, North–South and British–Irish) but it was the ancillary 'confidence building measures' – questions of early release of paramilitary prisoners and decommissioning – that created the greatest problems. The talks seemed in constant threat of breaking down. During one crisis that followed, the secretary of state for Northern Ireland, Mo Mowlam, controversially met with loyalist prisoners in the Maze in an effort to retain their support for the talks.

In early 1998 the two governments pushed towards settlement. On 25 March George Mitchell announced that he was setting a deadline of 9 April for completion of the process. There followed an intense round of dialogue that included the British prime minister, Tony Blair, and the taoiseach, Bertie Ahern, with interventions from the US president, Bill Clinton. Matters went to the wire, with the original deadline of 9 April missed by just a few hours. Following all-night negotiations, representatives of the two governments and the various parties met on 10 April to give their support to the Belfast Agreement, popularly known as the 'Good Friday' agreement.

The deal provided for: a devolved assembly of 108 members that would elect a multi-party power-sharing executive; a North–South ministerial council to oversee cross-border bodies; and a British–Irish council that included members of all the devolved administrations in the UK and Ireland. There were significant gains and concessions on all sides. The Irish government agreed to repeal Articles 2 and 3 of its constitution. The British government did the same with the 1920 Government of Ireland Act. There was also provision for the release of political prisoners within two years. The agreement was put to the people of Ireland north and south on 22 May 1998. Referenda were passed by 94 percent in the Republic and by 71 percent in Northern Ireland.

Despite the relief of all involved in bringing about the Belfast Agreement, it marked only the beginning of another process. Unionist unhappiness about the lack of republican decommissioning delayed implementation of the agreement. It was 18 months before devolved government was established in an executive led by the Ulster Unionist Party's David Trimble as first minister and the SDLP's Séamus Mallon as deputy first minister. Even then the administration was short-lived. On 11 February 2000 Secretary of State Peter Mandelson suspended the 72-day-old executive and restored direct rule. As time went on, successive elections saw support grow for the more hard-line political parties, including the rejectionist Democratic Unionist Party.

Ultimately, it was not until 8 May 2007 – just weeks before Tony Blair resigned as prime minister – that a power-sharing executive featuring all the major parties in Northern Ireland finally took office under the leadership of Ian Paisley and Sinn Féin's Martin McGuiness.

DECLARATION OF SUPPORT

1. We, the participants in the multi-party negotiations, believe that the agreement we have negotiated offers a truly historic opportunity for a new beginning.

2. The tragedies of the past have left a deep and profoundly regrettable legacy of suffering. We must never forget those who have died or been injured, and their families. But we can best honour them through a fresh start, in which we firmly dedicate ourselves to the achievement of reconciliation, tolerance, and mutual trust, and to the protection and vindication of the human rights of all.

'We are committed to partnership, equality and mutual respect.'

3. We are committed to partnership, equality and mutual respect as the basis of relationships within Northern Ireland, between North and South, and between these islands.

4. We reaffirm our total and absolute commitment to exclusively democratic and peaceful means of resolving differences on political issues, and our opposition to any use or threat of force by others for any political purpose, whether in regard to this agreement or otherwise.

5. We acknowledge the substantial differences between our continuing, and equally legitimate, political aspirations. However, we will endeavour to strive in every practical way towards reconciliation and rapprochement within the framework of democratic and agreed arrangements. We pledge that we will, in good faith, work to ensure the success of each and every one of the arrangements to be established under this agreement. It is accepted that all of the institutional and constitutional arrangements – an Assembly in Northern Ireland, a North/South Ministerial Council, implementation bodies, a British–Irish Council and a British–Irish Intergovernmental Conference and any amendments to British Acts of Parliament and the Constitution of Ireland – are interlocking and interdependent and that in particular the functioning of the Assembly and the North/South Council are so closely inter-related that the success of each depends on that of the other.

6. Accordingly, in a spirit of concord, we strongly commend this agreement to the people, North and South, for their approval.

CONSTITUTIONAL ISSUES

1. The participants endorse the commitment made by the British and Irish Governments that, in a new British–Irish Agreement replacing the Anglo-Irish Agreement, they will:

(i)   recognise the legitimacy of whatever choice is freely exercised by a majority of the people of Northern Ireland with regard to its status, whether they prefer to continue to support the Union with Great Britain or a sovereign united Ireland;

(ii) recognise that it is for the people of the island of Ireland alone, by agreement between the two parts respectively and without external impediment, to exercise their right of self-determination on the basis of consent, freely and concurrently given, North and South, to bring about a united Ireland, if that is their wish, accepting that this right must be achieved and exercised with and subject to the agreement and consent of a majority of the people of Northern Ireland;

(iii) acknowledge that while a substantial section of the people in Northern Ireland share the legitimate wish of a majority of the people of the island of Ireland for a united Ireland, the present wish of a majority of the people of Northern Ireland, freely exercised and legitimate, is to maintain the Union and, accordingly, that Northern Ireland's status as part of the United Kingdom reflects and relies upon that wish; and that it would be wrong to make any change in the status of Northern Ireland save with the consent of a majority of its people;

(iv) affirm that if, in the future, the people of the island of Ireland exercise their right of self-determination on the basis set out in sections (i) and (ii) above to bring about a united Ireland, it will be a binding obligation on both Governments to introduce and support in their respective Parliaments legislation to give effect to that wish;

(v) affirm that whatever choice is freely exercised by a majority of the people of Northern Ireland, the power of the sovereign government with jurisdiction there shall be exercised with rigorous impartiality on behalf of all the people in the diversity of their identities and traditions and shall be founded on the principles of full respect for, and equality of, civil, political, social and cultural rights, of freedom from discrimination for all citizens, and of parity of esteem and of just and equal treatment for the identity, ethos, and aspirations of both communities;

(vi) recognise the birthright of all the people of Northern Ireland to identify themselves and be accepted as Irish or British, or both, as they may so choose, and accordingly confirm that their right to hold both British and Irish citizenship is accepted by both Governments and would not be affected by any future change in the status of Northern Ireland.

2. The participants also note that the two Governments have accordingly undertaken in the context of this comprehensive political agreement, to propose and support changes in, respectively, the Constitution of Ireland and in British legislation relating to the constitutional status of Northern Ireland.

Annex A

DRAFT CLAUSES/SCHEDULES FOR INCORPORATION
IN BRITISH LEGISLATION

1. (1) It is hereby declared that Northern Ireland in its entirety remains part of the United Kingdom and shall not cease to be so without the consent of a majority of the people of Northern Ireland voting in a poll held for the purposes of this section in accordance with Schedule 1.

(2) But if the wish expressed by a majority in such a poll is that Northern Ireland should cease to be part of the United Kingdom and form part of a united Ireland, the Secretary of State shall lay before Parliament such proposals to give effect to that wish as may be agreed between Her Majesty's Government in the United Kingdom and the Government of Ireland.

2. The Government of Ireland Act 1920 is repealed; and this Act shall have effect notwithstanding any other previous enactment.

Annex B

IRISH GOVERNMENT DRAFT LEGISLATION TO AMEND THE CONSTITUTION

Add to Article 29 the following sections:

7.

1. The State may consent to be bound by the British–Irish Agreement done at Belfast on the ... day of ... 1998, hereinafter called the Agreement.

2. Any institution established by or under the Agreement may exercise the powers and functions thereby conferred on it in respect of all or any part of the island of Ireland notwithstanding any other provision of this Constitution conferring a like power or function on any person or any organ of State appointed under or created or established by or under this Constitution. Any power or function conferred on such an institution in relation to the settlement or resolution of disputes or controversies may be in addition to or in substitution for any like power or function conferred by this Constitution on any such person or organ of State as aforesaid.

3. If the Government declare that the State has become obliged, pursuant to the Agreement, to give effect to the amendment of this Constitution referred to therein, then, notwithstanding Article 46 hereof, this Constitution shall be amended as follows:

... (ii) the following Articles shall be substituted for Articles 2 and 3 of the English text:

> *'It is the entitlement and birthright of every person born in the island of Ireland ... to be part of the Irish nation.'*

ARTICLE 2

It is the entitlement and birthright of every person born in the island of Ireland, which includes its islands and seas, to be part of the Irish nation. That is also the entitlement of all persons otherwise qualified in accordance with law to be citizens of Ireland. Furthermore, the Irish nation cherishes its special affinity with people of Irish ancestry living abroad who share its cultural identity and heritage.

ARTICLE 3

1. It is the firm will of the Irish nation, in harmony and friendship, to unite all the people who share the territory of the island of Ireland, in all the diversity of their identities and traditions, recognising that a united Ireland shall be brought about only by peaceful means with the consent of a majority of the people, democratically expressed, in both jurisdictions in the island. Until then, the laws enacted by the Parliament established by this Constitution shall have the like area and extent of application as the laws enacted by the Parliament that existed immediately before the coming into operation of this Constitution.

2. Institutions with executive powers and functions that are shared between those jurisdictions may be established by their respective responsible authorities for stated purposes and may exercise powers and functions in respect of all or any part of the island.

... (iv) the following section shall be added to the English text of this Article:

8. The State may exercise extra-territorial jurisdiction in accordance with the generally recognised principles of international law.

Genesis Report to the Football Association of Ireland

*Preparation and planning for
the 2002 FIFA World Cup*

GENESIS CONSULTING LTD

Before 1988, the Republic of Ireland football team had failed to qualify for a single major international tournament. Sometimes they came close; more often they did not. Either way the end result was always the same: disappointment. The catalogue of failures meant that success when it finally came was particularly sweet. In 1986, Jack Charlton, one of England's World Cup 'heroes of 1966', was brought in to manage Ireland.

Having some outstanding Irish players, such as Paul McGrath, and others of Irish heritage brought in under the 'granny rule', Charlton's team broke with tradition by actually qualifying for the 1988 European Championship Finals in West Germany. The team did not make it past the first round, but that mattered little. If qualification had almost seemed victory enough, Ireland's 1–0 victory over England in the first match was a national dream come true. 'Jackie's Army' became overnight every other country's second team: the plucky boys in green, a gutsy bunch of upstarts, who would always 'give it a lash' (as the 1990 song went) without really hoping to win a trophy. Charlton seemed to concur. 'I'd love to win the competition,' he admitted, 'that would be terrific, but all we can really look for is to come out with some credit that we are capable of playing the best in Europe without any fear'.

Giving it a lash was the attitude that characterized Irish football during the Charlton era. For the fans, it was all a bit of a laugh and to be enjoyed for what it was. Not that there was anything wrong with having a laugh. The progress of the Irish team prompted a badly needed upsurge in national hope and pride after a particularly grim decade. Ireland's qualification for the World Cup in 1990 was even better still. Thousands of Irish fans travelled to Italy to support the team. Back home the carnival atmosphere was unprecedented. Ireland's matches, culminating in a famous penalty shootout victory to advance to the quarter-finals, became almost as much celebrations of being Irish as they were sporting fixtures. Many even condemned criticism of the team, such as that made by the RTÉ analyst and former international Eamon Dunphy, as unpatriotic. Ireland qualified again for the World Cup in the US in 1994. The European Championships two years later brought a remarkable streak to an end. Charlton stepped down as manager and was replaced by his former captain Mick McCarthy.

Under McCarthy, Ireland failed to qualify for either the World Cup in 1998 or the European Championships in 2000. With his job on the line, it was a relieved manager who watched his team win a World Cup play-off match against Iran to go through to the 2002 finals in Japan and Korea. Expectations were high, not least for captain Roy Keane – the Irish 'player of the tournament' at the 1994 World Cup. Although coming towards the end of his career, he remained a world-class player. As much as his skill, it was Keane's tactical sense and will to win that characterized his performance on the field. That relentless drive and unsmiling approach to the game, however, was often at odds with the spirit of the Irish team, which had relished its status as underdogs and 'good lads'.

A week before Ireland's first fixture, the team arrived at the Pacific island of Saipan. The idea was to relax after a long season, acclimatize to the region, and perhaps engage in a little light training. Unfortunately no one had told the captain. Even gentle exercises turned out to be difficult when it emerged that the kit was still making its way from Ireland. When it did turn up, the state of the practice pitch made training hazardous. Previously vocal about the Football Association of Ireland (FAI) and its treatment of the players (including making them fly economy class to fixtures while the FAI blazers sat in first class), Keane was furious at the 'shocking' facilities in Saipan, which were 'worse than a car park'. He lambasted the lack of drive and professionalism in the FAI and, crucially, in the squad. The attitude, he said, was one of 'We're the Irish team, it's a laugh and a joke. We shouldn't expect too much.'

Matters came to a head at a team meeting. McCarthy gave Keane a dressing down over his recent behaviour, which had included an unflattering interview in the *Irish Times* and on RTÉ in which he was critical of the situation in Saipan. Keane responded with an expletive-filled tirade, telling McCarthy: 'You were a crap player, you're a crap manager.' McCarthy sent him home.

Back in Ireland, the country divided between those who felt Keane's temper and obstinacy were misplaced and should have been set aside for the sake of the team, and those who felt he was right to take a stand. For some, it was about more than football. 'The essence of the differences between Roy Keane and Mick McCarthy', wrote Ronan Fanning in the *Sunday Independent*, 'is the conflict between ability and authority.' This was a clash of cultures between new and old Ireland. Even the taoiseach, Bertie Ahern, felt compelled to make an intervention, saying the nation would 'sleep happier in their beds' if Keane was recalled to the squad.

After the finals, the FAI commissioned Genesis Consulting to report on the preparations for the World Cup and subsequent events. The report concurred with much, if not all, of Keane's critique. Six months after Saipan, McCarthy resigned as Ireland manager. Two subsequent coaches failed to qualify for the finals of any major tournaments. In 2008 the FAI appointed Giovanni Trapattoni as manager on an unprecedented salary that was in part privately funded. In doing so it signalled the exchange of its amateur ethos for attributes more typical of the Celtic Tiger: a will to win and letting money do the talking.

Qualifying

The performance of the squad to come through the 'group of death' with Netherlands and Portugal, before going to win the play off against Iran was magnificent.

Preparing for Battle

No official structure and processes were set up by FAI to prepare for the 2002 World Cup.

'No overall plan was prepared with outcomes, milestones, and key tasks.'

In July 2001 the Travel Coordinator visited Japan to review 56 possible training venues in Japan and 30 in Korea.

In December 2001 a Working Group was set up made up of FAI staff and contractors. No-one in the group had experience of a previous campaign, and those with experience were not effectively engaged. If they had been, there may have been fewer problems with accreditation, as an example. The groups met infrequently and informally – no minutes or action plans were formally agreed and no overall plan was prepared with outcomes, milestones, and key tasks.

No dedicated budget was prepared for the 2002 World Cup. The FAI attempted to deliver everything that Mick McCarthy requested.

The Travel Agent/Coordinator was not given a budget for travel, although he did have a contract – he did deliver significant cost savings for improved standards of travel.

Plans were made to improve ticketing arrangements and these seem to have worked well.

Mounting pressure on staff resources was recognised by the Board with secondment, in March 2002, of 2 extra members of staff to handle commercial opportunities.

FAI staff attended a number of workshops run by FIFA in February and March 2002. In addition the Saipan venue for the first week's acclimatisation and relaxation was identified and visited by FAI staff including the Team Manager.

The main meeting covering logistics for training and equipment skips was held in March 2002. No minutes or plan or agreed action was prepared after this meeting.

Preparing the Team (after Qualifying)

Friendly matches were held with the following nations, after qualifying and before the week of departure:

- Russia, Denmark, USA

According to the players the first communication with them regarding the finals was at the first friendly match.

The team also played in Niall Quinn's testimonial at Sunderland the week before departing for Saipan. No letter or guidance note was ever given to players detailing arrangements for the World Cup. A briefing was held for the squad prior to the testimonial – Roy Keane missed this.

The final preparatory match was against Nigeria and the team travelled to Saipan the next day.

The overall quality of fixture chosen for the build-up was appropriate for Ireland, especially given the group for the first stage of the World Cup. Travelling such a distance after the game against Nigeria may have caused more physical problems for the players than actually occurred.

'Training for competition was not on the agenda.'

Saipan

Training for competition was not on the agenda, as Saipan was planned to be a week of relaxation, acclimatisation and light training. This was explained to and agreed with the players at the team (excluding Roy Keane) meeting the day before Niall Quinn's testimonial, itself in the week before departure for the World Cup.

Key staff arrived 2 days in advance to ease check-in and other arrangements, as is now common practice for the Irish squad.

The events of the week in Saipan are well documented. However we would draw the following conclusions:

- Saipan was a good choice of venue for acclimatisation and relaxation, but it added a disproportionately large complexity to logistics management who were already stressed

- It meant an additional 3rd leg to an already tiring journey (17 hours flying; nearly 30 hours total)

- Saipan was out of mobile phone/wireless contact, making communication difficult, exacerbated by the 3 hour time difference

- The Training Pitch was not up to the standards requested by the FAI and below that anticipated by the Team Management following their visit to Saipan earlier in 2002

- The Skips with training gear, official balls, medical supplies and drinks arrived on the Monday morning, 24 hours late. They left Dublin on 13 May rather than as originally planned (10 May). This allowed far too short a margin for error. The planned date of arrival was chosen to ensure that someone from the FAI would be present in Saipan to receive the skips

- The Pitch and Skips incidents were hugely more damaging than the technical impact they would ever have on the team's performance in the World Cup – they were the 'tip of the iceberg' for some. The training session on the first Sunday was a light stretching session which was added to the schedule by Mick McCarthy to help recovery from the flight. The players had equivalent kit with them and the balls acquired for the session, although not the official World Cup balls, were more than adequate for the light training 2 weeks before the first game

'The FAI support for their Press Officer and Team Manager was totally inadequate.'

• The FAI support for their Press Officer and Team Manager was totally inadequate to cope with a competition of this size, far less those events which occurred during the fateful week

• Consequently the Team Manager had no option other than to take control of media relations. Having started well, he subsequently lost control of events following the players' meeting on the Thursday and the subsequent press conference. He had little support from others

• The FAI had not planned any crisis management policy or procedures to fall back on in Saipan or at home in the event of any crisis

• As a result the events in Saipan exposed the flaws that were always there in terms of leadership, management and communication in the FAI.

Findings

Following our review and discussions with the Independent Chairman we find that:

• The Irish Football team, in achieving a ranking of 13th in the world, consolidated through their performance (12th place) in the FIFA 2002 World Cup, achieved a credible performance, delivered through

> Outstanding performance by a squad in good physical and psychological condition throughout the tournament

> Effective planning by the team management for the preparation for the tournament

• The much publicised incidents relating to the late delivery of skips and the quality of the training pitch in Saipan had little impact on the performance of the squad in the World Cup

> They did result in Ireland's Captain and arguably best player going home

> They were the final straw in a self fulfilling prophecy

• The seeds which culminated in the captain's withdrawal from the squad had been sown many years before and well nurtured over an extended period of time

> These symptoms had been totally ignored

• Many observers believed the potential of the Irish squad was not fully realised. We would concur with this view. The main factors which may have led to even higher performance include:

>   More positive action to recover the breakdown in the relationship between Roy Keane, the FAI team management and the FAI

>   Improved approach to and management of performance in the FAI

• The overall planning by the FAI was inadequate for an event the size and scale of the 2002 World Cup. The fact that the eventual outcome was positive (on the field and commercially) was more a matter of luck than effective management practice.

Footnote: The 2005 Genesis Report
In March 2005, Strategic Management Consultants, Genesis, presented a progress update on the 2002 report having been asked to carry out a review by the Football Association of Ireland (FAI).

Their overall conclusions from this review were that:
• Substantial modernization has taken place within the FAI since our original review in November 2002
• A more professional ethos now exists within the organization
• There is now a 'culture of discipline' in place, which was not evident in November 2002
• A robust and fit-for-purpose organizational structure has been developed to serve the organization
• There is evidence of considerable positive changes within the operating environment of the FAI
• The organization needs a more sustained period of stability, something that has not occurred since our original review
• The FAI needs to move on and to progress its long-term strategic plan for the game in Ireland, with the recently published Technical Development Plan at the heart of that strategic plan.

Index

Page references in italics denote illustrations

Illustrations

Acknowledgements

We wish to thank a number of friends and colleagues for their help in preparing this book. Maurice Bric and James McGuire were extremely generous with their time and advice. Stephen Kelly was an enthusiastic and capable research assistant. They, along with Kathryn Aldous, read early drafts. Errors that remain are of course our own. Kate Breslin was characteristically indispensable. Thanks also to Georgina Capel. Quercus have once again been a pleasure to work with, not least Publishing Director, Wayne Davis, who brought his usual energy and patience to the project. Rosie Anderson has been a most patient and encouraging editor and we wish her well in all her birthdays to come!

Quercus Publishing Plc
21 Bloomsbury Square
London
WC1A 2NS

First published in 2008

DESIGNER *Terry Jeavons*
PICTURE RESEARCHER *Caroline Hotblack*
PROJECT MANAGER *Rosie Anderson*
EDITOR *David Pickering*
PROOFREADERS *Fintan and Helen Power*
INDEXER *Zeb Korycinska*

DOCUMENT CREDITS p.12 The Board of Trinity College, Dublin (MS 52, Book of Armagh, f.22); p.17 British Library (MS Royal 13B. Viii, f.56v - from Giraldus Cambrensis, *Expugnatio Hibernica* Bk. II chapter vi); p.24 Library (Cotton Titus B.xi - Part II - f.78 r); p.33 The National Archives, ref. SP63/206 doc55; p.35 British Library (MSS.Dept.Lansd. MS.159, f.218 r); p.50–1 By kind permission of the Director and the National Archives of Ireland; p.57 British Library (C.115.d.8); p.64 Parliamentary Archives HL/PO/PU/1/1800/39&40G3n241; p.71 Parliamentary Archives; p.99 Courtesy of the National Library of Ireland, call number: Ephemera Collection – Abbey/1900-10/24; p.103 Ulster Covenant - first ten signatures (PRONI INF/7a/2/51). Director, Public Record Office of Northern Ireland, and the Ulster Unionist Council; p.108 Courtesy of the National Library of Ireland; p.114 Courtesy of the National Library of Ireland, call number: Ephemera Collection – Proclamations; p.120 The National Archives, ref. W095/1662; p.127 Courtesy of the National Library of Ireland; p.134 By kind permission of the Director and the National Archives of Ireland; p.142 Irish Newspaper Archives (www.irishnewsarchive.com); p.159 Courtesy of *The Irish Times*; p.170 Courtesy of the National Library of Ireland; p.176 CAIN (cain.ulst.ac.uk); p.177 Courtesy of the National Library of Ireland; p.188 The National Archives, ref. CAB129/162; p.194 article text © The Economist Newspaper Limited, London (16 January 1988)

TEXT CREDITS p.14 From *Patrick: the Pilgrim Apostle of Ireland*, Maire de Paor, Veritas Publications, Dublin, 1998; p.20 English translation from Irish Historical Documents 1172–1922, Edmust Curtis & R.B. McDowell (eds), Methuen, London, 1943 (Taylor & Francis Books); p.22 English translation from Irish Historical Documents 1172–1922, Edmust Curtis & R.B. McDowell (eds), Methuen, London, 1943 (Taylor & Francis Books); p.94 *GAA Rules and Bans*, Michael Cusack (1885); p.103 Ulster Covenant (D/1327), Director, Public Record Office of Northern Ireland, and the Ulster Unionist Council; p.148 Bunreacht na hÉireann, 1937, Preamble and articles 2 & 3: Reproduced under PSI General Licence No.: 2005/08/01; p.156 Courtesy of *The Irish Times*; p.164 The Republic of Ireland Act/Ireland Act (1949): reproduced under the terms of the Click-Use Licence; p.167 Extract from *An Irish Navvy – The Diary of an Exile* (Dialann Deorai) by Donall MacAmhlaigh, Irish translation by Valentin Iremonger is reproduced with permission from The Collins Press; p.172 Department Of Finance, *Economic Development* by T.K. Whitaker, 1958. Reproduced under Licence; p.180 By permission of Mary Maher; p.187 The Widgery Report, 1972: reproduced under the terms of the Click-Use Licence; p.196 © The Economist Newspaper Limited, London (January 16, 1988); p.201 The Good Friday Agreement, 1998: Reproduced under the terms of the Click-Use Licence; p.208 Reproduced by permission of the Football Association of Ireland (FAI)

PICTURE CREDITS p.19 The Print Collector/HIP/TopFoto; p.21 Dean and Chapter of Westminster; p.27 Getty Images; p.30 Getty Images; p.39 Bridgeman Art Library/Getty Images; p.41 Mary Evans Picture Library; p.45 Mansell/Time Life Pictures/Getty Images; p.47 Mary Evans Picture Library; p.54 Topfoto/Woodmansterne; p.59 Private Collection/ The Bridgeman Art Library; p.68 © Courtesy of the Warden and Scholars of New College, Oxford/The Bridgeman Art Library; p.75 Getty Images; p.79 Mary Evans Picture Library; p.89 Getty Images; p.92 Topfoto; p.97 Bettmann/Corbis; p.100 Hulton Archive/Getty Images; p.104 Corbis; p.108 Bettman/Corbis; p.111 Private Collection/The Bridgeman Art Library; p.116 Mary Evans Picture Library/Onslow Auctions Limited; p.123 Getty Images; p.131 Mansell/Time & Life Pictures/Getty Images; p.140 Corbis; p.146 Getty Images; p.154 William Vandivert//Time Life Pictures/Getty Images; p.162 Bettmann/Corbis; p.165 Express/Express/ Getty Images; p.174 Hulton-Deutsch Collection/Corbis; p.177 Topfoto; p.185 Mirrorpix; p.197 Eamonn Farrell/Photocall Ireland; p.199 TopFoto/ PA; p.206 Topfoto/PA